Important Note to Readers

P *rofiles in Hope* is a book of hope and hopeful stories of suicide and survival. These stories take the reader through very dark places before climbing the mountain of renewal. They include details of suicidality and suicide attempts, family and domestic violence, trauma, drug and alcohol abuse, anxiety and depression that could be very distressing to some.

If reading this book is distressing for you, please reach out for help.

You can contact Lifeline 24 hours a day:

By phone on 13 11 14
By text on 0477 13 11 14
By chat at www.lifeline.org.au/crisis-chat

There is also a list of other organisations that can help you access the assistance you need on page 303.

If you, or someone you love, is having a mental health crisis and is at risk of suicide, please call 000 or go to your local hospital, as they can help you access care.

And in Australia, in an emergency, if you are concerned for your or another's safety you can call 000 at any time.

An important note about writing about suicide

The way suicide is written about and reported is very important. Getting it right ensures we talk about suicide responsibly and don't hide it in a dark corner. Getting it wrong can cost lives.

For many years police would tell journalists when a death was a suicide not to report it. Journalists would mostly honour that request. After years of research and informed guidance, suicide is now reported, but there is one critical guideline that research stresses is very important. While it is appropriate to report that someone has died by suicide, the means of the suicide – the details of how the person took their life – should not be described in detail. Why? For people who are distressed, seeing a report with these details of how someone took their life risks the distressed person using those same means. So, in *Profiles in Hope*, you will not read specific detailed descriptions of how people tried to kill themselves.

Of great importance, too, is eliminating the phrase 'commit suicide'. You will not see this phrase in *Profiles in Hope*. The word 'commit' is associated strongly with crime.

Suicide is not a crime – it is a human tragedy – and the way we talk about it should reflect that. So, it is most appropriate to say that a person has 'died by suicide'.

Mindframe is a national program supporting safe media reporting, portrayal and communication about suicide, mental health concerns and alcohol and other drugs. Mindframe's guidelines on writing about suicide have been used in the writing of this book.

John Brogden is an Australian businessman, former politician, former Chair of Lifeline Australia and the Honorary President of LifeLine International. John's career in politics started when he became a member of the Parliament of New South Wales in 1996. In 2002, he was elected Leader of the Opposition on his 33rd birthday – the youngest person ever to lead a major political party in Australia. A global leader in suicide prevention and crisis helplines, John's passion for mental illness recovery stems from his own suicide attempt which marked a turning point in his life and reframed the public discourse around depression and suicide.

Fifteen Australians tell their stories
of surviving suicide and finding
the way back to a better life

Profiles in Hope

JOHN BROGDEN

hachette
AUSTRALIA

Aboriginal and Torres Strait Islander peoples should be aware that this book contains the names of deceased persons.

hachette
AUSTRALIA

Published in Australia and New Zealand in 2024
by Hachette Australia
(an imprint of Hachette Australia Pty Limited)
Gadigal Country, Level 17, 207 Kent Street, Sydney, NSW 2000
www.hachette.com.au

Hachette Australia acknowledges and pays our respects to the past, present and future Traditional Owners and Custodians of Country throughout Australia and recognises the continuation of cultural, spiritual and educational practices of Aboriginal and Torres Strait Islander peoples. Our head office is located on the lands of the Gadigal people of the Eora Nation.

A catalogue record for this book is available from the National Library of Australia

ISBN: 978 0 7336 5177 9 (paperback)

Cover design by Christabella Designs
Cover and internal images courtesy of Shutterstock
Typeset in 12/18 pt Baskerville MT Pro by Kirby Jones
Printed and bound in Australia by McPherson's Printing Group

MIX
Paper | Supporting responsible forestry
FSC
www.fsc.org FSC® C001695

The paper this book is printed on is certified against the Forest Stewardship Council® Standards. McPherson's Printing Group holds FSC® chain of custody certification SA-COC-005379. FSC® promotes environmentally responsible, socially beneficial and economically viable management of the world's forests.

Sam

Best wishes and safe
travels.

Contents

Important Note to Readers   1

Foreword by General the Honourable
    Sir Peter Cosgrove AK CVO MC (Rtd)   3

Introduction   6

Suicide in Australia   11

Chapter 1   Layne Beachley   17

Chapter 2   Matthew Caruana   41

Chapter 3   Pat Hall   59

Chapter 4   Preston Campbell   74

Chapter 5   Davina Smith   95

Chapter 6   Ben Farinazzo   113

Chapter 7   Nick Sherry   136

Chapter 8   Leilani Darwin   150

Chapter 9   Tom Boyd   168

Chapter 10 Jacqui Lambie   188

Chapter 11 Peter Moloney   207

Chapter 12 Ian Thorpe   222

Chapter 13 Annas Davids   244

Chapter 14 Ellia Green   260

Chapter 15 James Packer   278

Afterword from John Brogden   295

Contacts and Resources to Save a Life
… Or to Save Your Life   301

Helplines and Services   303

About Lifeline   305

Acknowledgements   307

Only if you've been in the deepest valley can you ever know how magnificent it is to be on the highest mountain.

– Richard Nixon, 9 August 1974

Foreword

by General the Honourable Sir Peter Cosgrove
AK CVO MC (Rtd)

What a remarkable book! It provides a riveting insight into the torment, the teetering on the brink, of a number of Australians – some of them extraordinarily well-known and thankfully all of them still with us. In doing so, it underscores the need, the work and the perpetual diligence of an organisation simply known as 'Lifeline'.

There wouldn't be too many organisations in Australia more admired than Lifeline. Since 1963, it has been for so many the reason for an alternative: a decision to live on, a reason to hope. So many Australians know of it because of the wonderful women and men who work under its banner – endlessly selfless, empathetic and profoundly non-judgemental. This is not their story, although in some ways it is, because it's the story of people who found themselves at one time or another or perhaps for months and years at a time, at a very low ebb – the sort of people who were looking for a lifeline.

My experience with Lifeline dates back to the days of my military service. In 1974, after my service in Vietnam, I was an officer serving in Holsworthy. Out of the blue, one night I received a phone call from a counsellor from Lifeline who had a very distressed and incoherent man on another line. Although the needy man was unable or unwilling to provide any details, the wonderful Lifeline volunteer worked out that he was probably a soldier from the unit of which I was part. After a brief discussion, I'd got enough information to act and with some soldiers went to the nearby army married quarters. Through the window, we could make out that the chap was alone inside, slumped comatose on the floor with the open phone nearby. We broke in and carted him off to hospital, where they brought him back. Another everyday miracle for Lifeline.

In *Profiles in Hope*, we read of the struggle and descent into despair of fifteen fellow Australians. These are short accounts but painful to relate to, painful (sometimes alarming) to read, but ultimately uplifting to know that despair could evolve to comfort, recovery and hope.

The interview style of the book is captivating: some of the dialogue is pungent and confronting but the authenticity and strength of the emotions behind each account is evident. Indeed, like me, you will come to admire the courage of those profiled who are so forthright with their stories – if you have clawed your way out of a deep hole, even with affectionate assistance, you wouldn't hold back both showing the angst and describing the effort, would you?

Like me, you will be particularly taken that John Brogden – himself a prominent public figure, a person who has been through a battle with his own demons – not only tells us of his own story but is the interviewer for the other participants in the book.

This is a major contribution to public awareness of the challenges and dilemmas so many within our wider community face. John has 'topped and tailed' the profiles with the sort of advice and exhortation we all both want and need, perhaps for ourselves or a loved one, perhaps for someone we interact with or chance upon, but fundamentally for all of us as citizens of the nation that prides itself on its sense of community.

It's important in closing to extend to John Brogden our heartiest congratulations and best wishes for the future of this important book and for Lifeline. My congratulations also go to the publishers, Hachette Australia, for their collaboration and empathy with this important project.

Read *Profiles in Hope* – you will find it most rewarding.

Peter Cosgrove

Introduction

Losing a friend, someone you know or, particularly, a family member to suicide leaves a dark hole. It changes your life forever.

Australia has matured enormously in the way we talk, feel and think about mental illness. However, we still struggle to talk about suicide. Many find suicide hard to understand and difficult to accept. And, in part, so we should. While we want to normalise mental illness as just another human illness, we never want to normalise suicide. We want people to choose life over death. We want them to know that no matter how dark life gets, no matter how hopeless things seem, there is a way back. That no human is beyond repair. The reality is that with help, support, compassion and love, suicide is largely preventable.

I wrote this book because messages of hope can help at a moment of crisis and save lives.

Suicide is easily misunderstood. Often, it is an act of impulse. We can live our lives with good mental health but, in a moment of crisis, come to a place where we attempt suicide. Fifty per cent of people who die by suicide have never seen a mental health professional. For some, when experiencing a crisis – a catastrophe in life – suicide becomes an option. And when the means of suicide are available, the chances of ending your life increase.

Some people who come through a period of suicidal thoughts or a suicide attempt never think about suicide again. For others, suicidal ideation (having suicidal thoughts) remains and can be a permanent part of their life. For them, like it is for me, the risk of suicide becomes a lifelong companion. So, it is important to learn how to manage crises and suicidal thoughts so you can live through them. It isn't easy. It takes mental and physical effort. And, like so many other treatments that require discipline and effort, sometimes it can seem too hard, and you give up. But it is better to start again than to give up forever.

Profiles in Hope tells the story of fifteen courageous Australians who share their journey of suicidality, attempted suicide and survival. I chose a question-and-answer format in this book because these aren't my stories. I want readers to experience these accounts of suicide and renewal in the words of the individual, without interpretation or explanation. Fifteen profiles in hope. Their stories show that it is possible to come back from the darkest place in your life, when suicide appears to be the best way to end your pain. They show that there is always hope, even when you feel most hopeless. I know all about that hopelessness.

I live with depression and suicidal ideation.

When I turned fifty I convinced myself it was not a time of great reflection – but of course it was. As I looked over my life, I realised that I had lived with suicidality for as long as I could remember, right back to my childhood.

For me, suicidal ideation means that when I have a severe emotional crisis, I begin to think about killing myself. In the really bad times, it means I think of a plan to kill myself. I've acted on those plans. It's not every day, week or month I feel like this, but it happens often enough to be a permanent part of me. Often enough that I've tried to take my own life.

In 2005, at the peak of my political career as Leader of the Opposition in the New South Wales Parliament, drawing even and at times ahead of the then-government in the polls, I behaved badly and said offensive things at an event. I apologised. In the aftermath, I resigned my leadership and decided to kill myself.

I was thirty-six. I was the youngest person in Australia to lead a major political party at the national or state level. I was possibly one election away from being the Premier of New South Wales – my life's ambition and obsession. But I was depressed, disgraced, ashamed and sorry for what I had done. I had brought great undeserved shame and embarrassment to my family, friends and supporters.

My career – and back then I believed that my career meant everything – was over. I wanted to die. I convinced myself that to kill myself was not just the only thing to do – but the best thing to do. To take myself out of everyone's life. To take away the shame and burden from the people who loved, cared for and supported me.

I thank God I survived.

I still live with suicidality. It is part of my make-up. I have accepted it will likely be part of my life forever. Accepting this hasn't been easy.

A few years ago, I visited the Riverina in southern New South Wales with a friend who was the local Member of Parliament. We visited schools and communities where I talked about my journey and about suicide prevention. At the end of the trip, at a community dinner, my friend's mother pulled me aside. I've never forgotten what she said to me: 'John – you will do more good doing this than you would ever have done as Premier.'

That was very kind. I never got to be Premier, so I can't compare, but fighting for the cause of suicide prevention is a very rewarding part of my life.

After politics, I went on to a career in business. My wife, Lucy, and I have three children. I live a life beyond what I ever dreamed possible as a child.

As the Chair of Lifeline Australia and then as President of Lifeline International, I have had the opportunity to advocate for suicide prevention in Australia and internationally. I have raised tens of millions of dollars for this cause and secured even more in government funding.

But whatever I have put in, I have received so much more in return. It is exhausting work, but I know that stories of hope encourage others to reach out for help. I know that stories of hope save lives. That is what has motivated me to gather those messages here.

I knew some of the people in this book before I approached them about appearing in these pages, and I met the rest during the writing. I chose people from a wide cross-section of Australia, so that readers would see something of themselves in these stories, making it easier to identify with them. Some of the people in this book are famous – household names. Others are unknown outside their world. But all are united in knowing now that life is better than death, and that you can survive to make a contribution on the other side.

Among the stories is that of Australian billionaire businessman James Packer, who shares his roller-coaster journey of success and failure in the public eye. Global swimming legend Ian Thorpe talks of the extraordinary weight of global fame as a teenager. Rebel Senator Jacqui Lambie takes you to her lowest point and shares her climb to become an important voice in national leadership.

Matt Caruana inspires with his sliding doors moment on a train. After Pat Hall's suburban life is shattered, she builds herself into a life-changing force for the poor and marginalised. Leilani Darwin shares her story of Indigenous trauma and how she is reclaiming her life.

All these people are sharing their profiles in hope to help others stay alive.

In 1956, US Senator (later President) John F Kennedy wrote *Profiles in Courage*. The bestselling, Pulitzer Prize–winning book profiled eight statesmen and politicians' courageous contributions to American public life.

This book, *Profiles in Hope*, is an homage to President Kennedy and *Profiles in Courage*.

Some people judge suicide and those who attempt it harshly. They see it as weak. Their religion may preach it is a sin. Their value system may see it as selfish. It is hard to believe, but in more than twenty countries in the world, suicide is still a crime. I ask that you never judge the most irrational of all actions rationally. Ripples of compassion, empathy and care along with adequately funded mental health services are all important in helping those who see only darkness and no way out. But critical to making a difference is ending shame, creating the safety to enable conversations about suicide and giving hope. Here, in these pages, are those ripples of hope.

– John Brogden

Suicide in Australia

In 2022 there were 1200 road deaths in Australia. In 2023 four people died in shark attacks. Road deaths are covered extensively in the media. Shark deaths lead the news bulletins here and internationally for days. And yet 3300 people die by suicide every year. On average, nine people – seven men and two women – every day. We don't talk about it. We rarely report it.

How many of us know that nine Australians die every day by suicide? Or that 65,000 people per year attempt suicide? And that one in six of us will have thoughts about suicide across our lifetime?

Suicide dropped by five per cent during COVID-19 but in the last two years has returned to pre-COVID numbers. Suicide rates in Australia are stubborn.

So why aren't we angrier about the number of Australians dying by suicide?

AGE

Every suicide is a tragedy, but probably none more than the suicide of a young person. We often hear that young people have the highest suicide rate in Australia. This is actually not true. While it is true that suicide is the leading cause of death among people aged between fifteen and twenty-four (in part because young people typically do not die from heart disease, cancer or other physical causes), the rate of suicide among young people has decreased in recent years. This is very good news. The reality is the highest proportion of deaths by suicide occurs in males in midlife, between forty and fifty-four years old.

Gender

Though males die by suicide at higher rates than females – seventy-five per cent of those who take their own life are men – that pattern is inverted when it comes to intentional self-harm and suicide attempts. Females are hospitalised at twice the rate as males for intentional self-harm, with and without suicidal intent.

In 2021 ambulance attendance numbers for suicidal ideation and self-harm were higher for females than males across the five jurisdictions where data is recorded – New South Wales, Victoria, Queensland, Tasmania and the Australian Capital Territory.

Aboriginal and Torres Strait Islander peoples

There are a number of population groups at higher risk of suicide than the general population, in particular Aboriginal and Torres Strait Islander peoples. First Australians die at suicide rates two times greater than the general population. Year-on-year, 'Closing the Gap' reports show that this rate is increasing. The suicide crisis among Indigenous Australians is already unacceptable, and is actually getting worse – and we seem incapable of stopping it.

Among young Aboriginal and Torres Strait Islander peoples, the rates are also markedly higher than those among non-Indigenous Australians. In 2022, among people aged from 0–24, suicide rates were three times higher than in the non-Indigenous population.

Defence personnel and veterans

When serving, permanent and reserve male defence personnel are less likely to die by suicide than their counterparts in the general population. But when compared to the working male population, they are at greater risk. And after leaving the defence force, ex-serving males are twenty-six per cent more likely, and females twice as likely, to die by suicide than their counterparts in the general population.

For those who voluntarily leave, the male rate of suicide is similar to the Australian male population. However, the rate of suicide for involuntarily medically separated ex-serving males is three times higher.

Too many women and men who serve to defend their country find life after service unbearable. We look to the recent Royal Commission into Defence and Veteran Suicide for answers and solutions, and to government to implement the Royal Commission's recommendations..

LGBTQIA+

More than seventy-five per cent of people in the LGBTQIA+ community have experienced suicidal thoughts, and approximately thirty per cent have attempted suicide in their lifetime. More than forty-seven per cent of people in the LGBTQIA+ community have seriously thought of taking their own life at some point.

LGBTQIA+ community members report having attempted suicide at a rate ten times higher than the general Australian population.

Solutions

So, what are the solutions? I am so sick of hearing 'the causes of suicide are complex and the solutions are not easy' being used as an excuse for slow action.

There are many solutions. They include:

- earlier assessment
- much more treatment in the community
- early detection and support for those with adverse childhood experiences
- significantly improved connections between services. Too many – far too many – people fall between the cracks of services rather than being passed on seamlessly between them
- standard follow-up after suicide attempts – like home visits by nurses to mothers after they leave hospital. Why can't we do the same for those who have presented to hospital after a suicide attempt?

We need a massive public campaign about the causes of suicide. We can do this because we've done it before. Look at our success in breast cancer detection and treatment – the extended lives and reduction in lives lost. Forty years ago it was impolite to discuss breasts in public. Well, we got over ourselves and got on with the job of saving and extending lives.

Ending the stigma associated with suicide is so critical to reducing suicide rates, and it is everyone's job. There is a strong view that in recent years we have increased the awareness of mental health, but not reduced the stigma. The same goes for suicide. This book will do some of that work. The stories told here, from Australians of different backgrounds, prove that suicide never discriminates. But so much more open conversation is needed.

Shared local data and responses from schools, police, ambulance, hospitals, medical professionals, community groups – netball clubs, football clubs – and local councils will save lives. If we know about clusters and hot spots quickly, we can act quickly. We are seeing more of this, but it needs to be formalised nationwide.

Work design is critical. Why do we employ people in jobs that we know are stressful and psychologically unsafe? And where we can't avoid it, in roles like the military and police, are we doing enough to train and support these personnel? We are required by law to have physically and psychologically safe workplaces. Look at the reduction in deaths and injuries on construction sites. Safe Work Australia's data shows that physical workplace fatalities have fallen because of increased awareness and training. But the same focus is not given to creating psychologically safe workplaces.

And, please – let's stop expecting the government to do everything. They have to do the heavy lifting in funding, but the community – all of us – are part of the solution. As John F Kennedy said, 'Ask not what your country can do for you, but what you can do for your country.'

I know I am in the minority in the suicide prevention community in proposing targets for suicide reduction. But let's put our feet to the fire. Because we need to do something radical to enact change. Targets focus the mind and create action. Having to explain in public why suicides haven't been reduced by agreed targets in an agreed time will force positive change. I know in my professional and political life having targets worked, and targets that an organisation or government has to achieve mean strategy, budgets and business plans to achieve them. Let's not just talk about change, let's make it happen.

But it all starts with understanding lived experience, and pulling back the curtain on suicide.

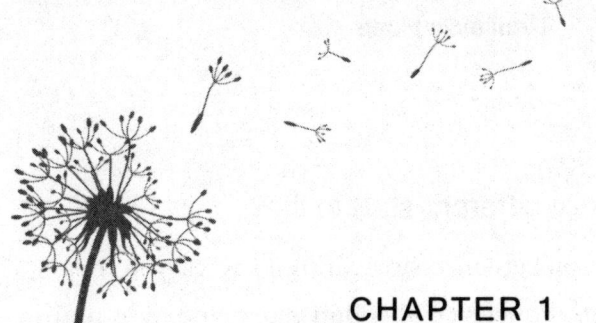

CHAPTER 1

Layne Beachley

The Surfer

Layne Beachley AO is an international women's surfing pioneer and seven-time World Champion. She is quite literally a legend in the world of surfing. Layne started life born with a different name, the child of date rape and the daughter of a seventeen-year-old mother who had to put her up for adoption soon after birth. Throughout much of her life - particularly in her early days as an international champion - she lived with a deep feeling of being unworthy. She fought and overcame mental illness and suicidality.

Layne has been my friend for twenty years. She and her INXS rocker husband Kirk Pengilly - himself a cancer survivor - inspire through their commitment to charities and the community. Layne looks as fit, strong and tanned today as she did at the peak of her professional surfing career. The surf is still her elixir.

* * *

* * *

Layne, you had a very different start to life?

I don't have the white-picket-fence story, if that's what you mean. I was adopted at birth, conceived through date rape. My mum was seventeen when I was born. She lived in Surry Hills, came from a religious family and they wouldn't let her keep me.

That was the early 1970s, it was proper working-class Surry Hills, Crown Street Women's Hospital, where women were sent when they'd been knocked up and the baby's father wasn't around. That's where Mum was. Her parents were supportive, but just wouldn't allow it. She wanted to keep me, but her parents weren't keen on the idea as they believed she wasn't old enough or mature enough. Which was the norm in those days. I am very grateful, of course, that I wasn't aborted and that I was allowed to live.

I don't think she ever contemplated abortion. More than anything, she wanted to keep me. She hoped, even right up to when I was born, that she could. Even though she'd been told all along that she was having the baby and putting it up for adoption, right up to the last minute, she thought, can I keep this baby?

It must have been traumatic for her?

There's an aspect of me that feels, metaphysically and cellularly, that I wasn't 'wanted'. She knew she wasn't allowed to keep me, so, from my perspective and cellular memory, it felt like there was no joy in the pregnancy, or the womb. The birth was challenging and traumatic, despite the fact I was six weeks premature. On a deep subconscious level, I must have felt this which may explain my premature birth – I just wanted the fuck out of there!

Immediately following my birth, I was placed into a humidicrib for the next six weeks of my life. No touching, no holding. No bonding. No breastfeeding, no connection. She was advised to stay away, to avoid creating a connection. She desperately wanted to hold me but to no avail.

So, you were adopted.

By Murray Neil and his wife, Valerie, who became my mum and dad, along with a newly acquired brother, Jason.

Valerie was a beautiful petite woman. Jason was five when I was adopted. Valerie had complications giving birth to Jason, and was rushed into an emergency C-section. Due to this complication, she wasn't able to have another child. So, that's when they chose to adopt. Ten months after submitting the application, Val picked me up with her best friend and her best friend's husband, because Dad was away working in New Zealand. When she arrived home with me, she called him and asked, what are we going to call her? And he didn't have a clue. Mum decided to call me Layne.

No-one knew anyone else called Layne. Well, there's quite a few of us now, many of them named after me! According to my birth certificate, my biological mum named me Tania Maris Gardner. That was my name. Tania.

We lived in Manly. Dad was working with Nestlé, Mum was a stay-at-home mum.

Very 1970s Australia.

Then we moved up to Balgowlah Heights. From memory, it was a comfortable and happy childhood. I grew up playing and having a ball, experiencing the freedom to roam. A 'be home once the streetlights come on' kind of childhood. I was super hyperactive. Always wanting to be outside. I was the epitome of a tomboy. Today I'd probably be diagnosed with ADHD. I didn't enjoy sitting still or being indoors.

When I was seven, Mum – Valerie – unexpectedly passed away. During the C-section to deliver my brother, apparently the doctors did a poor job of sewing her back up, so to correct the scarring Mum went in for cosmetic surgery and suffered a brain haemorrhage on the operating table.

What are your memories of her?

They are very limited. I recall sitting on her lap as a toddler, drinking the dregs of her coffee. That's the only coffee I've ever drunk in my life. Except in an espresso martini. I remember napping under a multi-coloured blanket on her bed. I've still got the blanket, which I believe her mother knitted. I've told the story so many times that I find myself less emotional and more pragmatic about it, yet sometimes grief takes me by surprise.

My parents' generation all grew up in this tough-love environment. Just do it and get on with it. Don't show emotion, don't deal with your emotions. Don't tell anyone if you're suffering. As a result, I suffered in silence because as a kid, I grew up feeling like I wasn't allowed to share my pain. When I was about nine years old, I headbutted the sand at Manly while surfing on my foamie and I felt my neck crack. When I came in and said, 'Dad, I hit the bottom and think I've done something to my neck', his response was to tell me to lie down, rest and that I'd be right.

Such tough love, just harden up.

One of Mum and Dad's best friends, Joan Tate, and her husband, Brian, became our carers after Val died because Dad still worked full-time. Joan was there after school. She would cook us dinner, bathe us and dress us. They had their own kids, but they were older, so they were empty nesters.

To me they were like a nan and pop. Joan said it took her eighteen months to earn my trust to hold her hand in public. I was a non-touchy-feely kid – always keeping people at a distance. Which I'm sure is a result of being thrust into that humidicrib. I never formed a bond or an emotional connection with my own mother.

The only mother you've had dies when you're seven. Is that where this real thread of toughness in you comes from? There is a bit of cement in there, do you know what I mean?

I'm not going to deny what I am. Losing my mum, growing up in a male-dominated, tough love household and playing male-dominated sports certainly toughened me. Yet, there's also a softness about me. Kirk [Pengilly, Layne's husband] calls me a refrigerated Caramello Koala. Tough exterior with a gooey centre. Now I'm getting older, I'm more room temperature.

When did you find out you were adopted?

When I was about eight, the kids around the street were beginning to ask why I looked so different to the rest of my family. My brother was tall, with brown hair and brown eyes. My dad is six foot tall, again with brown hair and slate-blue eyes. They're both quite pale skinned and burn easily in the sun. I, on the other hand, have dark olive skin, bright blue eyes, blonde hair, and I was three foot. Tiny. I looked at my family and thought, yeah, that's a good question.

Dad sat me down and told me straight out, 'You're my baby girl and you've always belonged to this family, but you're not a blood relation. You're adopted. You come from someone else.' It was very old-school language.

I quickly tuned out of what my dad was saying and tuned into what I was saying to myself. I'm his baby girl, I belong here, yet I've been rejected, I've been abandoned. My mother didn't want me. I'm not worthy of love. I felt so worthless in that moment. I felt like Alice in Wonderland. I remember I was sitting on a big, dark brown-and-white couch in our family loungeroom. It was deep, and like with Alice, the couch got bigger and bigger and it felt like it was swallowing me.

Was there a different way he should have told you?

I believe honesty from the start, from the moment I was brought into the family, would have been a better way to go about it, which would have given me the chance to create conceptual meaning about where I come from without being side-swiped by this information. Knowledge dispels fear. Had I known those things from the start, this may have prevented the longing and yearning that dominated my life for so long.

Did you ever experience what some adopted people say, which is the reverse? I'm special. I was chosen?

Yes, however, it took me a long time to get there. In fact, it was after I claimed my sixth consecutive world title.

When Dad told me I was adopted, that's when I decided I had to become a world champion at something. Anything. This is how I had defined being worthy of love – I had to be the best in the world at something, to overcome my feelings of worthlessness and being unlovable. Our deepest values emanate from our darkest voids. Today, I have the understanding and the appreciation that this all comes from within. But at the time I wasn't taught or educated about self-love. So, I just kept seeking it externally.

When I won my sixth consecutive world title, one of my friends asked why I was so driven. 'Is it because you're adopted?' The question felt like someone piercing a stake straight through my heart.

It resonated with me so powerfully. Like, holy shit!? It made total sense to me. Yes! I'm not going for six consecutive world titles for the titles. It's not the trophies I want. It's the feeling of being worthy of love. To achieve this, I had to become the most successful surfer in history.

Growing up, the most valuable lesson I acquired from learning to surf in Manly and then declaring as a fifteen-year-old that I was going to become a world champion was to say 'fuck you' to all of the critics and naysayers. You know, arseholes that told me I was never going to make it. Dream thieves, I call them. All you fucking dream thieves. Fuck you – I'll prove to you that I can.

When I was nineteen, I was working at the surf shop at Manly from 9 to 5, four days a week. I was working at Beaches Pizzeria three or four nights a week, making and delivering pizza from 6 pm to 11 pm. And two to three nights a week from 6 pm to 3 am at the Old Manly Boatshed, along with any other jobs available to me. Teaching people to rollerblade or surf, I'd take on anything to make ends meet.

I finished high school in 1989. I joined the pro-tour in 1990 and at the time, I was doing my own training. The lifeguards and the boys down at Manly gave me swim programs and training programs. I was committed. I had no idea about nutrition.

No idea about recovery. I ate a lot of shit and punished my body. I had no concept of self-care. In my second year, I went to Europe – in 1991 – and lived on frozen hamburgers and frozen pizzas. I really had no idea about how to cook or fuel my body.

I soon realised that to be the best, I had to surround myself with the best and learn from them. The current world champions were fit – they were healthy, they were strong, every one of them, from Tom Carroll, Martin Potter and Wendy Botha, and they all trained with Rob Rowland-Smith. So, I asked, 'Who is this guy? I need to meet him!' I didn't have my licence, and I lived in Manly. Early one Sunday morning I caught the 199 bus up to Palmy [Palm Beach], sat with Rob, and shared my dream of wanting to be a world champion. I wanted to be the best. And he told me what I had to do.

The training was ferocious. Once I started training with Rob, I had to show up at 5.30 in the morning, five to six days a week, no matter what the circumstances. In the middle of winter, in the pouring rain, sick as a dog, with the flu, I was there. I believed success had to be hard and I had to get this done.

Would you have said you were a feminist, blazing this trail?

It depends on your interpretation of what a feminist is.

Because I grew up as a tomboy, in an all-male dominated environment, I actually thrived in that world. It was familiar and comfortable so I just kept seeking it out. That's where I felt safe. The majority of my male friends were older than me. I never felt like I was going to be taken advantage of. I always felt like I was protected. The guys were always really supportive and encouraging. But I rarely felt like I could find that protection from women, because there weren't many around.

When I think about the one or two women that I did seek protection from on a consistent basis, they often rejected me, especially once I became a threat or when I became more confident or competent in my competitive career.

So, what are the men around you thinking? Here's this young woman. Look at this passion, look at this commitment. She works her bloody arse off, she's so committed. Let's get behind her and give her a hand?

One night, at three o'clock in the morning as I finished work at the Old Manly Boatshed, Grant McMinn – who was a co-owner – recognised how hard I was working, and how much I wanted to achieve my goals. He gifted me $3000 which was my ticket to Hawaii. Good luck. Go for it. He just wanted to see me succeed. So, I received more encouragement and unconditional support from the men in my life than I did from the women.

How was your mental health?

I was ferocious. Just fucking fiercely focused. Plus, this was a time when no-one spoke of mental health. Zero duty of care.

What happened when you lost?

I became desperately depressed and disappointed. I was inconsolable, just bawling my eyes out. I would always blame myself. I didn't blame anyone else. Then I'd go out and get smashed. Sometimes I would show up to heats drunk or hungover.

Then you get through it, get back on the escalator and win the next race.

Yeah. Occasionally.

In 1991, I committed to my first full tour year, and I had a shocking time. I was literally couch-surfing around the world. Lonely as hell. I felt like I had no support, no guidance. It was in Hawaii where I experienced the greatest depth of loneliness, because we were usually there for a month, and I had no-one to share the experience with. The mecca of surfing, you think I'd be able to share that with somebody?

I felt so abandoned and rejected by my peers as well. Mind you, I was also abandoning and rejecting them. As an adoptee, this is a common theme that runs through most of us. We have this massive fear of rejection, so we'll either behave in a way that gives people reason to reject us, or we maintain this illusion of control and reject them first. I was misunderstood. Everyone thought I was arrogant and a bitch. Fuck you, Beachley, was the common sentiment.

I felt like the outlier, the little black sheep that was just relentlessly focused on pursuing success at any cost. In 1992, I had a breakthrough where I made the final in Brazil, ultimately losing to Wendy Botha. Then in 1993, I won my first world championship tour event at North Narrabeen in Sydney.

I bought myself a pushbike with the prize money, which became my mode of transport to training and to work. That's the breakthrough I was waiting for. Now I have beaten the best, I believe I can become the best. And the following week I was diagnosed with Chronic Fatigue Syndrome [CFS].

How did you know? What prompted you to go to the doctor?

I was talking to one of the ironmen about how I was always tired and struggling to concentrate. I felt really bloated. I was just super uncomfortable all the time. He told me to go and see his naturopath. I went and did blood tests and food allergy tests, discovering I was allergic to everything. It was CFS. That was pretty hard.

Did that hit your mental health?

Absolutely! There weren't discussions around mental health until the late-nineties. But the CFS smashed me. I applied myself to healing. Fortunately, we caught it early so my recovery time was only six weeks by committing to a strict diet and limited movement. No gluten, red meat, dairy, corn, raw nuts, alcohol, wheat or anything canned or preserved. I'm good at applying myself if it means ensuring a positive outcome. I will do what it takes. I'd sit with a syringe in my arm and shoot 50 ml of Vitamin C straight into my veins, daily. The amount of energy this gave me was absolutely astonishing.

Six weeks later I'm back on tour. But my performance and results are super inconsistent, which is a reflection of my mindset.

Which was …?

Capricious. Some days I felt like I belonged there, some days I didn't. Some days I felt I had what it took, some days I didn't. I'd taught myself how to surf, so my technique was fundamentally flawed. In 1994, I won Bells [Bells Beach, Victoria], which was my second breakthrough event. I bought myself a car after that one, a Mazda 323 hatch, 1980 model from Rent-a-wreck in Manly.

So, parallel to all of this, you're on the front page of the newspapers and on TV?

Oh, no. It took winning my first world title to appear on the front page of the *Manly Daily*. Prior to this I became a media personality, because of my regular pieces on TV, on *The Footy Show* and *Wide World of Sports* on Channel 9.

You're getting recognised?

Every day. Mainly because of *The Footy Show*. I was actually more recognised outside of surfing than within it. I went to the supermarket with my best friend, and this chick is scanning the items when she looks up and says, 'Hey, I know you. You're that surfy chick on the TV.'

In 1995, I finished second in the world for the first time and was ready to quit. Because I was travelling, training, competing and working four part-time jobs, it was all too hard. I was only earning $8000 a year from my sponsor, and any money I earned was squirrelled away or invested into getting to the next event.

Around 1996, Billabong started a girls' brand. So, I went to them with a proposition and said, 'I want to be your number-one girl. I want to win. I'm gunning for a world title.' And they went, 'Alright, okay, do we have any say in it?!'

In 1996, I finished third in the world. Falling from second to third was deeply distressing and I was very disappointed in myself. But I was also in the throes of my second bout of chronic fatigue, which I was in complete denial of.

Why?

I didn't want to accept how I was feeling. I didn't want to accept the physical weakness, the mental confusion and the emotional rollercoaster. I was in a really bad place and I just wasn't willing to own it, because I was so focused on winning. I ended up depressed. I'd just signed with Billabong, and I wanted to earn my stripes there and show them I had what it took. I couldn't show them that I was sick. I couldn't show my peers, because they would beat me. Once again, I suffered in silence.

I started to question myself. I was looking for reassurance and validation from my peers, which was weird. I wanted people to tell me I was doing okay. I was constantly seeking external validation, which is a warning sign for me because I'm so intrinsically motivated. When I'm seeking external validation, there's something wrong but I'm not willing to acknowledge it.

At the end of 1996, I was completely rooted, but still training, still working part-time. Then in 1997, I went back to the naturopath and he affirmed what I knew. I was now in a much worse state. Mid-competitive season, I had to go on a yeast-free, wheat-free, sugar-free, dairy-free, fruit-free, alcohol-free, red meat-free diet. Again.

What did you eat?

Fish, chicken. Vegetables. Rice. Stewed apples and pears. I had to take an enormous amount of supplements. But before I received the second diagnosis, I fell into the deepest, darkest depths of depression. I had suicidal tendencies, for sure. I didn't have a plan. I knew I'd never go through with it. But the fact I was even contemplating it scared the shit out of me.

So, this was a combination of the worthlessness you felt, plus 'I'm not going to get there'.

The unfulfilled expectation. I'm sick. I'm fatigued, I'm out. I'm not going to fulfil any of my goals. This fuelled the sense of despair and depression that ensued.

Did you feel you were a burden on the people who'd helped you?

Yes, I felt I was letting them down. Yeah. All of that, totally. But I didn't talk to anyone. I'm a classic silent sufferer. I was drinking more. Self-sabotaging. Rejecting friends, withdrawing. I was in a really bad way. Super bloated. Poor concentration. Bad memory. Intense tinea between my toes. I had so much candida in my body, and I was craving all the foods that fuel it – sugar, alcohol, wheat, dairy. All that shit.

This was before I went on the diet. This is when I was in the depths of it. It was weird and obviously unhealthy, but fuck it, I just kept going. Just keep going. Just keep going. Then I woke up one morning and I started thinking of ways to end my own life. That was disconcerting. I wanted to be dead.

I wanted to be dead but I didn't want to kill myself. Actually, I wanted to be dead in order to end the pain, to end the suffering. I must have known that the way out of this was through more pain. So, prior to owning it, I flogged myself harder – training, working, competing. I was just so emotionally devoid of compassion and empathy for myself, I thought the only way to escape this was through more pain, more struggle, more suffering.

When you look back, were you at the lowest point of your entire life?

Yeah. Lower than when Dad told me I was adopted, I reckon. Very dark, lonely place. I cried a lot. Mainly because I didn't understand what was going on, and because CFS was labelled as 'yuppie disease' in those days. Externally, there was nothing evidently wrong with me so there was zero compassion. Intrinsically, I was broken, crying out for help, yet I failed to extend myself any compassion. And when we don't have compassion and understanding, we don't have empathy. Without empathy, we push away. So, I just denied and deflected.

My performance was slipping, training was challenging. Motivation was sinking. Self-care was absent. Even the way I spoke to myself about myself was harsh. I arrived at a point where I was so scared because I was thinking of different ways to hurt myself, so, I rang up someone I knew who had been through a similar challenge. Who I knew wouldn't judge me.

I rang Johanna Griggs [Commonwealth Games swimmer]. She was a good mate, and she'd been through CFS too.

I felt she would understand what was happening. She might be able to give me some counsel. So, I rang Jo and her response was, 'What took you so long?' Then I began the long slow journey of clawing my way out of that dark, black hole, and recognising that it didn't have to be that way. I took months off to rehabilitate. I stopped training, competing and touring. I also had to stop surfing. Which was hard. That was really challenging. I stopped looking out and started looking in. The only way out is within.

So, things picked up?

In 1997, I arrived in Hawaii. I was staying in a loft of a friend's house. I had a suitcase full of swimmers, T-shirts, shorts and supplements. I was on the strictest of diets. I was not drinking. I was not eating sugar. I was not having dairy. Still, I had to go much deeper. I was journaling daily, it was a brain dump, a release of unnecessary shit going on in my mind and life that I didn't have to harbour in my head. It helped me regain clarity. And it helped me have conversations with people I didn't want to have actual conversations with, if I wanted to vent, bitch or complain.

I sensed I was expanding again, like I was coming back into my own. I wanted to be world champion and I knew it was going to take nothing less than 100 per cent. I had to get my act together. I had to really apply myself to the supplements, rest and the diet. Intensely focus on nourishing my body, to then be able to perform the way I wanted to perform.

In Hawaii, I was lonely again. I paddled out at Sunset Beach and I saw Ken Bradshaw out there. He's a Texan, big-wave surfer. Looks a lot like Buzz Lightyear. I had written in my journal the year before, Ken is the kind of man I could easily fall in love with. And then when we came in, I found out he had broken up with his girlfriend. We just happened to have one of those moments on the beach where we just connected. So, we hooked up, and then world title number-one happened.

You're happy with yourself or are you still not worthy?

I'm twenty-six, I'm satisfied, but I'm still not worthy. The one thing I felt was relief, because I'd been claiming for over ten years that I was going to be a world champion. I think everyone else was relieved too. Like, fuck, she's going to stop talking about it now. And then Ken said, 'You're the best surfer I've ever seen. You can be the best of the best!'

I became the queen of self-promotion. I was happy to tell a story. Tell a story to anyone. I was very confident. But then also very insecure. It's funny. How can you be super confident and insecure at the same time? Maybe my confidence was arrogance masking my insecurity.

So, your health's back. You win the title. The relationship's brilliant. Loneliness goes away?

Completely disappears. But now I've decided that my peers don't understand me. And they don't respect me. So now I'm going to retreat from them and I'm just going to put everything into being with Ken. He can hold me and secure me and protect me. That way, I don't have to deal with the shit emotionally vindictive women can throw at me. But I'm desperate for their recognition and respect at the same time. I'm no one-hit wonder. It's time to get another title.

How did you win the second one?

The second one was an emotional roller-coaster because now I had achieved success, I then placed twice the amount of expectation on my shoulders to do it again. The worthiness thing. I didn't believe I was worthy of the success, unless it was twice as hard. So, I flogged myself. In the process, I tore my medial collateral ligament, fractured a rib and then I had a wave land on the small of my lower back and fold me in half, crushing my lumbar spine, but I just kept going, kept going.

But you still won?

I still won. Dragged myself through. And then the third world title …

How was your mental health during that up-and-down period?

If you looked at my competition result pattern, these provided a direct reflection of my mental health. If I'm winning, I'm in a good space. If I'm losing, I'm in a bad space. If I'm showing up to heats drunk, hungover or poorly prepared, I'm in a bad space.

Among all of this, there was one bit that I haven't mentioned. In 1995, I applied for my original birth certificate.

Okay. Why?

I felt that loneliness, that yearning. I wanted to know where I came from. Why I looked the way I looked. I'd thought about it for many years but I hadn't wanted to do it, but now the law had changed in New South Wales to make it accessible. I remember that very well. Finally, we adoptees were able to identify with where we come from.

It was liberating. Joan and I went to the office (births, deaths and marriages) and I applied for it.

Then, the birth certificate arrived and my roommate faxed it to me in South Africa, ten minutes before a heat. I paddled out with all that fresh information circulating in my head, and I almost lost.

It informed me that my mother was seventeen when she had me. I learned her name and my name, where she was living at the time and how old she was. But no contact details. She was born in Glasgow. Her name was Maggie. And she was seventeen. I thought perhaps she was a backpacker. No judgement at all, actually, I was quite resolved at that point. Okay, I thought, that answers my question. That closed a chapter for me. Then in 1999, I received the phone call from Dad. He said, 'Your mum called.' I was like, 'What the fuck?'

She went through the whole phone book, found Dad and rang him.

Wow, so she knew who they were?

She worked out who my dad was and rang him, and said, 'I'm Layne's mother and this is the circumstance.' And he said, 'Alright, well I'll leave it to Layne. Give me your details and I'll leave it to Layne to contact you.'

Did you want to meet her?

No, I didn't want a connection with her.

She was living in San Francisco.

Did she know you were a famous surfer?

She worked that out.

I'd told Dad I was searching for my mother and he was supportive. I decided to wait until I was in Hawaii to reach out to her, when I would be with Ken, so I'd have his emotional support. Because this is a really big step. Only she doesn't wait for me to call her. The next day she calls me at home because she wanted to hear my voice.

It was fucked up, because from the moment I picked up the phone, she tried to make up for the last twenty-seven years in the first five minutes. She said, 'I was date raped and I wanted to keep you.' She just vomited it all out.

Did you know about the date rape before, or was this the first you'd heard of it?

I knew nothing. The only information I knew was on the birth certificate. That was it. I knew nothing else.

I'm about to go back to Hawaii and compete. I'm in between events, about to win my second world title, and I basically wanted to tell her to fuck off, because it was just too much to take. I got really angry and almost hung up on her. All of my friends thought she might be a gold digger or a fame digger.

Yet, I was intrigued enough to want to meet her. I thought, I will give her the respect to meet with her. She gave birth to me. I wanted to connect with her. I really did. For some reason, I decided I wanted to meet on neutral territory. She was living in Santa Rosa, which is just out of San Francisco.

I was in LA on my way home from Brazil, so I called her and jumped on a plane to San Francisco and met her at the airport. I put very clear parameters around it. And, literally, when I first laid eyes on her, I thought I was looking into the mirror in seventeen years' time. There was no question that she was my mother. No question at all. And it felt like a couple of girls catching up. There were tears.

How did you feel?

Growing up and losing my mother, and then being told I'm adopted, I'd always placed firm boundaries around my heart. Protection mechanisms. I was always in this survival mode, fearing someone's going to either hurt me or disrespect me. Or, someone's going to die. So, I didn't wholeheartedly lean in and embrace the whole interaction.

Did she apologise to you?

Yes, she did. She was desperate to connect. Many years later, I learned her husband had recently died and she was left with a five-year-old daughter. She had very little money, she was HIV-positive, she was quite unhappy, and looking for something positive and happy to cling onto. My emotional state and focus on winning ensured I saw her as a distraction. So, I chose to push her away.

Ticked that box. We've met, now go away. You just wait there, and I'll be back when I'm ready.

However, she didn't want to wait. She randomly appeared at the final Hawaiian event and then she unexpectedly showed up at Huntington Beach in July the following year. And she just kept coming and kept coming. And I was like, fuck off, fuck off, fuck off. Then she started calling my friends trying to gain a connection through some of my girlfriends. She'd call me after a few drinks and ask random questions.

It was overwhelming. I don't know how to explain it other than she would come toward me and I would push away. Then, after interviewing her for my biography, I realised I had equated motherhood with loss and this was stopping me from connecting with her. As well as my judgement of her story. I truly did not believe that she was raped. I think that was her story.

Her excuse to give you away?

Yes. That was the story I had crafted. Whether it was really a rape. That was my judgement and I knew my judgement was preventing me from connecting with her.

I mean, I'm really grateful she gave me up. I'm so grateful that I grew up at Manly Beach and had the freedom to play, the love and the laughter, the support and the nurturing, and all those things I grew up with that made me a world champion surfer. So, when I came to this realisation, I actually admitted my wrongdoing. I wrote her a card and I bought her a necklace which said 'I love you Mum'. In the card, I said that I wasn't trying to prove you wrong, I was trying to prove myself right. And, I'm sorry, I hope you can forgive me. She wrote back that she didn't know how she was meant to take that. So, she rejected me again. Right as I reached out, as I offered the olive branch, I was completely shut down.

In the time since, I've had three men come forward, asking for DNA tests, all claiming to be my father. Three men.

Which also means they claim to have raped your mother. Or do they have a different story?

They've got a different story. That it was consensual. That it happened in Australia. After she gave birth to me, she moved out of here and went to New Zealand. Then she moved to San Francisco and married a gay guy to get her green card. They were lifelong friends and he left her his apartment when he died, and so she eventually came into money. On her death bed, she prided herself on telling me I had been written out of her will. She died several years ago from ovarian cancer.

How do you feel about all of that?

I don't know. Happy I met her. It was important that I met her. There are so many things I missed out on, but I reconciled that through a conversation we had before she died. I don't know if you've had a bedside vigil with someone that's dying – when you're present for that last spurt of life, that last spurt of energy. I thought she was going to come good.

I'm grateful Mum rang me to say they'd given her three weeks to live and to ask if I would come and say goodbye. I jumped on a plane the next day, to Spokane in Washington. I arrived there on the Monday night, visited her on the Tuesday morning with my half-sister Melissa. I was shocked to see how emaciated she was. We went again and saw her on the Wednesday which was the last time we spoke. We basically had a bedside confession.

'I'm so sorry, I love you, I forgive you.' And then she fell asleep and those were the final moments we shared.

A doctor once asked me if I thought my life was better off for trying to kill myself. And so, I'm asking you, did you have to hit the bottom?

No. We believe we have to hit rock bottom before we deserve more success or happiness. It's a fundamental misconception. It's a bullshit story we tell ourselves. I've won seven world titles. Six in a row. Five in a state of fear and two in a state of love. I know and have proven I can win in a different way. From a place of love instead of fear. But I also know at certain periods of time, I still believed that I wasn't worthy of love.

Were you angry with yourself?

I was, and I was disappointed in myself.

But you're at peace with all that now?

Totally, yeah. But look, to answer the question about what I have learned from hitting rock bottom, there's no way I would value my health the way I do today.

My health is critical. Vitality is my number-one value. Having the vitality to live a life that I love. If I don't have my vitality, then I have to look in the mirror and ask what am I doing to sabotage myself?

We've talked about the low and the suicidal thinking. Have you ever had that again in your life?

No, although I am susceptible to it and I am aware of it. My triggers are self-loathing, self-criticism, craving foods that are bad for me. Poor confidence. Seeking external validation or reassurance. When I'm experiencing any of those, I recognise I'm in a stage of burnout and fatigue. Something's gone wrong. Pushing too hard, demanding too much of myself. Not giving myself enough self-care. Not doing things that light me up. Putting my life on the backburner by serving everyone else.

So, these days, is that often because you're a giver? Working too hard in your business, foundations and other organisations? How does that come about?

At the moment, it's coming about because I'm caring for a father with dementia. I'm building a business. I'm a chairperson, I'm a director, I'm a charity ambassador. I'm a mental wellness advocate and speaker. I'm a wife. I'm a sister. I'm doing too much. And the more we give to others, the less we give to ourselves. I know now that for me to be able to show up and do what I do on a day-to-day basis, I have to do something for me. So, this morning, for example, I've been up since five o'clock doing a photo shoot at the beach. But I chose to not leave the beach until I'd spent at least ten minutes in the water. I have to be in the water. That's my happy place to rinse my mind, body and soul.

The ocean is my womb. That's where I feel held, that's where I feel nurtured. That's where I feel safe. So, I have to get back in the water. Back to where it all began.

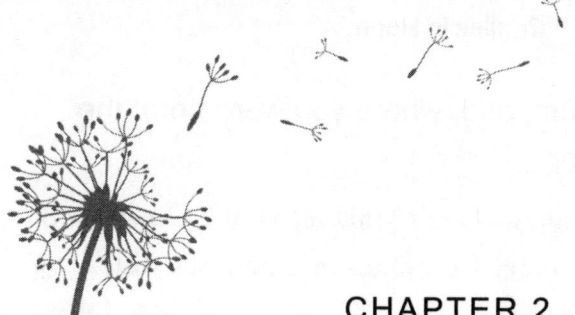

CHAPTER 2

Matthew Caruana

The Comeback Kid

Matthew Caruana is a young man from north-western Sydney who is using his experience to make a difference for others. I'd never met Matthew before I started researching for this book, but as I was about to meet a young man who was in a wheelchair as a result of his failed suicide attempt, I expected to encounter a person living with a permanent reminder of his suicidality and all that encompassed.

When putting this book together, during many of the interviews, I asked the question, 'Do you think your life is better for having tried to kill yourself?'

I asked Matt this with added emphasis. 'This is especially relevant to you, Matt, as you live every day in a wheelchair, having lost your mobility.'

His answer actually took my breath away.

* * *

Tell us about your mum, dad, where you were born, the house you grew up in.

I'm half-Greek, half-Maltese. Dad's Maltese, Mum's Greek. Both my parents were born here. I grew up in The Hills district of Sydney.

Dad was hard working, a carpenter, working for himself. He taught me hard work ever since I was young and what it meant to have discipline. I remember when I got my first Game Boy Advance, he was like, 'What is this? Come help me unload the truck!' A very practical man.

Dad grew up out at Kenthurst. They had all this land. They were always working. Ever since I was four I was downstairs with my dad, and ever since I was ten, during school holidays I was out working with him on site, and he'd pay me $50 a day.

He was teaching me the value of hard work from day one. As a teenager I didn't see that. But that's exactly what he was doing. Mum – I suppose we were a typical wog family – she stayed at home. Cooked, cleaned, washed, shopped. That was her thing. She helped Dad out with the invoicing and did the books.

I'm the eldest of three. I've got a sister, Christina, who is two years younger. And my brother, Alex, is four years younger.

Was it a happy family?

There was tension. Mum and Dad would fight a lot when I was growing up. I used to look at that and just step away from it. Wouldn't say anything. My brother and I would get into one another, as brothers do. My sister and I were pretty close. Out of everyone in the family, I was closest with her I'd say.

What were you hoping to do when you left school?

It changed over time, yeah. When I was a kid I used to love Michael Jackson. I used to look at him and think there was something about him. The way he would perform, capture the audience. I was like, wow! I still to this day vividly remember the morning he died. I remember crying.

I didn't want to be a singer, but for years I wanted to be a musician. I started by DJing, and then in Year 9 I was told that DJing is not an instrument! If you do music, you have to pick up something else. So I played guitar and that was my excuse to get out of Commerce. I didn't tell my dad, because he wanted me to get into business.

Did you go to Year 10 or Year 12?

I went to Year 10, but I had my suicide attempt at the end of Year 10. I went back to high school, but I didn't finish Year 11 and 12. However, I stayed until the end, finishing half of my subjects.

What led to the suicide attempt?

It's coming up on eight years. I was sixteen at the time, but I'd been thinking about it for a few years. At the age of twelve, I thought that I was worthless. Back then I never had a solid plan. I really started thinking about it a year later, looking at different methods, going online, doing research.

Why did you feel worthless?

That's a tricky one.

Growing up Catholic, I was always hearing that everything happens for a reason. Everyone has a purpose. I was asking myself, what the hell is my purpose? Why am I here? I came to the conclusion that I was worthless. I was living at home with my parents. I had no job. I was just taking up space.

I'm asking myself, what is the purpose of my life? I mean, it's a tough question to answer. If I was gone and dead would anything change? Do I actually add value to anyone else? And that's when I figured out that, well, no, I don't have anything to contribute. I feel like I'm just taking up space and that I'm worthless, at the end of the day. I was trying to fight those thoughts and come up with different answers to those questions, but nothing else made sense.

Also, at the age of twelve, I unwittingly stumbled upon a secret that impacted a family member. I was sworn to secrecy. Only I knew this thing.

Any family secret is a burden to carry for someone so young.

Yes. In between those four years – from twelve to sixteen – from the outside it looked like everything was perfect. Bodybuilding had become my way of showing people that I was doing well. That I was smashing my goals and all that stuff. I had this reputation at school of being the biggest kid. Because I was obsessed with the gym.

I was six foot, and built, because I'd worked my arse off.

That was your passion, weightlifting?

It was actually my insecurities playing out. Not feeling good enough. That I was worthless, needing to prove myself. I needed to be the man, be strong.

Everything on the inside is crumbling, so the outside at least can look like an edifice that's worth admiring.

In 2015, at the very beginning of that year I had this vision. I was on school holidays. I'm going to bulk up and get back to school, in like four or six weeks, and no-one is going to recognise me. I'm going to bulk up, I'm going to get cut. All for one photo to post on Facebook. I knew the exact pose. I knew everything, how I was going to look. It's crazy. I was going to the gym every day for an hour and a half, sometimes two hours, depending on the day. I put on 30 kilograms in eight months, all for that photo.

Were you happy with the photo?

Yeah, I thought it was perfect.

That was literally a week before my suicide attempt. I posted that photo on Facebook and everyone believed I was doing well. And you know, it sort of dawned on me pretty quickly that I put in all this work for this little photo, then people just hit 'like' and scrolled on past. I was worth nothing more than half a second of their attention. That's it. And like … all that weight I put on, put off, whatever.

You got to this peak that you'd trained for and gone through extraordinary physical change to achieve, and then a week later, you tried to kill yourself?

Out in public, people would stare, if I was at the beach. I wanted that. However, all the effort and all that attention was just feeding insecurity. At the end of the day you're not left with anything other than yourself. Just me, always looking in the mirror. I'd be flexing all the time. There was always something I was missing. I was never big enough, I was never strong enough.

I had a girlfriend. We'd been together since April 2013, when I was in Year 8. The night I tried to kill myself she was with her best friends, sleeping over, so I didn't talk to her or anything. I didn't want to disturb her. I was already feeling pretty shitty that day to start off with. At that point she was the closest person in my life. Right before, I sent a text to her – she was the only person I left a message for. And when you're at that point you don't hold back. Some of the sweetest things I ever said to her were in that text.

She was the only person from my contacts or Facebook friends that I thought would care the slightest bit. Even anyone in my family. I spent all this time just writing all my thoughts out, exhausting them. Except saying what I was going to do. I just said, this is it, I can't take this anymore. Then I sent the message, left my phone on the bed. I didn't want anything to hold me back because I knew for certain what I was going to do. I visualised exactly, this plan for over a year of, how I was going to do it. The time of day, where. I just didn't know when.

So, at the same time as you are bulking and cutting, you have a plan to kill yourself in parallel?

Yeah, happening at the same time. I was always thinking about killing myself. I'd be in school and just zone out. And even just leave school and think about it. I'd even go to where I was going to do it. I knew exactly what I was going to do. It's like I wrote a fucking script for it and it played out.

It was eleven o'clock at night. No-one around.

I wanted to die. A question I commonly get asked is, 'Matt, do you regret it?' The only thought I had when I did it was, *Finally*. It was a sense of relief. I remember the night vividly.

I was found at around six o'clock the next morning.

You were there for seven hours?

Something like that, yeah, because they were doing construction there. The tradies found me.

My dad woke up and saw the door to the garage was left open. Where's Matt? He's already thinking, shit, where's Matt? I don't know what was going through his mind. I used to sneak out, they never knew. But they were panicking. They didn't know what to think, yeah. After he'd searched the house he called the cops. The tradies had already called the cops, so then they put two and two together.

My girlfriend didn't see the text I'd sent for about half an hour. After which there were non-stop missed calls and texts from her. She tried all throughout the night to get a hold of me and it wasn't until five o'clock in the morning, she actually said fuck, I think he's done it.

I woke up in hospital, two weeks later, having been in a coma.

Do you have any memories of when you were in that coma?

Not really, no. It was just a black period for me. When I first woke up I thought it was the afterlife at first. The Intensive Care Unit [ICU] was a big blur. Conversations there I don't remember. The only thing I remember was a CD player. Because my family knew I loved music they brought in a CD player, and when people came to visit they would buy CDs they knew I would like, and they would play music and all that.

It's the only thing that's really stuck with me. Along with the thought that, if I was worthless beforehand, how pathetic am I now?

I quickly realised I couldn't feel or move anything below my waist. I was heavily medicated. I couldn't even sit up. I had no ab muscles. I couldn't move my legs, they weren't working. I had tubes going through me, a neck brace, a cast on both arms and boots on my feet, in a hospital bed.

I remember when they broke the news to me, when I was in the spinal ward, which was a month later. They brought in this MRI of my spinal cord. It was in two. I'd severed my spinal cord at T12. The bottom thoracic. There was a clear cut. They told me this was the reason I would never walk again. That this is the highway of the nerves connecting the brain to the body, and wherever it's injured on the body, everything below it is affected. Sensation, function, bladder, bowel, sexual function. All that stuff. Look, if there's ever a nightmare at sixteen years old, knowing you'll never get it up again is pretty much up there.

You come out of the coma. It's all a blur. You remember music. People come and go, it's not registering. But what did register is you're still as miserable as you were before. Did you feel like trying to kill yourself again?

I was constantly thinking, alright, what's my next out?

The greatest indicator of a potential suicide attempt is a previous suicide attempt. If you've made an attempt before, you are more likely to try again. We used to just discharge people from mental health clinics. Thanks for coming, see you later. They'd often just walk straight out and take their own life. Now, thank god, there's a program to help people when they leave hospital.

I just felt like suffering at that point. As if I wasn't already doing it tough, finding out that there's no hope, that was the hardest part of all. Then it was like, why didn't I do it properly?

I just kept thinking that.

How long were you in the spinal ward?

The ICU, one month. Spinal ward, three months. They kept me back because of my mental health. Physically, I was ready for rehab way before. Thankfully I was quick to adapt, being young, and also my physical shape beforehand gave me a huge advantage, although I broke both my wrists with my injury, so that kept me back a little bit. I was in casts for a good two months. Then I finally got them in splints, and they only got them off a couple of weeks before I left.

I had a brain injury as well. They shaved the top and sides of my head, left the back. I'm like, come on, finish the job! It really affected my memory at the time, and also my problem-solving skills. They had this test. They'd come in every day. 'Hey, Matt, what's your name? Where are you? What time of day? Here are three images, remember them for tomorrow morning.'

I was on suicide watch almost the entire time I was in hospital. For the first two months, twenty-four hours. Then after that it was sixteen hours a day. Then it was eight hours when I was in a chair. It was only the last week I was in hospital where I didn't have someone watching me. I wasn't allowed outside the hospital grounds unless I had my mum or girlfriend with me. They were the only two people I was allowed to have. There was only one day in hospital where I actually had a little bit of freedom. I went and got a coffee and went to a local physio clinic.

The first wheelchair I was in, I wasn't allowed to push or control myself. They wouldn't get me a motorised one, someone else had to push me. There were no handles, no push rims, just little wheels the size of my hand. That drove me nuts.

They were worried that, being independent, you'd be free to try to take your own life again. Were they asking that question, are you still a threat to yourself?

That was a question they'd ask pretty often. I mean, I was seeing a psychologist so much. Twice a day for quite a while. I was refusing all antidepressants. A week before I left they gave me an ultimatum: Matt, we can send you to the psych ward or you take at least one of them, which I did.

What was happening with school and family? Did they tell the other kids at school that you'd tried to kill yourself?

Word got around pretty quick, at least within my grade, that I tried to kill myself. There were rumours going around about all these different things. People were saying I'd overdosed on steroids. All this bullshit. My year group was pulled aside at the very beginning of Year 11. They said, look, Matt's not going to be at school for a while. I do know that my close mates, my girlfriend at the time, my brother and sister, they all got counselling from the school counsellor, often.

Did the doctors think you were going to make it out of the coma?

They weren't too sure. When I was in the coma, my sister brought this little journal for anyone that wanted to write a message to me while I was unresponsive. I remember when I came out of the coma people telling me, 'Matt, you should look at this journal. You know, read it.' I knew it was there, but I never wanted to look at it. People would bring it up every now and then, and I would say no.

Years later, I'd forgotten about the journal and my brother one day suggested we go upstairs to my old room. I was sleeping downstairs at the time. So, my brother wheelbarrowed me, as kids do, and we got upstairs. I hadn't been up there since my injury. This was now four years later. There was my old little cabinet. I wanted to know if there was anything still left in it, and there was that journal. The first page I opened was the back. Of all the fucking people, it was my dad's message. That broke me. It was half a page of questions. *'What did I do wrong? What could I have done differently? What did I miss? What didn't I do? I'm sorry I failed you.'* Dad was the one guy that I never see cry. Never. In hospital was the first time I've seen him get teary.

It was never anyone's fault. I chose to do it. No-one made me. It's a fifteen-minute fucking walk from my place to the place. There was plenty of time to have a second thought, but I was the one who did it.

When was the first time you decided you wanted to live, that you didn't want to kill yourself?

Four months after I'd first come into hospital, I was with my mum and we went to Penrith, because I wanted to get some piercings. I was obsessed with piercings at the time.

I wanted to get two dermals in my eyebrow. I got them and it was like I'd achieved a goal in my own mind. I was feeling good about myself, and then on the train trip back, this guy, probably in his fifties, a complete stranger, got on. Never met him before. A real down-to-earth Aussie bloke. Before he even sat down he saw me in my wheelchair, and he asked, 'What did you do to yourself?' He was real loud about it too.

I don't know whether it was how loud he was or how I felt with these piercings, but I just told him I had attempted suicide.

He was the first person I told. Everyone who had asked before, I said I'd had an accident or a fall. I'd never told them the truth. His response was, 'Well, that was pretty fucking stupid, wasn't it? Look at you now.'

Then he sat across from me and said, 'So you've attempted suicide and you're in this wheelchair. What are you going to do about it now?'

I didn't know how to respond. But that question left a mark on my mind.

This complete stranger wanted to have this conversation and I didn't know how to respond to him. He got off the train and Mum was like, 'What was all that about?' She'd sat silent the whole time. She was in shock.

What an extraordinary story. That bloke could have missed the train or got on another carriage. How incredible.

I never so much as got the guy's name.

Would you like to meet him?

I would love to meet him. I don't know who he is.

What would you tell him?

I'd just say, thank you. You gave me a gift that I never knew I needed. That one question, what are you going to do about it now? At the time it meant nothing to me, but the next morning I felt lighter for some reason. I went and saw my social worker without her chasing me up. And this was the first time I was open and shared with her. I told her everything about the guy on the train and how it made me feel. She asked me if I thought it was a sign. I said, 'What are you talking about?' This is what she said: 'Matt, you'd been lying to people for four years about how you were feeling. You've now been lying to people for four months about what's happened. The first time you actually told someone the truth, you felt lighter. What if you opened up to the people close to you in life? Could you potentially strengthen the relationships you already have with them?' I remember those words so clearly, because I just didn't want to hear it. 'What if you were to open up?'

I cut her off. I didn't like that idea, I never had. But my girlfriend came to visit that afternoon, and everything just came out. She was asking how I was, and I said, I'm not doing well. For the first time in our relationship, I was being honest with her. In that moment I was able to see the world as though I was standing in her shoes. She was the same age as me, sixteen. Just started Year 11, and every day at three o'clock she was jumping on two buses to visit me. Every afternoon. Every day in the holidays.

She was supporting me at a time when I didn't want any of it. I was pushing it away. I remember how emotional I was. I was just in tears. I mean, just saying all this stuff to her. I pulled out my phone and scrolled to that photo on Facebook where I was ripped. I said, 'What are you doing? That's a man. Why are you still with me? Here I am, I'm in a wheelchair.'

I loved her, but it was like, what are you doing? I don't have any of the muscles anymore. They melted quickly. And not only that, I'm in a fricking wheelchair. I can't feel or function or anything from my abs down. There's nothing there.

But she kept coming?

She told me that in the photo I had all the muscles, that I looked great, but she'd never seen a bigger man in front of her than the man I was in that moment.

So this random stranger boarded the train, told you to wake up to yourself, and then got off the train. And that's the turnaround. That's an incredible story.

And asked that question: 'What are you going to do about it?'

The kindness of strangers. In this case, the honesty of a stranger.

My mum was asking, 'Matt, why did you do it, why did you do it?' She just wanted an answer.

That same social worker asked me to come back for a meeting at the end of 2016, not even a year after my injury. They said they had this program at the hospital aiming to prevent trauma in youth and would I be open to sharing my story? I never liked speaking so I was like, nah, I think I'll pass. But then she reminded me of the guy on the train and what it did for me.

That played in my head. As that guy on the train said – 'What are you going to do about it?' I used to just feel sorry for myself. But the world doesn't stop. Those people are moving whether I'm alive or not. The sun's going to shine tomorrow. No-one gives a shit.

So, when she reminded me of the guy on the train, it was like this voice just said yes for me. I didn't even think about it. What if I helped someone? How would that feel? So the first time sharing was the beginning of March 2017. The manager of the program was just asking me questions to prompt me, to get it out. I was shaking afterward. But these thirty or so kids, same age as me, came up to me and said thank you. I'd inspired them. Some said they wanted to help their friends after hearing me speak. I remember that vividly, because that was the first time I heard that I wasn't worthless and believed it. These were someone else's words. Not just mine. They didn't know me, why should they tell me this? They were just thirty or so kids from a local high school.

And what are you doing now?

I figured I wanted to follow through with speaking. What it was really about at the end of the day was being an example of hope for others. That's what it was. And if people are coming to me and saying 'you inspired me', it's like, well, wow. If me sharing my story can do that – what else can I do? At eighteen I found a mentor and started cold-calling schools. 'Hi, my name is Matt Caruana. I attempted suicide at sixteen, I turned my life around. I'd love to speak to your students about mental health and suicide.'

That's a hard pitch to knock back. What was the success rate with schools?

Zero. For ages. So, I gave up knocking on doors and I started picking up the phone. They would ask me to send them an email. That was the polite way of saying no. I probably came off as very brutal and up-front. The first gig I ever got was Glenwood High School in 2018. I'll never forget that.

About 200 students in the school auditorium. I had a few slides with me. I was given an hour. When I got to the Q&A, no-one had their hands up. They were just uncomfortable. And maybe me too. Then I spoke at Pittwater House [a private school on Sydney's Northern Beaches]. That was the school that brought the thirty kids to my first talk in the hospital. They asked me to come.

What was different about that gig was that people started sharing and asking me about what they could do to support themselves and support their friends as well. On the drive home Dad asked me, 'Do you see yourself doing something with this?' And I thought yeah, I want to take this somewhere.

When was the last time you thought about suicide?

The way I'd like to answer this is I'm in a different mindset now. It's not something that I consciously think about. I'm aware if the thought comes up. And the thought hasn't come up in, I would say about eight months. It's like I'm sitting at a cafe and I watch a car go by. I see the car. I know it's there. But then it's gone and I don't see it anymore.

You know how to deal with it? You've learned how to let the thought come and go?

The body that I built before my injury was a great representation of all of these strengths I had inside me. Ultimately that goal wasn't great, but it took a lot of discipline, hard work, self-belief, persistence and consistency. The difference is that today I take those strengths and I don't use them for my insecurities, I now direct them toward what's purposeful.

Before, my thoughts defeated me. The moment I tried to kill myself, my spirit had died. There was no turning back. Those thoughts had conquered me. Now, when the thought comes up, I don't feel like I used to feel. It's just a passing thought.

Do you feel worthy now, Matt?

Yeah, I do. I'm just very blessed to be in the position I am now.

This question is particularly relevant to you because you've lost part of your mobility. Is your life better because you tried to kill yourself?

Absolutely. It's the one thing I'm most grateful for.

At this point, Matt wheeled himself back from the table we were sitting at. Without saying a word, he lifted his right leg, bending it at the knee and raising it around 20 centimetres. Then he lifted his left leg 10 centimetres. It actually took my breath away.

I've lost part of my mobility, but I am going to walk again.

This morning I was at Royal Rehab in Putney. They have this robot called the Lokomat. It's the world's leading medical device for physiological gait rehabilitation. There's a treadmill and there's a hoist for a bit of weight support. I put on the harness, which connects to the hoist, and it supports my stance as I 'walk' on the treadmill.

Royal Rehab also have this thing called the Exoskeleton, which is like a wearable mobile machine. I was on that for a year and I started on the Lokomat this week. I call it the Everest of my goals, but walking again is what I want to do. As far as I'm concerned, I'm already walking in my mind, I'm just waiting for my body to catch up.

Everyone must be so proud of what you're doing.

Yeah, they are, thankfully. I always live by the motto: 'What are you going to do about it?' Because there are always going to be new challenges in life. I'm continually turning my goals into tangible achievements, whether it be a successful Guinness

World Record, representing Australia in the emerging Aussie Rollers or being a part of two start-up companies.

And you are the living, rolling definition of inspiration.
Thank you for sharing your story.

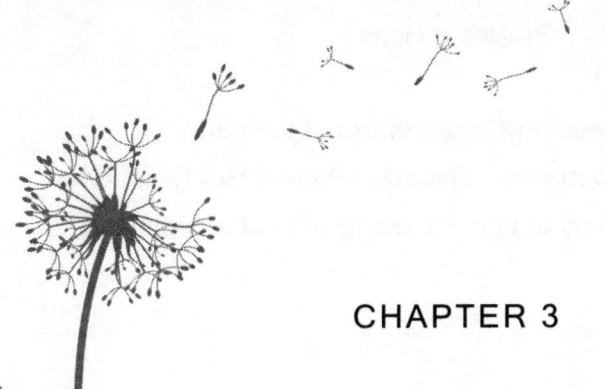

CHAPTER 3

Pat Hall

The Local Champion

Patricia Hall OAM grew up in a traditional Australian working-class home. Born in the 1950s into a loving, hard-working, Catholic family, she married young, had three sons and was a loyal housewife, as was the norm at the time. Her life could almost be called ordinary.

Then her husband left her for another woman and her world shattered in tiny, irreparable pieces. Seeing no way forward, she tried to end her life.

But she survived.

It's what Pat has done in the second half of her life that is anything but ordinary. In Warwick Farm, Liverpool, in suburban Sydney, Pat started helping some of the poorest people in Australia. Migrants, refugees and people trapped in real poverty and disadvantage.

Today she is the CEO of Liverpool Neighbourhood Connections, a not-for-profit centre transforming lives by lifting people out of poverty through social enterprises that help them start their own business and take control of their life.

But you've still probably never heard of Patricia Hall OAM. I went out to southwest Sydney to see Pat doing what she does best.

* * *

Before we dive into where the Pat Hall story starts, can you give us a snapshot of where it ended up, at the worst moment?

I don't know whether it was rejection. I don't know whether it was that I'd lost everything. Perhaps I'll never know. But I knew I couldn't survive. I thought, I can't do this. If anyone ever says you've got to stay strong for your kids, that's the wrong thing to say. I wasn't any good to the kids. I couldn't get out of bed in the morning, I couldn't exist. I don't believe I was selfish. I've heard that said, but I don't believe it. I just didn't want to be here anymore. If something hurts you, you try and stop the hurting. If you've got a pain in the head, you take a Panadol for it. I had a pain in the heart and I had to stop it.

Can you tell us the story of that pain. Where does it begin?

I led a very, very protected life. I grew up in Bass Hill. My father was in World War II, my mother was a real hard worker, and my grandmother was a card-carrying member of the Communist Party. I was the youngest of three kids, and the reason I'm telling you this is because that sets the scene for why I didn't cope. I grew up in this family where you couldn't swear in front of Trish – they called me Trish – you weren't allowed to do anything in front of Trish. I was the golden child. It was a very stable house, a wonderful life.

I met my husband when I was fifteen. His family were very middle class, a lovely family. His mother was different to my mother. My mother liked to bet, my father had greyhounds and was an apprentice jockey before the war. My husband's family wasn't like that. They were a very wholesome family. We got married when I was twenty-one. I'd never even had sex before, I was one of those people who did the right thing. I still do the right thing too much now. I was just that sort of person.

I went to business college, and then I got a job as a junior secretary at Selleys chemical company. I ended up being the secretary to the New South Wales State Manager.

At that age, did you see your purpose in life as getting married and having kids? Like your mum?

I'm not like my mum. When my mum died, I found out that she and my dad were never married. I was really shocked.

I didn't want kids. I was really good as a secretary and then they offered me this job as assistant to all the sales managers. I was so excited to take it, and then I found out I was pregnant. It happened by accident. That really changed the course of my life because I wasn't maternal, but I had a son and was very happy. Three years later, everything started to go wrong. We had a second son and I got really sick the week after he was born. They thought I was going to die, thought I had some sort of rare leukaemia. I didn't get to see or hold my new baby until he was three months old because I couldn't look after him. He was taken off me. My liver was failing, I only had seven white blood cells left.

The first night in the hospital they told my husband I would die, and then they said the same thing for five more nights, that I wouldn't survive. But I did. My father hated hospitals, yet he'd leave work to come and sit with me every single day. I used to say, I'm dying, and he'd tell me I had to stay alive for my two boys.

Mum stayed with me when I got out so I could bring my little newborn home. My father took one look at my baby boy and said, 'Look at the little fellow, let me give him a kiss.' That was on the Friday. Dad died the following Tuesday of a massive heart attack.

Dad was fifty-eight, and he died on my birthday, which is really hard because I was so close to him. People said that he died so I could live. So many people told me that, but my mother, who was obviously heartbroken, said that while Dad loved me, he certainly didn't give up his life for me.

It nearly killed me. The specialist wanted to put me back into hospital, but I was adamant I was going to Dad's funeral. They weren't going to take that away from me. I think a psychologist would look back and say that Dad's death was probably the first thing that had affected my mental health and me as a person.

Mum really suffered after my dad died. She used to fight with Dad all the time, but once he died she had no-one, and said she didn't want to live. It was really hard for the next two years. She had cancer and never told anyone. I had no idea. I decided that I was going to have another baby, even though they said I couldn't have any more. I got pregnant, but I didn't tell my mother because I knew she'd be upset and worried. It was about then I started to suspect she was sick. I finally got up the courage to tell her I was pregnant and, as predicted, she wasn't happy with me. She thought I might die in childbirth. My baby was due early February, but Mum died on 30 December, so she never got to see her third grandson.

Did that affect you?

Not as much as when Dad died. I gave the church away, I couldn't believe in God anymore. I couldn't read a book – and I used to read a book every week. I couldn't even read a magazine. Because my mother suffered, I was glad when she died, because she was such a strong woman and I hated to see her reduced to how she was when she died at sixty-two. So, I'd lost both my parents. But life goes on. For a little while it was hard, but I got through it. You've got to when you've got kids.

Were you a working mum?

I didn't work until my youngest son was six years old. I saw a job in the paper for a clerical assistant at a neighbourhood centre. I didn't even know what a neighbourhood centre was, but I thought, I can do this, and so applied for it. I got the job, and really liked it, and it showed me what community work does.

When my youngest was six years old, my husband told me that he didn't want to be married to me anymore. He told me he was attracted to a woman at work. I cried on the shoulder of a friend across the road, and it turned out she was who he wanted, not me. I asked him to go to marriage counselling, but he wanted none of that. I'll never forget the night he left me. I was sitting in the lounge room with the three boys next to me. He walked out, said he was going, took his golf clubs and that was it. I really didn't cope. They say it was because I lost my mother, father and husband within ten years. My security was all gone.

How old were you then?

I was thirty-nine. There was this occasion when I woke up in the middle of the night and I had this thing about cutting myself. It was just something in my head. I can't tell you why.

I was telling everyone I was okay, but I knew I wasn't. I went to the local doctor and he got me into a psychiatrist straight away. He told me I needed to go to hospital immediately and I said, 'I can't go to hospital. I've got three kids.'

I told him I was suicidal, but I didn't tell him about wanting to cut myself. I made a deal with him to wait until the next week, when I could organise the kids and then go to the hospital. But the whole time I was planning for my husband to have the kids so I could kill myself. I didn't have any doubts.

I knew what I was going to do. I was thinking, I'm going to kill myself when he takes the kids. I'll do it then. I'll work it out. Everyone was hovering over me, the neighbours, my sister, and my best friend. I convinced them all not to worry about me so that in that time, no-one would twig what I was going to do.

They were worried you were going to kill yourself?

I don't know that they thought that, but they were certainly worried about my mental health. It's interesting how you can plan all this even though you are in this terrible state, but when you get into doing it, you're in some kind of void.

I was working toward this. Finally I had control over something. I'd had no control over my life, but I had control over taking my life. So, when my husband took the kids this one day, first of all I rang my sister and said, 'I'm okay. I'm fine.' That was her off my back. Then my neighbour from across the road came over to see how I was and I told her how good I was. I said that my husband had the boys and I just needed everyone to give me some space.

I then locked the house completely so no-one could get in. I had tablets to take, but I actually wanted to hurt myself. They say a lot of people want to hurt other people, but mine was self-inflicted. I got a knife, but I couldn't find a sharp one and I'm thinking, no wonder he left me – I can't even get this right. My husband had bought me a Eurythmics CD which I was playing. It was all these songs about love and so I had that going on too. I had the heater on, which I was sitting next to. I had the drugs. I had the knife, but I didn't know how to do it. I was in a void and I remember thinking when I started to bleed, I haven't said anything to my kids. That was sad.

You didn't think of writing a note?

No, I didn't think to do any of that but when I started to bleed I got a bit of paper and wrote 'I'm sorry kids', then simply signed it 'Mum'. That was it. I thought, they're better off without me, I can't function. I can't look after them. How can I do anything? And this is where fate kicked in.

My sister had called my best friend, who rang another friend and said, 'I'm really worried about Pat, we've got to get to her.' I thought I had put everyone off the track about what I was going to do. I swear that I'd locked every door and window in the house so no-one could get in, but I hadn't. As long as I'd lived there, I had never, ever opened my bathroom window. Never. Never, never, never. But for some reason, that bathroom window was open.

I didn't check it because I'd never opened it before. So, the girl next door, who had been at the end of the chain of phone calls, hoisted her twelve-year-old girl up so she could climb through the window. She said to her, 'Don't look anywhere else, go straight to the front door and let me in.' They told me I had to go to hospital, but I wasn't going. With the phone in her hand, my girlfriend gave me the option: I was either going with her or she was going to call an ambulance.

Were you upset they found you?

I was angry because I didn't want to be here.

Were they distressed?

Yeah, especially my best friend.

At the hospital, they said you either have to admit yourself or be scheduled. I thought, either way I'm gonna be stuck in this place, but all I was thinking was: I'm gonna get out of here and finish this. So, they put me in there and I met a nurse. She was a psych nurse. She was so out there, wearing big hats with daisies. She was a hippie. She had been through suicide – the same thing happened to her. She used to put an empty chair in front of me and say, 'That's your husband. You tell him what you think.' In the end she had me swearing at the chair. She saved my life.

She broke all the rules after I got out of hospital. She took me out, she took me into the city, she showed me a lot I hadn't seen before. Now remember, I was a good Catholic girl that had never done anything out of the ordinary, and now here I was with this nurse and we were in Balmain, dancing 'til four o'clock in the morning with two gay guys. She showed me a side of life I never knew existed.

And that was quite deliberate? She wanted to take you out of your old life?

She did. The psychiatrists said my parents loved me too much, they didn't let me experience any heartache. They didn't let me worry about money. They didn't let me experience life. So, I did that for a while and then I went to outpatients for a couple of months.

Pat, when did you stop wanting to kill yourself?

The hospital was the worst place for me. The first night there was very scary. Patients were all lined up for tablets. It was winter, pouring rain and dark. I thought, what the hell am I doing here? Where am I? What have I done? I'm locked up now and I still want to kill myself. It hit me.

I didn't want to be there. They're the ones that worked out what was wrong with me. They said I had no self-esteem, no confidence in myself, and they were right. They made me do a course on building up my self-confidence. And I can honestly say that with the course, the support I got from work at the neighbourhood centre and the hippie nurse, all those things came together.

When I came out of it after ten weeks, I wondered why the hell I'd done that. I think I had to get to that point in my life to turn it around, because if I didn't hit the bottom, I would have never gained that self-confidence I have.

But you wanted to die.

No shadow of a doubt. I wasn't doing it so people would feel sorry for me. I didn't want to be here, I wanted out. I didn't want to face this anymore, I didn't want to get up in the morning. But, I got over it and I started to have a life.

I went to university, did this course at UTS, a Diploma in Community Management.

Was that the first time you'd sat down in front of a book in some time?

Yeah, I was forty-something. Absolutely loved it. That's when I met my second husband. We were introduced about two years after my marriage broke up. Like me, he was going to take his own life. He was devastated when his wife left him, so he got in his car one night to end it, but somebody stopped him.

So, then everything's great. My new partner becomes engrossed in his life and he works seventeen hours a day and he moved in with me. Bad mistake. He's living with me, but I never see him. He coaches grade cricket as well as running an indoor cricket centre. He worked himself to a state of nervous breakdown. He was probably still dealing with his own demons. Things started to go wrong, we were breaking down. I had kids, his kids were older, all grown up and he wanted to run away. He hated what he was doing, and he kept saying to me, 'If it was only you.' I said, 'Well it's not only me, I can't.' So, we split up, and once again I fell into that spiral – and it was a deep and dark spiral.

Did it happen quickly?

Very quickly. He moved out and here I was again. I was so bad that I remember thinking about suicide, but then I thought, no that's not the answer, that's not gonna change it. I know I can get better, I know that. But I stopped eating, which is something I do when I'm stressed. I can go two weeks without eating. It happened when my husband left me, it happened then, and

68

it happened when one of my sons was diagnosed with mental health issues.

I went to my doctor and he gave me sleeping tablets, which probably wasn't the answer. I wasn't sleeping, I was crying all the time, I was a mess. I lost all this weight again.

I had to re-enrol in uni. It's funny how life does these things. The train broke down. I was stuck on the train for two hours. As I sat on the train, I thought, I can't do this. I can't re-enrol in uni. I have to work my life out because I'm spiralling down and I knew I was going to get to the point where I would be suicidal again. So, the train breaking down, it was like God watching over me.

So that represented a pause?

I knew I had to let my partner go. We left as friends. He went to New Zealand and I decided to go see my aunty, who's a lovely woman. She was in Bundaberg. I needed to be with someone who was non-judgemental, and that's my aunty to a tee. That's what I needed to heal my heart and make me stronger.

My girlfriend and I went out the night before I left, and I was happy for the first time. I'd had a good time out on the town. The next morning, I hopped in the shower, bent down to wash and condition my hair and that was it, I blacked out. I passed out in the shower. I must have fallen under the spot where the water flows because I burnt myself badly.

My son found me and I went to Westmead Hospital, to the Burns Unit. I was there for nine and a half weeks with burns to seventeen and a half per cent of my body. It was in there that I grew again. I'd grown when I'd tried to kill myself and I grew again now. This time, the burns I sustained made me tougher. They changed me to become very, very resilient.

Are you better off because you got burnt?

I think so. I look horrible in places I'm not going to show you, but I'm better off.

All my life experiences made me stronger. I thought, I'm not going to kill myself. I'm not going to let this get to me. When I got out of the hospital, my skin wasn't fully healed, I was still healing. I wore burn suits for two years. I had to have a nurse come in every second day. I had to take a big jelly cushion everywhere just to be able to sit down.

This psychiatrist in the hospital was bloody brilliant; he taught me so many strategies. When you come out, you're very scarred and you're very red. Now, it's white and it's mangled, but not red and ugly like it was when I first got burnt. The psych wanted me to look in the mirror every single night. He wanted me to find something that looked good to me. I thought, well, nothing looks good. Because I had burnt my arm badly, I had to go to the gym all the time and as a consequence, I built up these amazing breasts. Every night I used to look in the mirror and I would think, bloody hell, I've never had those in my life before! That psychiatrist was so right!

Even though my partner had been gone six months, his photo was still next to my bed. It was time for me to shove it in the drawer. Not long after, I was down at the cricket centre and he walked in. I had no idea he was back in the country. He didn't tell me. I could have killed him. I had never hit anyone in my life but I was ready to smack him in the mouth. I was thinking, how dare you come back, just when I've got my life back together? Of course, I still loved him and so I didn't hit him or tell him any of that. Instead, we got back together. I was just friends with him to begin with, then after a year or so we got back together, and we've been happily married twenty-five years now.

When did you begin to climb the ladder at Liverpool Neighbourhood Connections [LNC]?

After I finished uni there was a locum job going to be a coordinator. I was going to go for it, but then I thought, well it's only a temporary job and I don't want a temp job now that I am qualified, I want a real job. I thought, I'll stay where I am. Then this job came up, to be a coordinator here. It was me by myself, a lone worker.

You ran the whole thing?

Yeah. A coordinator had been here before, but there was nothing really happening. This was a hall that was leased out by the community. I decided I had to change things. This community was very needy, dealing with third-generation unemployed, druggies, housing commission types. The worst possible area.

There was a playgroup over here. It wasn't our playgroup, but I really wanted to do everything I could and I did a roster up for them. They were so rough that when I gave them this roster, this woman said to me, 'You know what the fuck you can do with that?!' She ripped it up in front of me. I thought, welcome to Warwick Farm.

How did you gain the ability to sell yourself, sell the programs and ask for funding?

My parents taught me that you didn't ask for money, you didn't do any of that. However, I'd been put in a role where I had to ask for money for the centre to survive. This is how the scholarship idea came to be. My idea was if I could give a woman a scholarship to learn something, rather than the government just give us $5000, then I could say, look what you are doing for this woman, you are changing this woman's life, rather than improving the centre. You're going to give that woman's kids the role-modelling to understand that Centrelink payouts are not a wage. Kids are going to see that Mum's earning money. Mum's going to be happier that she now has tools to get out of her situation. I thought, if I can develop that model, I can keep it here and then I would feel okay about asking for money. That's how I did it. And that's how the scholarship model developed.

And this extends to your belief in enterprises rather than just giving people money.

Yes.

Is the focus on women because of what happened to you?

The Neighbourhood Centre made me believe in myself. I said to myself, I'm going to help women, and I think I have.

And here they're from all over the world.

They're all from different countries. These people are just dirt poor. I guess I'm very passionate about helping women and you know what? I see how it changes their lives.

When did you hear about your Order of Australia?

I was really shocked about it. It was during COVID. I got a letter to say I'd been nominated, and I had no idea. I thought, *I won't get it*, but I was wrong. It was very humbling. People who get those awards should be volunteers, who give their time. I don't have time to volunteer cause I'm too busy working.

With Lifeline, I often say that the best outcome is that you never need to call us again. Is the best outcome for you that these people go off and have a working life and don't need the centre anymore?

Yeah, I feel really good when that happens.

You're dealing with people that most Australians don't even want to know exist.

These people out here, they've got nothing. Nothing. They can't speak English very well, so they're disadvantaged.

They've got cultural disadvantages. They've got language disadvantages. Some of them are domestic violence victims, but we can help them get away if they've got their own job. So, I believe however you can help them, it's good.

Pat, would any of this have happened if you hadn't tried to kill yourself?

No, none of it.

If you could go back to that day, just before you locked yourself in that house, and give yourself some advice, what would it be?

If I knew then what I know now about what I could achieve, I would say, think about what you are going to do in life. But you don't think about that at the time. Turns out, it was the best thing for me.

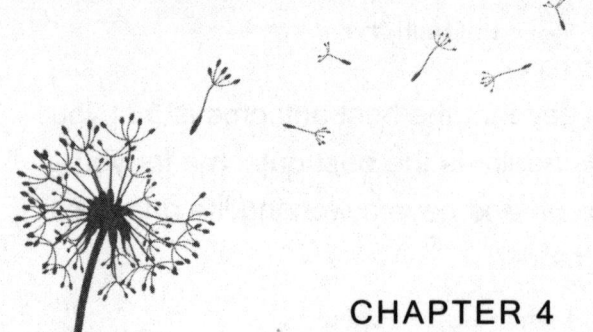

CHAPTER 4

Preston Campbell

The Rugby League Legend

Preston Campbell OAM is a legendary football champion, but it is through his work as a community leader and sports ambassador that he has really made an impact. When he was nine years old, Preston played his first proper game of Rugby League. He got knocked out cold. After that, he played soccer.

Preston went back to Rugby League at sixteen, playing for the Inverell Hawks. Five years later, in 2001, in his first full year playing first grade for the Cronulla Sharks, he won the Dally M Player of The Year — the award for the most outstanding player of the NRL premiership season. He is one of only a few players in the 45-year history of the award to win it for playing in more than one position.

For a sportsman, an award like this should be a triumph, but within months of winning it, Preston tried to end his own life. He survived. In 2003 he was part of the Penrith Panthers grand final-winning team. Since his suicide attempt, he has rebuilt his life and dedicated it to preventing suicide, focusing on Rugby League players and Aboriginal and Torres Strait Islander peoples especially.

* * *

Where did you grow up?

I come from the Northern Tablelands of New South Wales. I was born in Inverell, but grew up in Tingha, about 20 kilometres out. At the time, there would have been barely 800 people there. Tingha's one of those spots that'd be great for any young person to grow up in. Imagine a place where the landscape is your playground. Once an old tin-mining town, people came from all over the world for the tin, gold and different gems.

Brothers and sisters?

Younger brother and an older brother, two younger sisters and an older sister.

What did your mum and dad do?

For as long as I can remember, both my mum and dad worked on the CDEP [Community Development Employment Program]. It was a work-for-the-dole program, just for Aboriginal people. As a kid I didn't realise it was a government program, but it was what I wanted to do when I left school. That was my dream, to go into CDEP, because my mum and dad worked there. My brother and my sister worked on it at one stage as well. So did my uncles and aunties. I wanted to work on it because every time I saw them working together, they always had smiles on their faces. They were really happy to have a job, and they got to do training. Dad had multiple tickets on multiple machines. So he had qualifications. He was a hard worker, Dad.

So, good role models?

Definitely. That was the case for most young people in town, that they had a mum and a dad going to work on the CDEP. When the CDEP was in town, even though we did have our issues, the crime rate and the issues we had were pretty low.

Was Tingha your traditional area as well?

Yeah, yeah. They call that Gomeroi or Kamilaroi country.

And when you grew up, did you feel different or did you feel that you belonged?

I didn't see any difference. There wasn't a lot of talk about being Aboriginal, about culture, customs, language or traditions. We didn't dance. There were no stories. At least, I didn't experience any of that.

You didn't hear anyone talk about being a Gomeroi man?

No, I didn't understand that. It wasn't until later on in my life, when I did a lot of travelling around that I delved into that sort of stuff. There was a bit of an identity crisis when we eventually got a TV because we'd see people from the Top End, painted up, dancing, and speaking the language. I was the same colour as them, I kind of looked like them, but I was struggling to understand why I couldn't do what they did. At one stage there, as I got older, I would look at Aboriginal people and I'd think, I don't know if I can be like them.

When did footy come into your life?

Footy has always been around. Tingha's pretty famous for Rugby League players. Up in the Northern Tablelands people know of a lot of players that have come from Tingha. The Tingha Tigers is one of those footy clubs that has a history of over 100 years of Rugby League.

I had my first real game when I was nine. I was a small kid, so my mum didn't really want me to play contact sport. I got knocked out in my first game and it kind of scared me a little bit, so I changed and played soccer. It wasn't until I was sixteen that I went back and played Rugby League seriously.

And how about school? Did you like school?

Loved it, but more for the social side of things. I didn't understand why we had to go to school. I was told to go to school, but no-one told me why. I already had my idea of what I was going to do in life. I was never going to leave. I was going to spend the rest of my life in Tingha, working on the CDEP.

Did you experience any racism as a kid?

I don't know. I don't know whether it's because I was ignorant or whether I subconsciously ignored all that sort of stuff? Looking back, I know there was a bit of division between Aboriginal and non-Aboriginal people in the community. But I didn't understand that, and I still don't understand it. I know racism is a form of discrimination. I just don't know how I feel about it.

When people ask me, I say I don't know, but it's one of those conversations that some people are really, really sure about. I think if I'm not looking for it, I won't find it. Or if I'm not looking for it, I don't see it. Maybe it's because I don't like conflict all that much? I do look at other Aboriginal and Torres Strait Islander people and I see how hard they fight. And how loud they talk. They just want to be seen, you know. Want to be heard. I understand why they need to do it. But that's never been me.

What took you back to League at sixteen?

I had a cousin that I was playing soccer with – Nathan Blacklock. He'd play soccer in the morning, and Rugby League in the afternoon. He ended up playing for St George. We were playing soccer together, and then he stopped coming. I missed him, so I followed him across to Rugby League and started playing there.

The famous Tingha Tigers?

I never actually played for the Tigers. I was at the Inverell Hawks.

So, you went back to play with Nathan in Inverell?

We got to play juniors together, in the under-18s, in 1994. After that, he and a few others came to Sydney and Newcastle to try and forge a career in Rugby League at the elite level. They'd been scouted by the late Arthur Beetson [one of Rugby League's legendary 'Immortals' and the first Indigenous captain of a national Australian sporting team].

I had a lot of respect for Arthur. Amazing man. Not just as a Rugby League player, but the work he did afterward. Just a great human. I didn't really know who he was until I first met him in Wollongong.

I ended up making the NSW Country team when I was eighteen. We played against the City team, back in the day when it was City versus Country. We had a guy in the team playing hooker for us, and he had already been signed for the Roosters.

Arthur Beetson came in after the game, sat down next to me and started having a chat. I didn't know who he was. We got smashed that night. He was checking in on me and just told me to keep my head up. That was my first encounter with Arthur Beetson: him singling me out and me not realising who he was. Years and years down the track you figure out that was a pretty special moment.

When did you decide you wanted to be a professional League player?

A recruitment officer for the old Coast Chargers asked if I wanted to go up there for a trial. I'd never thought about leaving Tingha, but I thought I could be a chance, so I figured I might as well give it a go. I'd started to see Tingha in a different light as I was getting older, although I don't think the town was changing, I think I was the one changing. So yeah, I saw it as an opportunity and just went for it.

I played a couple of games and they said they wanted to sign me. That's how it worked back in the day. Then you shook hands, and worked out a contract. I signed for two years. Back then it wasn't an NRL contract, it was the ARL [Australian Rugby League] during the Super League war.

How did you adjust from little old Tingha?

Without a doubt, the hardest thing I had to do in my younger years was leave my home and family. I didn't realise it at the time, but the connection was so strong. I think for a lot of young people – man or woman, Aboriginal or not – they tend to feel the same way. Especially country kids. It's just a different culture. On the Gold Coast people walked different, they talked different.

They wore different things. They did different things. It was a strange feeling. I was also going into a culture where there was a big party lifestyle. You come in after a game and they've got three or four eskies full of beer. It was something I wasn't used to. After that, they wanted to go clubbing. I'd only go out because I was the designated driver. I didn't drink at all. After a while they started to respect that I wasn't a drinker, but in the beginning it was difficult.

Any mental health issues that came out of leaving home?

I cried myself to sleep for months, just wanting to come home. I was lucky that I had Mum and Dad telling me that if I came home they were going to boot me in the bum. So, they were really tough – at least, that's what I thought. I thought I'd ring them and they'd say, 'Come home,' but they encouraged me to stay and to give it a go. I'm glad they did. It's one of the biggest obstacles for any young person, leaving home.

I caused a lot of trouble in the early days because I thought that if I got myself into trouble the club would send me home. There would be days I wouldn't turn up to training. It was intentional, because I wanted them to send me home. But they had faith in me.

I was thinking, if it works out, it works out. If it doesn't, well I'll just go back home. There wasn't any real plan on my part to be a Rugby League player. I've always had that attitude, I wasn't too worried about if it didn't work out. I could just go back.

But the Gold Coast went well for you.

It did. I went there in late 1996 and I debuted in 1998 in my first game, against the Balmain Tigers at Leichhardt Oval. It's still my favourite place to play. We got beat that night, but it's still my favourite place. It was the start of the NRL [National Rugby League] that year, because the ARL and Super League had merged, and the war was over. I was twenty, turning twenty-one. It was a pretty quick turnaround in terms of the way my footy career was going.

And your salary was going up?

No. We're talking back in the late nineties. It was just enough to get by for young players like me. Most players worked all day at another job and then came to training.

When I was a kid, all the League players were either garbos for the local council or cellarmen at the club. They all had jobs, usually with or around the club.

I was ground maintenance. So, where I lived, I'd step out of the door and I was at work. I looked after the gardens, I looked after the pool. It was a pretty cool job.

Then at the end of 1998, in forming the NRL, they streamlined, got rid of five or six underperforming clubs, the Chargers being one of them. I was ready to head back to Tingha when the club got a call from Johnny Lang, coach of the Cronulla Sharks. In the last game of the season we'd played Cronulla and I'd set three tries up. I had a pretty good game. Once Johnny heard that the Chargers were out of the competition, I got a phone call and was asked if I wanted to come down to Cronulla.

I had a yarn with my girlfriend, Lee, because we had a daughter by then, Tayla. I was a young dad with responsibilities. My priority was to take care of my family. As long as I did that, I was happy. It didn't worry me whether I played for my state or for my country. Taking care of my family, that was my goal. They'd been back in Tingha while I was up on the Gold Coast, then they'd joined me. Now it was a case of, do we want to go to Sydney?

So, down to Cronulla?

Yep, we all moved down. One-year contract with the Sharks. A very surfy-style place, but living on the Gold Coast was a good stepping stone. I think I might have struggled if I'd gone straight to Sydney from Tingha.

And was Cronulla the next step in your career, getting more serious?

The year we came down, I got Reserve Grade Player of the Year. On the basis of that, they signed me for two more years. I was now playing First Grade in my second season, and 2001 was when I sort of broke out and became a household name. I won the Dally M Medal, the NRL Player of the Year. Same as the Brownlow Medal for the AFL. That's when the pressure came.

I didn't notice it at the time, but there was this change in me. Suddenly it became less about taking care of my family, and turned into an addiction to the attention. I'd gone from being the unknown boy from the bush in '99 to being named best player in the competition in 2001, and I kind of got caught up in that hype.

Did it go to your head?

Definitely. It can be addictive. I think that's why a lot of men and women, when they come out of their chosen sports, struggle with that transition. It's there, and then it's gone all of a sudden, so there is a lot of struggle.

And that's when the problems came?

Life was great. Football was good. I was having fun playing football, taking care of my family. Life was awesome. It was my last year of my two-year contract with the Sharks. I was in negotiations with them. I wanted to stay, but I'm just a country boy – I never realised I should have been thinking a bit bigger.

That maybe you could get more pay at another club?

Being the person I am, I was just happy to put food on the table. So, I signed again with the Sharks.

They got you cheap, is that what you're saying?

Looking back now, somebody like Andrew Johns was probably on $700,000. When I won the Dally M, I got $80,000. That's a big difference. But again, I just asked for what I needed, and that was it.

So, another season with the Sharks?

I got to talk with the incoming coach of the Cronulla Sharks, Chris Anderson. He was going to be the coach for 2002, as Johnny Lang had gone off to Penrith. I sat down and had a conversation with him. I signed thinking I was going to be playing halfback or in the back line, but during this conversation, he mentioned that he'd signed another player to play in the position I was looking at, and that I would be playing hooker. I didn't really think of it that much. Again, I just went in with that attitude of mine: it's alright, I'll give it a go.

It wasn't until I jumped back into the car, directly after the meeting and was driving back home that I started feeling angry.

I was punching the steering wheel. By the time I got back home I was furious. It wasn't fair. I signed to play halfback. I can't remember what I said, but Lee could tell I was mad. But in all of that, I felt like I had to suppress the way I was feeling, because I didn't want it to be a big thing. I just wanted to play Rugby League and take care of my family. But then it turned into something else.

So, suddenly it's gone from you rolling with the punches, enjoying it, to things being serious.

I felt mad. I felt angry and I didn't know where that was coming from.

From there it just went downhill. I lost respect for the club. Lost respect for the people at the club. Lost respect for the coach. I just hated everyone. I'd come home from training or a game, throw my bag on the floor and go to bed. I disconnected from everyone, not realising I was doing it. I was angry, I was depressed. So many different emotions. But that was my way of dealing with it.

Then there was the drinking. I started writing myself off, and it affected my football. I was in the starting team, first round of the season against the Dragons, playing hooker. I can't remember what round it was, but soon enough I found myself in reserve grade.

Lee must have noticed the change?

Lee was the only one who did, but then, I did a great job in hiding the way I really felt.

Did the footy media look at it and say, this doesn't make any sense?

Yeah, but it didn't help me. I was thinking to myself, yeah, they're right, this shouldn't be happening. It was this ego-driven thing.

But you buried how you felt?

I did. Yeah, I did. And that's why I had to go to my bedroom and stay there, because I was always angry.

I never drank at home. But drinking was easy to disguise because again, it's part of the culture. You have a drink to celebrate or a drink to drown your sorrows. It's just a normal thing, nobody is going to think or know any different.

So you're down to reserve grade?

During this time, I asked for a release because I just wasn't happy. I wasn't going to play football anymore, but my manager had other ideas. I was going home to Tingha. I just wanted to go back to a place where I felt safe, somewhere I felt comfortable. And it would have been easy just to go home.

The Sharks eventually released me at the end of the season. Johnny Lang was coaching Penrith and he rang to see what I was doing. Even though I'd have been happy to go home, I still needed to take care of my family. So, I signed a contract to go and play with the Panthers.

Were you still angry?

I was a broken person by then. I'd been like this for over twelve months. Things at home weren't great. I thought it was fine, but Lee had other ideas. We'd been in Penrith probably a month or two when Lee upped and left with the kids. We'd had Jayden at Cronulla, in 2000. So, the family of four quickly became just me.

I couldn't understand why she wanted to leave. I was mad at her, and I was in this state again where I hated the world. Soon enough I got to a point where I thought, why am I doing this? The reason I'm playing football is gone now, so what's the point?

Did you hate yourself?

I didn't think of it that way. I was stuck in a loop of it being everybody else's fault. Lee was up in Ballina with her parents. I went up to visit a couple of days before Christmas, hoping that maybe we could work something out. When she opened the door I just saw the look in her eyes: 'What are you doing here?' She knew I was coming, but she didn't want me to be there, yet she understood that I needed to see the kids.

Did that make you angrier?

I don't think I could have gotten any angrier. When I saw that look in her eyes, it was like a lightbulb moment for me. I knew I'd lost her and I'd lost the kids. When I knew it wasn't going to work out it was like, nah. I jumped in the car.

Did you want to die? Did you want to kill yourself?

Yeah. I drove the car off the road. I wanted to injure myself so badly in the hope that I wouldn't wake up. But I did. I woke up in the helicopter flying to hospital in Lismore. My first thought was, you idiot, what are you doing? By the time we got to the hospital, I'd flipped. I was angry that I was still alive, and I was thinking of ways to kill myself.

When they asked if I wanted to contact somebody, I gave them Lee's number. I thought she'd feel sorry for me, but it was the opposite. She was mad at me. She brought her mum and they were both really angry with me. They were really upset that I'd done it.

Was it clear to them you wanted to kill yourself?

Lee knew, she put two and two together, but she didn't say anything. Neither did her mum. No-one else knew, not even the ambos. I told everyone it was an accident. I said I'd been training down the beach and on the drive I'd passed out. They didn't have any reason to think I'd done it on purpose. I mean, I had this public image, Preston Campbell, he's a good person, he's not going to lie, he's not going to hurt himself.

I didn't know how to tell people. It was the way I thought at the time. When you have a broken mind you think a little bit differently. I didn't want to be perceived as being weak. I didn't want to be thought of as less than a man, so I guess that's part of the reason why I didn't tell people.

Three days in hospital, then my cousin came and took me back to Penrith. He stayed with me for a week. He didn't know I'd tried to kill myself. It was good having him there. Good having family around. But when he had to go, it just left a big void. A couple of weeks into my recovery, I was telling the doctors I needed painkillers. Not long after, I woke up one morning, took a painkiller, then I took another one, and another, and another. I decided to kill myself.

Then there was this knock on the door, interrupting me. I waited a little while, in the hope they would go away. I reached down to get another painkiller and the insistent knock on the door kept going. I answered the door, wanting to get rid of whoever it was so I could do what I needed to do. When I opened the door, my coach Johnny Lang was standing there.

Was that fate?

It was, yeah.

He saved you?

Yeah, but he doesn't know that.

You haven't told him?

I've told other people, but I haven't directly told Johnny. He said, let's go for a ride. He had his car parked out the front.

Do you reckon he knew you'd been suicidal?

He definitely knew I needed help. Because I respected him, I got in the car and didn't ask any questions. We drove to Parramatta. On the forty-minute ride to Parramatta, not one word was said. By the time we got to Parra I was high from the painkillers. A proper high. We went up to the first floor of this building, got out of the elevator, went to the reception desk. At this point, I had no idea what we were doing there.

At the desk Johnny said that he'd made an appointment for Preston Campbell. I looked at him, and he told me it was going to be alright. Johnny had organised for me to see a counsellor. So, he definitely knew I needed help. Five minutes later, somebody called my name. Johnny looked at me and said, 'Away you go.' Johnny Lang's got a lot of words, he likes to talk, but on this one day, he barely spoke ten words to me. And that's where my journey began.

So, were you high throughout that first session?

Very.

Did the counsellor work it out?

I think she knew. And I think that's when I realised that I needed help. In the beginning, I was a bit hesitant about telling the truth, but by the end, I was crying. The floodgates had opened. I think I was just so mentally exhausted.

This was before the season started. I had been training, but I hadn't been eating, and I wasn't sleeping. It was a real battle getting up to go to training, and the same when I was at training. There were days where I'd go without eating. Days I'd go without sleeping. Just way out of whack. I was just so exhausted, mentally and physically. I told the counsellor about this. She helped me understand that what I was feeling was normal.

So you started eating and training properly? Did you start playing well?

Four or five rounds into the season I started to feel good. I started in the Penrith NRL team, playing on the wing.

John Lang signed you and put you back into first grade?

Johnny has always helped me out. He's like one of those wise old uncles. He's always had faith in me. He's always seen something in me.

So, this begins to turn your life around?

Yeah, I was understanding what I was going through, and finding ways to manage it, without drinking and without constantly feeling angry.

I'd lost the feeling of joy in life. But I soon played football again, because of John Lang. I wanted to play football for him. Outside of that and seeing the psychologist, there wasn't much else going on. Still, I was just playing football, I was on the wing and I was starting to feel happy about it.

There was no ego involved. This is what seeing psychologists helped me understand. I learned that it wasn't about the externals. It was internal, it was me. I blamed a lot of people and made a lot of excuses for myself, and that was me in denial.

So, I'm getting better, I'm feeling better, and I'm starting to understand that I played a massive part in the way I was feeling. I said sorry to Lee, but not to the point where I was begging for her to come back. I totally understood why she needed to leave.

Did she see the change in you?

She did. And I think that's why she came back. She said, 'I didn't leave because I don't love you. I left because I didn't like the person you were.'

Are you still together?

Still together. We had another boy, Jake. Obviously it wasn't all rosy. We needed to work on things.

All this time I'd been working on myself. I was still struggling a little bit with self-confidence and anxiety, but at the back end of the year, we made the finals. I was starting to feel like I wanted to live. I was starting to feel this joy. We went on to win the grand final in 2003, which was a great achievement for a footy club, for any footy player, but especially for me.

I played four years at Penrith, then in 2006, I moved back to the Gold Coast, playing five years with the Titans. I was thirty-four when I finished up, and by then, I looked at Rugby League differently. It wasn't just a way of taking care of my family – maybe it was somewhere I could make a difference in others' lives.

In 2013, we lost two young Rugby League players to suicide. Twenty-year-old Mosese Fotuaika from Wests Tigers, and Alex Elisala, also twenty, from the North Queensland Cowboys. At this stage, I was working in the community arm of the Gold Coast Titans, doing a lot of travelling around, carrying out work in the community and schools. The passing of those two young men hit pretty hard. I felt really sad for their families. I felt sad for all involved. Two young men that were here one day and then, just gone. Back then, there was no awareness about this stuff. No education.

Because the NRL were inundated with phone calls about these two incidents, I think they felt the need to do something. They were looking for somebody to share their story of how to tackle this and as uncomfortable as I was, I put my hand up to tell mine. There was a segment on the popular Thursday night Channel 9 *Footy Show*, when it was still around. They did a piece on mental health with myself and a number of others, and it really sparked a conversation.

Live on television you talked about this. Had you talked about it before?

No, this was the first time.

Did you talk about the suicide attempts on air?

Both of them, in particular the car smash. We went back to film in Ballina, at the location where I'd crashed the car. I shared the story roadside. It's weird, because we were there that day, setting up, and in the middle of the interview, somebody pulled up on the other side of the road. I thought we were in trouble with the authorities, but I recognised who it was as soon as I heard his voice, even though we hadn't talked in eleven years.

It was the man that was first on scene when I crashed my car.

Just passing by at that very minute?

I walked over and gave him the biggest hug. I thanked him and got a bit emotional.

After sharing my story on the show my phone went crazy. People had no idea this had happened. A number of people felt upset and guilty.

Did they say 'Why didn't you call me? I would have helped you.'

See, it's not something that we did back then. I don't know when people started seeing psychologists and being able to get through situations like the one I went through, but certainly not back then. I knew that more people needed to understand, needed to know. This was something we needed to talk more about. Even today, there's still not enough talk about it.

That's why this book's important.

It's very important. That's why I agreed to be involved. Talking about mental illness is not attractive, but we need to.

Was anyone angry that you tried to kill yourself?

Oh yeah, my mum was angry. I could understand why. But when I sat down and had a conversation with her, to help her understand why, it made it a lot easier for her to understand why I felt like that. Even so, she said, 'But, son, you didn't need to do that.' No-one gets angry at someone if they get cancer, do they?

When I tried to kill myself it was because I thought it was the right thing to do, that everyone would be better off without me. That's what it does to you. That's why it's so devastating, because it has you thinking you're doing the right thing.

So, Preston, how did you take all that into what you're doing today with your foundation?

Simply put, it's about connection. Connection can mean so much. A lot of it comes from our understanding of how important connection is. And connection is relationships. Our relationship with technology, especially youngsters online with social media. Connection is about our relationships with other people. It's about our relationship with alcohol and drugs. It's important to understand the relationships we have with everything. Without relationships and connection, we, as human beings, we're nothing.

I know there's no simple answer to this question, but why do you think suicide rates among Indigenous Australians are double those of non-Indigenous Australians?

Because we feel like we don't have any connection, to anything. We struggle with alcohol. We struggle with drugs. We struggle with gambling. We struggle with violence. We're just disconnected. We're disconnected and that's something that I've come to understand is really, really important. It's actually not just us though, it's all peoples, all around the world.

And it looks different for some people. What's important to you might not be as important to me, but what should be important for the both of us is that understanding. That there is real value in positive, meaningful connection and relationships.

I don't like separating First Nations people and non-First Nations people because we all have issues. I think that until we can all speak the same language around this, we're still going to have trouble. We're always going to have trouble, but not if we can work together.

Do you think your life today is better because you tried to kill yourself?

Well, it definitely would have been different.

Did you have to get to that point to be where you are today?

Don't most people? We don't realise the beauty of the world we're living in until we go through something pretty significant like that. I don't know if it has to get to that point for a lot of people, though. Some people just get it. They lose a loved one, and get inspired, or depressed. It can go either way. For some of us, we just need to go to the extreme to get that inspiration. I often think, if I didn't know what I know now, would I just be back in Tingha, and content with that life? I don't know. That's a difficult one to answer.

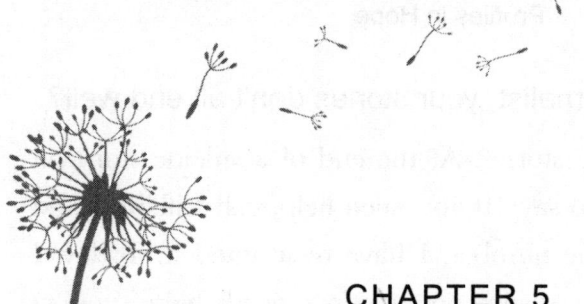

CHAPTER 5

Davina Smith

The Journalist

Davina Smith may be a familiar face to some of you. She reads the daytime news across Australia for Channel 9. Whenever Davina interviews me about suicide and mental health she always finishes by saying, 'As someone who has called Lifeline myself, I encourage anyone watching who is in crisis to call Lifeline on 13 11 14.'

While talking to Davina for this book, I found out she is an Ambassador for the Gidget Foundation Australia, who provide free psychological support to new parents. I also finally got the chance to ask her why she needed Lifeline. Why an outwardly successful, articulate, bright woman needed to make that call.

Davina shared with me (and now you) how her public success masked internal self-doubt and worthlessness. And how Lifeline saved her life.

* * *

Davina, as a TV journalist, your stories don't all end well?

No. Especially suicide stories. At the end of a suicide story on Channel 9, we used to say, 'If you need help, call Lifeline,' and we'd put up the phone number. I have re-scripted it. Today, I say to camera, 'If you or someone you love needs help, support or hope, call Lifeline. If it's an emergency, call 000. As someone who's been there, I know. I've been through it, I've suffered post-natal anxiety, I've suffered post-traumatic stress. I've had depression. I've had anxiety. I still live with it.'

Let's start with your family story.

I've got two little brothers, who are not little. They're bigger than me. We grew up on a farm in Toowoomba. It's an old dairy farm. It was my grandparents'. Everyone lived within a stone's throw of each other. My cousins were down the road. I couldn't have asked for a better childhood. Everything was perfect.

I was as tomboy as you can get. I swam. I was just mad keen to be outside and around the animals, all the time. That was my joy in my life. Life was Toowoomba and life was the farm.

Dad was a sales rep in town, but we had the cattle on the side as well. It was my grandparents who ran the farm as a full-time job. We had dry times and terrible times, so the farm was never really a full-time job for our family.

What about your mum?

She's a nurse. My parents are incredibly hard-working and have always been an example of a great work ethic. Every morning Dad would be up and on the go at 7 am. He'd come home at

5 pm, get into his farm gear, walk down to the cattle and look after them.

I feel like my family life was as good for my mental health as anything is. Mum was the nurse and she always did night shift, so that she could be with us during the day.

We could not have asked for more. My father is the most generous, wonderful man and my mother is the absolute model of the perfect housekeeper, the perfect cook, and so intelligent. They're still there on the farm.

When did you first want to become a journalist?

When I was at school, I was torn between law and a passionate obsession to be an actress, and I've always loved to write and tell stories. When I finished school I went into the industry via a university degree, which I did in Toowoomba. I did three years at uni, Bachelor of Communications in journalism with the aim of being a TV reporter.

Did you have to refine the way you spoke to get that TV newsreader speak?

Yeah, I'd spend the day at uni and then drive my little Hyundai hatchback back to the farm, parroting what I heard on the radio to get that voice, to get the intonation, the flow and the speed, trying to sound older, with much more authority than my nineteen-year-old self. Because who would believe a nineteen-year-old girl telling a terrible story?

I don't think I'm someone who has ever been very good at anything. But I am someone who is just very persistent and will plug away. And I'm a perfectionist. So, I've always been the one who has had to work ten times harder to get to where I am.

I must have sent away 100 different show reels over the years to get a job as a reporter in Brisbane or Sydney and was always told, no. Finally, I got one.

I did three years in Rockhampton, working up there as a reporter.

How was leaving home?

It was a big deal. Dad's only cried twice in his life, and that was one of them. I remember him crying. I bought a TV to take to Rockhampton and it wouldn't fit in the back of the car. I was trying to slam the boot down and Dad was trying to push it in there with me, and we had this massive argument. I just said, 'I don't want to leave.' Then he cried as well and I just remember thinking, *Oh my goodness.*

During those first three years in Rocky at WIN Television, you'd go out once a month, to somewhere like Emerald, and spend forty-eight hours out there, shooting as many stories as possible. It was a three-hour trip. Just me and the cameraman. I'm still great mates with some of those cameramen today. They were like older brothers and dads.

What was the next big thing?

Ideally it would have been Brisbane. That's where I was sending my tapes, begging to be picked up. Somewhere where there was a competitive news environment. I had no ambition of leaving TV news. I'd found what I loved.

I love telling people's stories. Even on the traumatic days where it's awful, there's something so humbling about someone welcoming you into their home to share their story.

Did any of the stories affect you?

I don't think at the time I realised it. Rockhampton is in the middle of nowhere, on a highway. There are a lot of car accidents that we would show up to as the police and emergency services were arriving. There were plenty of occasions where in the middle of the night, the police needed our camera lights so they could search for bodies, and the paramedics needed them for illumination to help revive people. Often we wouldn't be shooting anything, but just holding our lights up.

That must have been traumatic?

It's different. I think it's very personal. I would be there in these moments with people who were taking their last breath. When someone passes away, it is such a deeply personal place, for everyone who goes on to live. It never sat well with me that I was there and experienced that moment.

There were plenty of times where it did affect me and I'd have a good cry, but because news is such a fast-paced world, you move on. But then you come back to the court case a month, six months later. There was a terrible plane crash outside of town. I was with the cameraman. The investigators couldn't get to the scene that night because it was in the middle of nowhere, so they asked us to film the scene. That was an incident that sticks with me. The next day I woke up and was deeply traumatised, but didn't know where to place what I was feeling, so I called the cameraman who was with me and had a cry with him.

There were no formal employee assistance programs? Were you meant to tough it out?

This was just the job and, isn't it awful, isn't it sad? But you've got to show up and do the job again tomorrow, and you've got to smile and look okay. I know throughout my career, one of the things that's probably saved me is the make-up and the hair and the clothes. Putting all that on becomes very much like putting on a mask. It's not until you go back home and wash it all off. That's when you break down because it all drops away and it's just you. The whole world of television becomes this mask that you can bluff your way through. And that helps you cope with a lot of the trauma.

Did you report much on mental health in those days?

No. I can vividly recall, whenever it was something that was mental health–related, the prevailing thought was, 'we won't report on that'.

Particularly suicide. The old rule of the media - don't report suicide.

Yeah, absolutely not. That's how it was for domestic violence, suicide and mental health. If it was a court case and something terrible had happened in a family, but a submission had been made to the court that it was mental health–related, I didn't touch the story.

So, you're hitting your mid-twenties. Another move?

I'd met my husband Mark in Rockhampton. He was working one of the rescue helicopters up there. I would often be at the helicopter base interviewing him or interviewing his boss, and he'd be making starry eyes at me.

Then he joined the army, and it was all very higgledy-piggledy for a few years, but in that time we got engaged and he ended up getting a posting order to Holsworthy in Sydney with the 6th Aviation Regiment with the Black Hawks. And he said, come.

I'd never had any ambition to work in Sydney. I worked with plenty of people who did. It's thought of as the pinnacle. If you're going to make it in television, you want to be in Sydney, but it was the last place on earth I wanted to work. I knew nothing about New South Wales. I was a typical one-eyed Queenslander.

However, there was a job going as a producer at Channel 9. I half-heartedly threw my resume in and got a phone call saying, come meet with us. They didn't have any on-air work as a reporter, but told me that if I worked hard and proved myself, I could end up there. I was probably taking a bit of a backward step coming to Sydney. But it was a foot in the door.

I desperately wanted to report, but that wasn't an option at the beginning. My boss said, 'Prove it, prove to me that you can do it,' and within six months I was reporting. While I was nervous about the move, it paid off because I worked my absolute arse off in that time.

It wouldn't be uncommon for me to be there at five o'clock in the morning and still on the road at seven o'clock at night, then turn around and get up at three the next morning and start all over again.

I don't think I'm ambitious. If any sort of ambition is driving me, it's because of my perfectionism; myself and my standards. Not the prettiest, not the smartest.

That's a high bar, perfectionism.

Yes, it's terrible.

If you fall short of it, what do you do?

Any mistake I'd make would eat me up. I'd be reading the news and stumble, the bulletin would move on, the auto-cue would move on, but my head would be stuck on that mistake I made fifteen minutes ago, or four hours ago. I had to learn very quickly, in making a transition from reporting to presenting, that shit happens. It's live TV. There are mistakes, things go wrong, and you need to push through.

You were married at that stage. Did that add a lot of pressure?

I was very happy on the road as a reporter, but there was a four-month window where I didn't see Mark because of his job, coming and going, and me coming and going.

It just felt wrong. It just felt like I wasn't there for him and he wasn't there for me, and we just weren't seeing each other. It was after the Queensland floods, when I was up there reporting and he was up there working. We were both up there for this month-long period and in that month, we would pass each other at an airport, and it was a quick peck on the cheek, and we kept moving.

How was your mental health at this point?

I was fried. But I didn't realise it. It was anxiety. I was running on 100 per cent adrenaline all the time. I had no balance in my life, because I figured I had to work and work, and work and work, and work to prove myself.

I started suffering panic attacks. I would be in the hotel at night, after I'd been out on the road all day. I'd wash off the make-up, get into my pyjamas and end up in bed in the foetal position, crying, racked with a real physical wave of anxiety.

I thought I was sick. I'd lost feeling in my forearms, and I thought I was having some sort of stroke. It was because I was so locked up and had so much tension, I'd lost feeling. But I wasn't dying, I wasn't sick, and I had to go to work the next day. I wasn't going to miss a day of work, because I loved my job and had to keep working.

Any panic attacks at work?

No, I was always poker-faced. Hair and make-up, expensive clothes. I was fine. But the moment I'd take it all off, I would crumble. Occasionally people might have thought me a little withdrawn. I didn't feel I could complain. I didn't know anyone else around me who had anxiety. Everyone in television is so perfect, and everyone's so kind and polite. I just felt I had to be the same.

So, you've got a job at the pinnacle. You're married, but not seeing enough of each other. You're beginning to feel the effects of stress and pressure, and anxiety, but not understanding or acknowledging it.

In 2012 we both had the option to go to Queensland. We jumped at that because we thought: this is a chance to slow down a little bit. Mark was going to be in Oakey, and I was going to be in Brisbane, two hours away.

My job was to present on weekends and three days during the week. He was full time at the base. We'd come to the conclusion that we would spend more time together that way than staying in Sydney and never seeing each other. Queensland was a bit of an escape. We didn't know whether it was forever or whether it was just a reset.

We were seeing more of each other, but I wasn't particularly happy in Brisbane. To a certain degree, the TV reporters are a little bit like celebrities up there and I didn't like that. I was being recognised in public and that added to my anxiety. I never had that in Sydney. We'd get invitations to red-carpet events, which were the last place I wanted to go. I would much rather be at home with Mark.

By 2014, after two years in Brisbane, the chance came for us to come back to Sydney and for me to be the daytime weekday presenter. It is quite a long shift. You're at work from 7 am through to 5 pm. It's four days a week but it's a long day, you're on all day really. You're back and forth between the camera at least a dozen times during the day doing news updates and bulletins, as well as social media. It was an era where breaking news became such a big thing. There'd be a terror attack overseas. Quick, go live!

I listen to you and can feel your growing anxiety, but you went straight into the fire.

I like to be busy, I don't like to stop and think.

What happens if you stop and think?

I'm annoying and terrible and procrastinate and spiral. The best thing about my job as the daytime presenter is that you do not stop all day. You go from commitment to commitment to commitment. That attracted me because I'd had my days in the newsroom in Brisbane where nothing was happening and I didn't have a story, and the anxiety of sitting at my desk and not really knowing what to do. This was the solution to that problem.

To me that feels like a very pressured job?

Oh yeah, there's huge pressure.

Our marriage was suffering, and that was the turning point where I thought, I'm a bad person. I am becoming difficult to live with. Mark is this happy-go-lucky guy and he's got this high-pressure job, I thought, he can cope and I can't. So, I need to get some help.

But that help only came after a series of very traumatic breaking news events in 2014 which I worked on. The last one was the Martin Place siege, which I was on air for all the way through.

I can remember when I first started seeing a psychologist in 2014. It felt like a secret I had to keep, in case work found out that I wasn't coping. I was terrified that they would take what I loved away from me.

Did you tell any friends or Mark?

Mark knew. My parents didn't know. I didn't want to tell them. I didn't want to worry them. None of my friends knew. To the point where I would go see a psychologist and I would make sure it was on the weekday I had off during the week. I'd look around going into the GP clinic where the psychologist was based, terrified that someone I knew would see me coming or leaving. And the reason I picked that psychologist was because she worked at a GP clinic, so I could easily say I was seeing a doctor.

How did you go with the psychologist?

It was such an eye-opener. She told me I wasn't a bad person. Because I felt like I was turning into this awful witch of a wife. She told me this was clinical anxiety, that I wasn't well, that she could get me better. In some respects, it felt like a weight lifted off my shoulders because I felt like I was a terrible person. But, I would have to take medication and I would have to come back and see her.

Then the next problem became, oh shit, I've got this secret I'm going to have to keep now. And I think for a long time I felt like I was getting worse before I was getting better, because I had so much anxiety about the anxiety and keeping it a secret.

Were you taking medication?

No, I wasn't. I wouldn't let the GP write a mental health plan for me because I didn't want it to go to Medicare. That's how paranoid I was.

I went on medication when I fell pregnant, because at that point I had come across a fabulous GP who knew the psychologist. Together, they sat down and said, 'This is causing stress on your body. You're pregnant and any risk from the medication is nowhere near as great as the risk of the physical anxiety you're putting your baby and your body through.'

Within three months of having the meds, I realised what a game changer it was. I still felt like me. I still got nerves going on air. I still had all the emotion of life. But it just took that edge off. The panic attacks stopped. That constant running-on-adrenaline that I felt all the time, that made me feel like I was going to crack, the shaking, that just subsided. I just remember thinking, why didn't I do this sooner? This has changed my life.

Had you ever had thoughts of suicide up to that point?

Yeah, I had. I'd felt very low and very anxious. A burden to people. A burden to Mark. I had fleeting thoughts of suicide, but I wouldn't say I was suicidal. I found a lot of comfort in thinking that I just wanted to disappear. The minute I thought about removing myself from the world, I would find a degree of comfort. But I didn't connect that with suicide.

Your baby arrives. How long were you on maternity leave?

I took about seven months. Rose was a very hard baby. She had silent reflux, a lot of food allergies and intolerances. I could not put her down, as she would just start screaming. It was really bad. It became paralysing because I couldn't leave the house. There were weeks on end where I would lock myself in the bedroom. She would only sleep upright on my chest. I'd have to be on one of those fitness balls, bouncing.

I was so tired, I was so mentally not well at that point. I was blaming myself, saying this is my fault. I've done this to this baby. I got given this beautiful, perfect child and I did this to her.

Did you speak to the psychologist about that?

I didn't recognise it as postnatal anxiety, because I was so used to anxiety being panic attacks and this real physical wave would come over me. It took a while for me to recognise that I wasn't well again. The meds needed changing and I needed more sessions with the psychologist. I had also started seeing a psychiatrist by that point, because by then I was suicidal. I'd got back to work, and I used to think about driving off the road as I was driving home.

The wheels came off badly when I went back to work because we were not sleeping. We were in the trenches. Rose went from having reflux to a sleep condition known as parasomnia, where she woke regularly through the night, screaming. She was like that through until the age of three.

Was work your sanctuary?

One hundred per cent. I felt like I was such a failure as a mother, and a failure as a wife. The one thing I could do on autopilot was my job. That's why it became so important.

Did your mental health improve?

I think after taking a lot of heavy sleeping tablets. There was a lot of trial and error.

The postnatal anxiety was there probably for a good twelve to eighteen months after Rose was born, and the ultimatum eventually came from both my psychiatrist and psychologist. They wanted to put me in hospital for postnatal anxiety.

By yourself, or with Rose?

No, by myself.

That's a big call.

One of the hospitals in Sydney now has a ward where mums can go with their babies. That's a game-changer.

Until a couple of years ago, there wasn't a single bed in New South Wales for mother and baby. As if it wasn't enough that you felt bad about the anxiety, then you had to abandon your child as well.

I needed to be in hospital, but I didn't go. Hospital didn't scare me. It was leaving Rose. That's what terrified me. What I learned through postnatal anxiety is that with the right support and the right people, you can get through it.

I think the only good thing about the anxiety and what I'd been through was that Mark learned very early on that he couldn't fix me. He's a man, he's in the army. He figured he'd make this better. What he learned is that he couldn't. And I didn't want him to make me better either. I just wanted him to hold me and hug me, and just be there for me. And he was. In the most extraordinary way.

Adversity brings you together, which is fantastic. So you were surviving, but not thriving?

We weren't thriving, but we were getting better, bit by bit.

Mark got sent to Afghanistan for six months at that time. So, there were stressful periods. He got home from Afghanistan at the end of 2019 and was immediately posted to Queensland. The initial agreement was that Rose and I would stay in Sydney and then we'd play it by ear. Then COVID hit and the borders shut. This great plan that we would fly back and forth and see each other every second weekend went out the window.

So, I spent most of 2020 in Sydney with Rose, working full time. Rose was at day care and preschool. We'd been trying to have another baby without success. I think I felt really good mentally. I felt like I could protect myself from postnatal anxiety the second time around. I'd do everything right and would manage the situation. We were going down the path of IVF. We had a great doctor who was very supportive of that, and I fell pregnant in September of 2020 – while Mark was in Queensland and I was in Sydney.

We had an extreme family trauma when I was seven weeks pregnant. It had been a couple of weeks after everything had gone to shit and we were in Sydney, in lockdown. We were a family unit of three, with Mark back home. I was terrified and so scared about the future. I spent a lot of time in bed.

I was living with the fear that other people would find out about this family trauma. I was scared financially for the future. I was scared for our marriage. I was scared about our relationships with other people.

And a day came when I was spiralling. I called the GP. She wasn't there. I called the psychologist. She wasn't working. I emailed the psychiatrist, didn't get a reply. I could feel myself going down and down through the course of the day. I kept telling myself this was all my fault, and that it was all going to explode.

I was off work at that time because of everything that was going on. I just completely blamed myself. If I was a better wife, a better mother. If I didn't do the job I did, none of this would be happening and this was all my fault. Mark and I argued that night. Despite the trauma, we had been rock solid looking after each other. However, this was a really, really bad day. It was the combination of not being able to get any help, having an argument, and not wanting to call my parents and worry them because they couldn't do anything anyway. I couldn't confide in anyone.

Rose had gone to bed, it was about eight o'clock at night. I left the house, got in the car and drove off intending to kill myself. I made up my mind that everyone would be better off without me. Mark's life would be easier. Rose would be upset, but she'd have a better life. I was in such a frenzy and so wrapped up in the trauma of what was going on, I'd almost forgotten I was pregnant.

As I was driving, I got hit by this wave of nausea, and it was like, oh yeah, that's right, I'm pregnant. It was the nausea and the baby that made me pull over. I called the 24-hour veterans outreach service. It was a disaster of a phone call. It was a young woman, who could obviously feel how panicked, upset and traumatised I was, and she freaked out. She was as scared as I was. She suggested I take up knitting or find a new hobby. It was the last roll of the dice. I was really, really upset. Ninety-nine per cent of me wanted to just disappear and end my life. But that other one per cent was the baby, and that was what was stopping me. With that one per cent, I rang Lifeline.

I felt such lost hope, because that last phone call had gone so badly. I thought, this is not going to help. I'd been triggered because of the phone call I'd just had. The engine was running and I was pulled over at the side of the road, and this woman I spoke to at Lifeline just brought me straight into the present. It was the calmness that came from her. She didn't try to fix me. She just wanted to make sure I was safe. Where was I? Was I in any harm? The two calls were like chalk and cheese.

We spoke about the baby, and she gave me a plan to get back home. We started talking about how a shower was something I found comforting, and wearing pyjamas. She asked me how good a shower would be right now, and how good would those comfy PJs be. She just found the right things to say. I decided to go home, have a shower, put my pyjamas on, get into bed and tomorrow, I would call the GP. I wasn't going to take no for an answer. I would get an appointment with the doctor.

Do you think your life is better today because you reached that point, because you'd hit bottom?

I think you realise, first and foremost, that your family and friends are not better off without you. That they need you. I think how if that had been my full stop that night, if I had taken my own life, I would have missed out on everything that's happened since. That baby was born, her name is Hope. She's the most extraordinary little girl. She is so full of happiness and joy and fun. If she hadn't come into the world, what a gift the world would have missed out on. And what joy I would have missed out on, not being around her. I think of the dance concerts and the swimming lessons that Rose has done. I think of the good and bad times that Mark and I have had as a couple and I think about where we are today. It wouldn't have happened if I wasn't here. I think about the good I can do at work, talking about mental health.

There are days when I don't put myself out there, because I'm not mentally in the right space to do it. But on the days that I do feel strong enough to talk about it and mention it at the end of bulletins, the messages I get are from people who tell me that I seem like someone who's got their shit together, that I look perfect. They say, 'If you're struggling, it's okay for me to struggle too. And if you got better, I can get better too.' It's people saying, thank you.

And that means the world to me. To know that every time I mention it, there is at least one person who reaches out. You tell your story in the hope that it saves one person. Because one night, I left our family home, got in the car and drove off intending to kill myself. And that night, someone saved me.

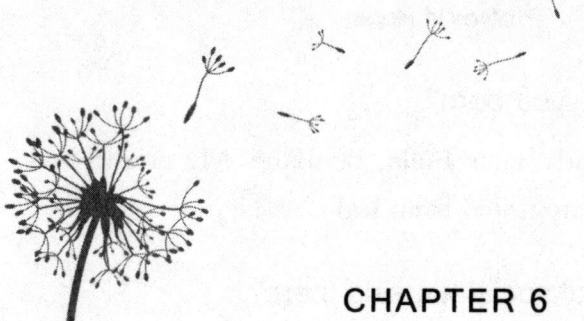

CHAPTER 6

Ben Farinazzo

The Soldier

B en Farinazzo shows little of the physical and mental trauma he has experienced. His smile and humility shine through. There is nothing ordinary about him. An Australian with a rare combination of Italian and Aboriginal heritage. Army officer and East Timor veteran. CEO. Athlete. Gold-medal winner in rowing and powerlifting. Husband and father. Ambassador for Australia Day, Lifeline, Soldier On and many other causes.

Through all of this Ben has battled post-traumatic stress disorder, depression, anxiety and a broken neck and back. At his lowest, he decided to take his own life.

He came back from his physical injuries and learned to live with mental illness. He lives with – not through – his mental illness. This gives him the perspective to understand the journeys of others, speak for them and live a life that inspires.

* * *

Tell me, where were you born?

I grew up in Richlands, near Inala, Brisbane. My nonno and nonna and my father migrated from Italy.

Inala. Is there a lot of social housing there?

Yeah. Very low socio-economic area. A lot of migrants. In those days the whole street was Italians, with the vineyards and all that out the back. We made our life selling vegetables and fruit at the local markets. It was a wonderful upbringing as a kid.

How many brothers and sisters do you have?

One brother and two sisters. I'm the eldest of the four. Mum and Dad met at high school. All Mum's family lived around the corner in a place called Ellen Grove. You can tell it's where we used to live in Richlands because it's actually named Farinazzo Street!

So, Mum's side, it's a large family, lots of brothers and sisters. My grandfather worked in the British police over in India. He came to Australia with his two sons. Met my Nana, and they got married and had five kids after that.

And was she Indigenous?

Not that we knew. Mum's mother comes from a place called Caroona, near Quirindi in New South Wales. Something happened. Nana got sent away to work for a white family somewhere in Brisbane, and they kind of fostered her, and kept her on. She fought very hard to not be seen as Aboriginal, so I'm not clear on the details.

She didn't want to be known as Aboriginal?

No. She carried that through her whole life. When she met my grandfather, she then went back on the Aboriginal missions where she came from and my grandfather ran the mission. She was the Matron there. On these missions. Without telling anyone she was Aboriginal.

At her funeral two weeks ago, there was no mention of her Aboriginal heritage, something that she had fought her whole life to get away from. It has been a tough topic for our family. But my work with a lot of Indigenous kids in recent years has encouraged me to move my way through that as a way of healing.

Did you feel Aboriginal as a kid?

No. I grew up feeling more Italian because I didn't know about my Aboriginal or other parts of my heritage. I was running around in Brisbane with only a pair of shorts on. Never got burnt, dark skin. The kids at school would call me black boy. But really, I didn't have any idea.

Wasn't raised, wasn't talked about?

No. It wasn't until I was a teenager. And then we still really didn't understand it. I think a part of this healing is learning more. Part of the challenge with that, people look at me and say, you're a Farinazzo, you're Italian. I say, yes, and more. I find the best way to communicate that is to say look, in the end I'm a proud Australian, but I've got Italian, Aboriginal and mixed heritage like a lot of Aussies.

You've made a decision to embrace being Indigenous.

Absolutely. I reached a stage in my life where I wanted to understand a bit more about who I was and who my family were. There was one pivotal conversation that I had with a kid at Canberra Grammar School, when I went and did some mentoring for their school program.

We went around the circle and had to say which country we were from, what town and what our family name was. And I found it hard to answer. I said I knew I was a Kamilaroi man. And the fellow next to me said, 'I'm from Kamilaroi, too.' He goes, 'Whereabouts?' I couldn't answer the question. He said, 'Uncle, we need you to know this and be proud of that, so that we can know it and can be proud of it too.' That conversation changed me.

So, what was your household like growing up?

I'd be out on the tractor as a ten-year-old, driving the tractor while my nonno was down stacking the grapes in the back. It was a wonderful life. I mean, I'd run around. If I was hungry, I would just pull a mango off a tree, or grapes off the vine, or rip tomatoes off the vine, crack a rockmelon on the ground and just eat it. It was great.

Did you like school?

Yeah. I went to a Christian school growing up. After we moved to the Gold Coast I started at the Southport School. It was fantastic. Then Dad and Mum divorced. And it was like the world changed overnight. As soon as everything started to implode I just said, I'm going to go to boarding school. Mum said it broke her heart. I didn't want to be part of it all. And so I moved from being a day boy to being a boarder.

Did they have cadets at Southport?

I absolutely loved cadets, and I loved rowing.

So, then came the end of high school. I had done art, film and television, and I thought maybe I'll become a painter when I leave high school. My parents weren't too sure. I really had no idea. Dad had me meet with a Lieutenant Colonel. We had a bit of a chat, we signed some papers and next minute I'd been accepted to go to the Australian Defence Force Academy [ADFA].

ADFA is army, air force and navy. It's males and females, it's all mixed. I loved that because that was a little bit different to boarding school. In fact, it was in that first year I met my wife, Jodie.

What did you study?

I did a Bachelor of Arts. I was a sixteen-year-old, walking in there. It was tough. But I remember going out bush for the first time, patrolling with a weapon, and I fell in love with it. It was one of those moments. I felt deeply connected to this. After three years there I went to the Royal Military College [RMC] at Duntroon. Army officer training. That was a year, then back to ADFA to do Honours.

Were you commissioned as an officer?

Yeah, at the end of RMC. I went to the parachute infantry, and then Jodie and I got married.

We then went to the School of Languages down in Melbourne. I did Indonesian, Bahasa, and absolutely loved that, then got posted to Darwin.

We were doing stuff up in the Northern Territory and across Northern Australia, then East Timor happened, and I got a message: 'Captain Farinazzo, be in Townsville by eight o'clock tomorrow morning.'

It was 1999 and we were looking at sending in an International Force into Timor-Leste to restore law and order following the humanitarian and security crisis that had taken place. My boss became the Australian Force Commander and the commander of all land forces. My job was to go with him as a liaison officer and interpreter.

Did you feel a risk of death when you went over?

Before I went over I did consider that as a possibility, and said my farewells. Put it this way, on landing, I wasn't strolling. I was running out the back of that plane looking for a place to get down low, so I didn't get shot.

It made you so bloody proud to be an Australian. It was one of those moments where you feel like everything you have done in your life has led you to this one moment. I even thought to myself, if something happened to me right now, and I didn't come back or survive, I'd be fine with it. If this is what I was meant to do and achieve, then I'd be happy with it. It was that sort of conviction.

We moved from Dili down to Suai on the southern border. On arriving, I was sent out with a group of guys to find out what this place was all about. There was no-one in the town. Dead quiet. Every government building had been ransacked, burnt down. Everything was wiped out. We saw this old church, and as we're walking toward it we could feel and hear this clinking. We were walking through spent bullet shells, all the way leading up to the church. That's a lot of rounds that had been fired there. They weren't ours. Inside the church there were bloodstains up the walls and all over the floor. You could see where they had dragged bodies onto the back of trucks. It was horrible. I'll never forget the smell. Going through the adjoining school and classrooms, it was the same.

No-one alive?

There was one kid, with a bandana on, the side of his face burnt off. He was probably seven years old. He ran over, hugged me, and just cried and cried. He'd been looking for his mum and his sister, but all he could find was their jewellery.

What we'd walked into was the aftermath of the Suai Church massacre, which took place on 6 September 1999. It is impossible to know how many people had been killed by pro-Indonesia militia.

This kid was laying under the priest's bed. He'd run and hidden, and the bed was on fire, melting onto his face. Deciding he couldn't stay there any longer, he rolled out and ran to the hills, hiding for god knows how long. He said some people got away and that they were all up in the hills. As a young kid growing up in Inala, going to boarding school on the Gold Coast and that, I would never have pictured something like this. It was something you'd only see in movies. But to be in the middle of it made me wonder – 'Is this humanity? Is this what we're up against? How can people do this?'

Our Padre held the first church service in Suai, following the massacre. As the service was taking place, people were coming down from the hills dressed in whatever bloodstained clothes they had left. The Padre said to me, 'Can you ask the locals if they'd like to say anything?' As the interpreter, I walked over to a lady and I said, 'Is there something you'd like to say?' There was this quiet pause for a bit, and then she started singing the Hallelujah Jesus Christos, and then everyone joined in singing this hymn. It was like the sun then opened up through the clouds. A surreal moment. And the soldier next to me said, 'Boss, I'm not sure I believe in God, but if there is one, he's with us here today.' I thought yeah.

Your job was helping to translate every story – so you were the first to be told?

It seemed like every person we met wanted to talk to me.

I was very clinical about it; it was a job. I then got involved in the church and started speaking there regularly on a Sunday, initially as an opportunity to share information about what was happening around the country. It was a major entry point into East Timor from the south. So the church services became massive.

It wasn't long after that when I did my Christmas farewell at the church. We needed them to handle things themselves. So they organised a church service and invited me – they called me Captain Ben – to come and speak one last time.

What happened then is all blurred in my mind now. At the end of my talk, the whole front row of people burst into tears and came running forward. These older ladies were holding onto me, crying and crying. Behind them were a group of blokes who were angry, demanding to know why we hadn't got there before everyone was killed in the church. They were all running toward me.

I just remember falling down, people on top of me. I didn't know whether I was fighting or fleeing. I had no idea what was going on. The next minute, one of my soldiers grabbed me by my shirt and just dragged me out, threw me into the back of a Land Rover and got us out of there.

It wasn't long after that, that I returned home. I borrowed a satellite phone, called my wife and asked her to pick me up from the airport. When we arrived, the plane opened up, I walked out, looked around and gave my weapon to someone. There was no customs, no nothing, just my wife. I said, 'Let's go home.'

No health assessment, mental or physical?

Nothing. I went home, had a shower and we went out for lunch. A couple of weeks later someone suggested they get me in for a debrief. How are you going? That sort of stuff. I told them things weren't totally right. They told me not to worry, it would get better. And that was it.

I'd never come back from combat before. How do you process this sort of stuff? I was back in a surreal world. To me, it wasn't the world that I left. I was detached. I'd go into the supermarket and I'd see some East Timorese people in there but I couldn't talk to them. I was like, wow, my worlds are mixing here. I cannot do this.

I got posted down to Canberra and got made an instructor at the RMC. Our first son was born. And it was then I realised the wheels were beginning to fall off.

I couldn't sleep anymore. Terrible nightmares. All night. Up until that point, I had a real optimistic faith in humanity, that there was a goodness in the world. What I'd experienced just totally ripped the arse out of that. I thought, you go to war, and in my mind you know, it's blokes on blokes. And that's fine. It doesn't involve burning kids in churches. I mean, who does that? Well, they do. And not just them. It's happening around the world. This wasn't just East Timor, it wasn't limited to just that conflict.

That really hit you.

I was waking up, bawling my eyes out. Then being anxious about doing stuff. Feeling disconnected from the world around me. When people would come over to the house, I would sit in the backyard by myself because I didn't want the noise. I was so aggressive. If there was too much milk in a cup of tea, I'd just lose my shit. This wasn't me. I was a calm and easygoing guy.

So, I went and sought help.

Was that a big move in the army, admitting you needed help?

Back in those days there was no national mental health conversation. There was no helpline number at the end of *Home and Away*. There was none of that. The only people who had PTSD were Vietnam veterans. I didn't know what was happening. I walked into the office of this psychologist and explained what was going on. He said I should take everything I'd told him, put it in an imaginary box, put that box on the top shelf of a locker, push it right to the back, lock it up, throw the key away and never, ever visit it again. 'If you go into it and it comes out, you'll not only lose your job here, you'll never, ever get a job on the outside again. You will be unemployable for the rest of your life.'

He was trying to look after your career, not your mental health? Did that make sense to you?

I thought that was bloody good advice. Block it out, move on like a man and get on with it. I went home and resigned from the military. I was so angry. I was angry at everything.

Nobody mentioned PTSD at this stage?

No. I'd kind of heard of it, but it was Vietnam vets who had it. It couldn't happen to me. Anyway, I got out of the army and started working in financial services.

How was your mental health at this stage? Was it all in the box, in the locker?

Toxic waste was coming out around the edges. I was still not doing well, but I kept moving. I was now a security adviser working up in central Java, in a village by myself. Looking out for local terrorist groups and policemen taking money, extorting Exxon. Middle of nowhere sort of stuff.

Were you getting on the grog?

Every night, smoking two to three packets of cigarettes a day and drinking like a dozen cups of coffee, to keep me up. Then drinking alcohol all night, and eating chilli all day. I'd come back home to Jodie and my now two kids, and I was drinking whisky and smoking cigars at six in the morning, out in the backyard. Everywhere I drove my car, I was speeding. I didn't believe in rules anymore.

You hadn't talked to anyone? Just kept it all in and pushed it all down?

I had offloaded to one mate. He wanted to punch me in the face, and told me to stop being a pussy because I hadn't really seen any action. I thought, fuck, he's probably right. Then I'm sitting with this psychiatrist, massively offloading, and he's rolling his eyes. At the end of it he said, 'Well, Ben, I don't think there's anything really wrong with you. It's just a case of work–life balance. I think you need to go home and look after your wife and your kids. Be a bit more present with them. You know, there's legitimate people who have got PTSD, like our Vietnam veterans, and then there's others just making it up in order to rort the system. Is there anything else I can help you with?' It sounds ridiculous now, but I was very happy with his advice.

So, then we moved the whole family over to Jakarta. I'm now in the expat life, where it's okay to be on the piss. By this stage I was putting on weight. I was tired. I couldn't run anywhere because of the smog and all the rest of it. Three kids now.

Did the bad sleep and the drinking continue? Did you feel you were spinning out of control?

It was like waves. I'd reach a really bad point and then I'd think, 'Oh my god, what am I doing here?' I'd have to pick myself back up again, stop drinking, stop smoking. I'd go to the gym. I'd work myself really hard to get on top of it, and then I'd go back down again. It was a constant cycle. Sometimes it coincided with changing jobs, sometimes when we moved. It was really hard to pick. After another job change, and surviving dengue fever, we came back to Australia.

Were you physically and mentally exhausted?

I had no idea what was going on. I was just done. We moved back to Canberra. I started up my own coaching and consulting business, took on a CEO role for a training academy, and at the same time took on another CEO role for a recruitment company.

So, you just kept loading on the pressure?

It all looked good. I'd got a house, two CEO roles, got my own business, wife, three lovely kids and all the rest of it. Meanwhile, I was going downhill again, drinking myself to sleep, waking up and starting work at four in the morning, smoking, drinking ten cups of coffee and just getting through each day.

I remember, we were at home, it was a Sunday. I had some argument over who was unpacking the dishwasher and taking the bins out, something minor. I stormed out of the house, didn't know where to go. I went to my office. We'd done some mental health training. I was standing outside having a smoke while scrolling through my phone, and here I am reading up on anxiety and depression. Then I get to the questionnaire and fill it out. It was really high, that score, and it literally said, 'You need to call your GP or Lifeline. Now.'

It was Sunday, so my GP wasn't there. I thought about Lifeline, but wasn't that if you were about to kill yourself? Still, I called Lifeline and a lovely lady picked up the phone.

'Hi, my name is Ben. I don't really know why I'm calling.'

'That's okay, Ben. That's normally how this conversation begins.'

I lost my shit. I fell to the ground and sobbed my eyes out. I can't really remember much of what happened. All I know is that someone actually heard me. God bless that woman, whoever she was. She helped me put into place the course of events which saved my life. Because from there I then organised to go and see my GP. I was fortunate that my GP had military experience, a lot in mental health. She'd known me for twenty years.

'Hey, I don't want to waste your time, I just want some sleeping tablets.'

'Sit down in a chair and tell me why you think you need sleeping tablets.'

'I can't stuff around. I've got a board meeting in half an hour. I've really got to get going.'

'Sit down and let's have a talk.'

And after the talk, she said, 'Ben, I think you might have post-traumatic stress disorder [PTSD].' That was the second time that week I just lost it.

Was there a feeling of relief when that happened - a weight off your shoulders?

No, not at that point. I was just totally confused. Like, what is happening in my life? I remember her saying I had to cancel my appointments, and that I couldn't be left alone. 'We need to get you under some immediate supervision.'

She was worried about the potential for suicide?

I guess. This was uncharted territory. I wasn't even thinking about that. My world was just collapsing. I didn't know what was going on anymore. I'd crossed a threshold. I ended up going and seeing a psychiatrist and a counsellor, and I was formally diagnosed with anxiety, depression and PTSD.

I thought I was just going to knock this over in a few weeks. Go on meds for a week or so. So, we kept it very private, apart from letting my parents and Jodie's parents know. I carried a lot of shame. I remember ringing up my dad, I was dreading the moment.

'Dad, I'm so sorry. I've got PTSD.'

'What are you so sorry for, my son? I love you. Have you got help? Do you need us to come down?'

After a while, we thought I'd recovered, at which point I got ischemic colitis. That's reduced blood flow to part of the large intestine. Almost had my bowel cut out. It's like a heart attack in your stomach, so that forced me to cut out the grog, cut out everything. I stopped all medications. I felt like I was on top of everything and everything was fine. I was like, 'You beauty, I'm back!' I took on a new job as CEO of an outdoor education company. But it didn't stay that way.

On the way to work one day, my wife rang me up and told me to check my emails and to call her straight back. I did. There was a suicide note from one of my close mates.

Ex-army guy?

Yeah. I rang Jodie back. I said, 'I've got to go.' She said, 'I thought you'd say that. I've booked your flight, it leaves in thirty minutes.' The police found him. I went to the hospital and sat there for a couple of days until he was conscious. I remember us just hugging each other. We'd shared stories. He was one of the blokes I'd spoken to. Anyway, his family then arrived and I had to get back. I remember thinking on the way to the airport, how easily the roles could have been reversed.

As I sat there on the plane, my arms started bouncing on the armrests, uncontrollably. I got the shakes. I wrote it off as adrenaline. I got home and Jodie told me I needed to sleep. I tried, but it felt like an electrical current was running through my whole body, shaking the whole time. Every time I shut my eyes, I'd startle. I was already aware of suicidal ideation, from all the work that I'd done with my counsellor. I could see it coming from a distance. I realised I'd had these thoughts before. You just see it coming.

I just needed to rest my brain. I needed to take a tablet or something to switch it off. I was just going down this track. I wanted to get away. I couldn't stand being in my skin, thinking, I hate this, I'm a bad person, they'd be better off without me here. All this irrational bullshit was coming into my head. Just stop, stop. Shut your eyes and go to sleep.

For two days I couldn't sleep. I couldn't even shut my eyes. My emotions were flicking all over the place. Finally, I crawled into the shower, turned the taps on and curled up in a ball on the shower floor. I needed some sort of relief, just the water running on me. I was thinking of every way to kill myself. I was losing control and would not be able to stop myself. I called out to my wife, 'Get me out of here.' Luckily she was there. She took me to hospital. They took my shoelaces and my belt off, drugged me up to the eyeballs and threw me onto a concrete slab in a cell.

They put you on suicide watch.

That's all they had until they could transport me. Then I was on a minibus and next I was somewhere else, sitting on a windowsill alongside people who were bandaged up, talking to themselves.

Are you still medicated?

Absolutely. My wife walked in and she was mortified. My psych was on overseas holiday and so was my doctor. She didn't know where to go. I told her to call John Bale, the CEO of Soldier On. And so, John spoke to the blokes at the St John of God Hospital in Sydney, which was very confronting. I thought, I'll do a weekend here, but then I've got tons of work on.

You thought everything would get back to normal quickly?

The fact that I couldn't talk probably indicated it wouldn't. I was shut down. I was gone. Years of just trying to get through, just collapsed. The world collapsed. The nightmares that I had no longer just stayed in my dreams. Even when I was awake, all of a sudden stuff would happen. I didn't know if I was asleep or awake. It was the first time I accepted that I might have a mental illness, that maybe I did have PTSD.

I sat down with a Padre while I was there, who I tried to avoid because the last thing I wanted was to have God shoved down my fricken throat. But, he was persistent. He sat me down, God bless him – literally.

'Ben, I've noticed you've been doing the physical training sessions, all the counselling sessions. You've been going to the art therapy room, walking every morning.'

'Yeah, it's because I'm going to conquer this thing.'

'What if it never goes away?' I felt like I had been hit in the head with a sledgehammer.

'I don't know, I've never thought about that.'

'How about instead of you trying to conquer this thing, you see every day as an opportunity to learn more about yourself, your illness and how to connect with the world around you. How would that sound?' I said that sounded pretty bloody good.

'Why didn't I speak to you earlier?'

'Because you kept running away.'

I spent a year in a mental health hospital, off and on. Every time I came home in those early days it was like staring into the sun. I could only hold my gaze for a minute or so, and then the world would collapse in on me and I'd have to go back.

I was then looking down the barrel of no job, no house, no nothing. I came home at Christmas. It was absolutely fantastic. I'd been wanting a mountain bike for about three years and I got one for a Christmas present.

A few weeks after, I go for a ride up in the hills behind my house. It was a beautiful day. I was chasing the shadows between the gum trees, down the path. I could feel my heart rate speeding up and my breathing picking up. I also had a lot of drugs in my system. I started getting light-headed. As I came down the hill, around a bend, across a creek and over a little footbridge, my front wheel slipped off the edge. I threw my foot down to try to lift it back on, but the pedal got caught and instead, it just catapulted me over the top, headfirst off the bridge, and into a rock.

I came to in darkness in hospital, feeling like I was in a tomb of pain. Even the air was throbbing. The doctor told me not to move. 'You've broken your back in three places, and your neck in two places. If you move, you could be a quadriplegic or die.' I was so pissed off. I was just overcoming wanting to take my own life and now my life is almost taken away? I thought, what if I could live one more day? If it's come down to this now, then every day counts. I remember my dad telling me that whenever he's in a bad spot he says the Lord's Prayer, and my mum said, just ask to be granted grace. I was afraid. I couldn't move. All I could do was stare at this one little dot on the ceiling. That's burnt into my mind. And so, I said the Lord's Prayer and I asked to be granted grace.

What happened next?

I fell away, into the darkness. Up ahead of me was this small light, and I was moving toward this light. I was looking at it.

It was just like a small spark. The only thing I had control of at that point was my breath, enough to blow on this spark. You know how you start those little fires? If you blow too hard, you blow the bloody thing out. So, I was blowing, nice and gentle. I kept blowing and the spark turned into this little flame. Then there was this realisation – 'Oh my God, this flame is me. I need to gently nurture this flame back to life.' Now, I don't know if this was the drugs I was on or what it was, but this was a very clear image in my mind.

I'm still thinking, grant me grace, grant me grace, and return to life, return to life. It kept drumming through my head. I wondered what it would look like? Wouldn't it be good to be able to use my arms again, because then I could hug my kids again. Imagine if I could sit up and give my wife a kiss on the side of her face. Imagine if I could sit on the grass at my house, just after it had been mowed and have my dogs come up to me. It was like these little snippets of my life. Not big things. Just the little tiny moments that piece it together. Then I thought, imagine sitting in my rowing boat again. Imagine seeing the sun come up in the morning at five o'clock and the birds singing as the day begins. Imagine if I could do all that? Those thoughts really galvanised me, and then the healing process began.

How long were you in hospital?

Only a few weeks. Then in rehab in a full body and neck brace. Which I must say was pretty fucking hard and scary, because every time I moved for about six months, I felt like I was going to die.

How was your mental health through all of this?

All over the shop. But I think that was a turning point for me, not wanting to kill myself anymore. I thought, fuck it, I'm going to live.

So, at the point where you could've died from your severe physical injuries, you decided to stop thinking about taking your own life and to live.

It was at that point, at my lowest, when I had nothing left to lose and I could have died, that I thought, life is fragile, I could die any minute anyway. Why would I take my own life?

We were still going to lose our house, there was no income coming in, but I was still alive and I still had my family. Between 2015 and 2018 my wife did a massive amount of heavy lifting. She pulled it all together. She kept everyone together. I was trying to learn to walk. I was trying to learn how to lift up a broomstick. I was trying to learn how to lift my head up without being scared that my neck was going to break.

Even though I wasn't a CEO anymore, I came up with the idea that I would be the CEO of my life. So, who is on my board? I've got my psych, my counsellor, I've got a physio, I've got my dietitian, I've got my sleep doctor. First, I went to my psych and said, 'Tell me why you're a good psychiatrist. Show me your numbers. How many clients have you got, how long are you going to stay in business? Because I am not changing psychologists. If I pick you, you're going to look after my life for the next few years. This is a two-way thing, I'm not just here to bleed out and tell you what's happening with me. Are you on board or not?' Then I went to my counsellor and said, 'What are your credentials?' She said, 'If you don't like me, you don't have to stay, you can just leave.' I said, 'I'm with you.' And then – this is critical – I got back in my rowing boat.

I was sitting there, just off the jetty at five o'clock in the morning, minus five degrees, watching the sun come up, bawling my fricken eyes out. It was at that point I realised I'd made it back to life. I thought, I'm alive. I'm alive. I'm alive!

I started training with other veterans. They had a learn-to-row program through the RSL and then Soldier On. So, I ended up with these other veterans, sharing similar stories. One of them goes, 'You should try out for this thing called Invictus.' 'What's Invictus?' I said.

It was explained to me that it's an international multi-sport event for wounded, injured and ill veterans and their families. Founded by Prince Harry. 'It's like an Olympics for wounded veterans.' I was happy to do some training with these guys, and then a year later I put my application in.

Which event did you put in for?

You had to pick a couple of sports. I put down indoor rowing and powerlifting, as I'd been working out in the gym. So, I showed up at the first selection camp, at the Australian Institute of Sport. Next thing I know, I'm standing out at Sydney Olympic Park dressed in green and gold, getting ready to represent Australia. I'm like, 'What the hell?!' And this thing is massive! When my kids came with my wife, they were given green t-shirts for the family members to wear. Now, my kids were teenagers and there was no way they were going to wear these t-shirts, but when they see Team Australia families walking past wearing the shirts, they put them on.

What happened next just changed my life. I was getting ready for the start of the indoor rowing, doing the warm-up with my headphones on, listening to the *Gallipoli* movie soundtrack. I was thinking to myself, all these poor bastards. All these guys, I want to do it for them. All these mates that I've met. The seventy-two other Australian competitors. The 500 wounded people around the world that are here competing. I just want to do it for my family. For my wife. For myself. I've just got to walk out there and just do my best.

So, as we're walking down the corridor to start up the indoor rowing event, these six foot eight, 180 kilogram guys are leaning on my shoulder going, 'Hey, little Aussie, how do you think you'll go? Ha-ha. You've already lost.' I'm freaking out, wondering why they all sound like Arnold Schwarzenegger. But, I'm just so bloody proud to be Australian. And then the light opens up and the arena erupts. I felt like a gladiator, walking into the Colosseum. It was a deafening noise. I look up to the left, as I'm walking toward my machine, and my whole family has flown down from Brisbane. I didn't know they were coming. My sister had made up these stupid bloody t-shirts with my face on them and 'Go Ben!' So, I got on the machine and rowed to my race plan, finishing it off as my coach instructed, like a human hammer.

I won the heat! I'd got my personal best. I was so happy. It was the first of two heats, after which they tally up the times of both heats and work out the top three placings: gold, silver and bronze. I ran over to my wife and my kids while the other race was on, then I was asked back down for the medal ceremony. I was like, shit, what, I'm in the medal ceremony?!

There's no podiums at the Invictus Games. No flags. No anthems. Everyone is equal. We're all the same, but I've got my

Aussie gear on and then it's announced: 'Farinazzo, gold for Australia.' I went on to win a second gold in another rowing event.

After the Olympics, the Commonwealth Games and the Invictus Games, the Royal Mint – who make the medals – ask one or two competitors to come back and talk to them about what the medals mean. I was invited to come and talk about what the medals meant to me. I said, the first one was for my wife and my kids, because they won that. I would not be alive or here today if not for them. The second medal takes me back to just sitting in that rowing boat, off that jetty as the sun was coming up, because it reminded me that the sun will rise, even after the darkest night. That medal's for me.

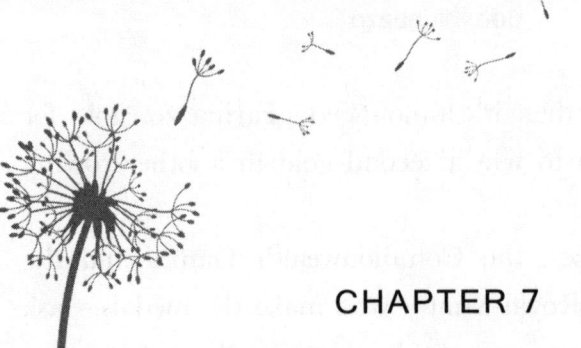

CHAPTER 7

Nick Sherry

The Minister

I first met the Honourable Nick Sherry in Parliament House, Canberra, in 1993 at a young political leaders' event. He was a Labor senator and junior minister in Paul Keating's government. I was the New South Wales Young Liberal President.

Nick doesn't remember meeting me, but I remember meeting him. He struck me as one of the most arrogant people I'd met in politics – and considering some of the people I've met in politics, that's a big call.

Thirty years later we are friends (and he isn't arrogant anymore). He is a very successful businessman and a global expert on superannuation and pensions. But not before a crisis in Parliament over twenty-five years ago led to a suicide attempt that made him realise that raw political ambition is not as important as living.

* * *

Nick, I remember you telling me you were pretty much born into a Labor family. Your dad was a Member of Parliament?

All through my teenage years and then later, up until I went into politics at the age of thirty-five, the Australian Labor Party was just part of my life. I grew up with it. And many of my activities, my work ambitions, were centred around being in parliament, being a politician.

Dad – Ray – was born during the Great Depression, in Glebe, in working-class Sydney. He was an orphan; his parents died in a motor vehicle accident. He came from a very challenged background back then in the 1920s and 30s. He had very little formal education. At the age of fifteen or sixteen he signed up for the Merchant Navy, which was during World War II. After that he became an actor in Stratford-Upon-Avon, where he met my mum. They came back to Sydney in 1956.

Mum was in the theatre too. When they returned to Australia in the 1950s, getting work in theatre was pretty challenging. Dad got offered a job as the first newsreader for the TV station in Hobart. That's how we ended up in Hobart. Then he went into politics for Labor. He failed to get into the Senate in '67. Then he was a Federal Member from '69–'75, and a State Member from '76 until '80.

He was a real humanist. He found some of the cut and thrust of Labor politics, and politics in general, hard to deal with. I think I learned a lot from that. He was very idealistic.

He was always very practical. His view was that government has an important role in people's lives. But, because of his background and experiences, he never believed government could solve everything; there were limitations. Government is there to help people with wages and conditions, housing, health, education. That was a very strong influence.

Mum was interesting because she worked either full time or part time, which was relatively unusual for that time. She was much better educated than Dad. I think they were ahead of their time, but because she worked, Dad always used to do the washing, ironing and all the washing up. Dad worked full time for the TV station, Mum worked part time at the TV station and for theatres. She was very active. It wasn't a traditional family in that sense.

Was it a happy childhood?

Oh yeah, yeah, lovely. Fantastic childhood. Very supportive family. Lots of fun. A good life. Comfortable. Mum and Dad bought an old colonial house in Richmond, outside Hobart, because it was cheap. Now it's worth an absolute motza. But you know, people didn't want colonial houses in the sixties. They didn't admit to anything to do with colonials or convicts.

So, we grew up in the country for my teenage years and I would catch a bus into Hobart and go to high school. A very happy life.

When I was at university I wanted a job, so I ended up working at Wrest Point Hotel Casino as the night cashier auditor. I really only intended to take the job for a few months, but I ended up working there for four years and became active in the old liquor trade union.

There was a big internal fight in the union at the time and I thought, I can do a better job than this mob, so I stood as State Secretary in a by-election at the age of twenty-three, and was elected. It wasn't a career I'd initially thought of, but because of the relationship between unions and the Labor Party it was sort of related.

One of the good things about being a union secretary is you're in touch – and I hate this term – with everyday people. You get to know what their attitudes are, what their aspirations are. The Wrest Point Hotel Casino paid people pretty well, but in the broader areas of hospitality – restaurants, clubs and hotels – it's low-paid, tough hours, shift work.

The union gave me much more direct contact with people in their everyday struggles. The members were mostly room attendants and housemaids cleaning rooms in hotels, who were working part time. I'd meet with them and hear their stories about why they were working. Supporting their families.

I worked night shift for the four years I was studying at uni – not doing a lot of study, but I did get my degree. I was Secretary of the Student Union as well.

You were involved in the Tasmanian Council of Unions too, weren't you?

I was the President.

You were the most powerful unionist in Tasmania at that time?

Yeah. In the Labor Party as well. Senior Vice-President for a period of the State Party. Everything was focused on my political life. I was a significant Labor figure in Tasmania, but also nationally.

At the expense of everything else?

Oh yes, that was my total life.

Even though I was very focused on the union, I stood for State Parliament – didn't win. I was only twenty-three. Stood for the federal seat of Franklin in '87 and didn't get elected. Then there was a Senate vacancy in the 1990s. So I went into the Senate at the age of thirty-five.

Were you so ambitious for politics that it didn't matter where you got into Parliament?

It was all about politics and Parliament. I had a very limited social, personal life. So that was the centre of my life. Too much the centre, as it all turned out.

After the first three years Paul Keating made me a Parliamentary Secretary, even though I didn't support him against Bob Hawke, and I told him that to his face. I stuck with Bob Hawke. Anyway, Paul Keating rang me up and he said, 'You're a bloke with some ability. I can't just reward everyone who supported me – it wouldn't be a good look.' He told me that because he'd served in Parliament with my father. They were both elected in 1969 and they shared an office in the Old Parliament House. Anyway, he got on well with my father.

Was your dad still alive at this stage?

No, Dad had died in '89. Just before I went on to the Senate. It was very sad. But he knew I was going to get there. So, anyway, Keating rang me and said, 'I knew your dad well, I always liked him,' and he was very cultural. Which wasn't a great part of my focus in life. He said, 'I'm going to make you Parliamentary Secretary for the Arts.'

That was 1993, and then in '96 I became the Deputy Leader of the Opposition in the Senate.

I've always thought that was remarkable. You were barely forty. Not that that's necessarily young, and you're from a small state. Being Deputy Leader puts you straight into the shadow cabinet and the leadership group in six years, right?

Six years, yeah, and I thought, well, you know, in that political sense, fantastic. And having my own area of policy and responsibility, plus all the economic responsibility in the Senate. All that work. It was a big workload. Big promotion. And I was very happy with the role.

I first met you between 1993 and 1996. I remember your supreme confidence, on the verge of arrogance. We formed a friendship over time and a policy interest at the same time. And then the suicide parallel as well.

I don't think I've ever been an arrogant person. I enjoy what I do, and I enjoy an outcome. That to me is the satisfaction. Not talking about it.

Were you restlessly ambitious or ruthlessly ambitious?

I don't think I was ruthless. I'm a person who believes you keep your word in politics. You are frank. You call it as you see it. I'm still very comfortable in doing that. I don't think I'm in any way devious or scheming. I don't like that. My father never liked it. I don't like it. I was feeling very happy in what I'd achieved to that date.

By 1996 there was only one more position for you to get, which was Labor Leader in the Senate. All of a sudden you're one step away.

Yeah, and I had that expectation. I was told that's where I would end up. I didn't want to go to the House of Representatives. I didn't want to be Prime Minister. I was very happy in the

Senate. I could do what I wanted to do and focus on the policy areas I enjoyed in that role and have significant influence.

It's the exercise of power. Power's not a dirty word, it's what you do with it. So, applying power and influence for the policy areas I was interested in.

In six short years you're in this extraordinary position of power and influence.

I'd achieved everything I could possibly achieve, in my view. Short of being in government.

How long until the suicide attempt?

It was about eighteen months. October 1997. I always remember it, because it was a week before the AFL grand final. Which Geelong wasn't in, by the way. I think Adelaide won it that year, they beat St Kilda.

So, you're at the top. Then there's the travel rorts affair.

It was a government own goal. It just blew up out of nowhere. There had been incorrect claims for travel and accommodation. Transport Minister, John Sharp, was caught for sleeping in his car or something, and claiming it as a hotel expense.

Other Howard government ministers were tied up in it and had to resign too?

These Howard government ministers were all falling over. Then they hit on me for claiming expenses in Hobart, because I stayed privately at my mother's house, but Mum didn't live in Hobart anymore. She lived in Canada. She was a resident of Canada. She'd remarried. She kept her house in Opossum Bay, which was an outer suburb of Hobart, because she returned to Tasmania three or four months of the year. I stayed there and still claimed the allowance.

I knew politically I was finished. Three Liberal ministers had fallen over, so I was going to fall over politically.

You had to resign as Deputy Leader and Shadow Minister?

That's right. I could read the tea leaves. I felt a great disappointment in myself for being stupid.

I couldn't see a way through this politically for myself, and also, it directly hurt the Labor Party, which was very important to me. So, there was a great sense of disappointment.

We met as a leadership group on the Thursday night, where we were discussing it. Kim Beazley, who was the leader of the party at the time, Bob McMullen, Gareth Evans, who was Deputy, Simon Crean, Jenny Macklin I think was there, and John Faulkner. They hadn't said to me, you've got to resign, but I sensed what I had to do to end this – literally – what the right thing was. We finished dinner and then I went back to the flat. I came to my decision after that meeting.

And Nick, were you highly distressed? Were people worried about you?

No, I don't think they were worried, because I was keeping my shit together very well. Very composed and rational.

I had a flat in Canberra, where I lived alone. I went back to the flat, thinking back over the events of the week and what I thought would be the inevitable outcome.

My conclusion was that was the end of my political career, so, consequently, that was the end of my life. They were both connected. Which is why I made the decision to take my own life, because there wasn't anything else there for me. That's it in a sort of brutal nutshell.

There was no-one to walk through the door and stop you?

No, no, because I wanted to succeed.

You wanted to die?

Yeah, oh yes. And I'm told it was very close. I lost an enormous amount of blood. The police found me. I could vaguely hear a door knock and they smashed it down at about six or seven o'clock in the morning.

I was taken to Woden Hospital. I was semi-conscious and then became unconscious. Eventually, I woke up late morning at the hospital. It was just me and a male nurse. They wouldn't allow me any communication with anyone.

People must have been worried about you?

They'd contacted my family. Mum came back from Canada. Helen, my ex-wife, was still alive – she sadly died of accelerated dementia a few years ago – and my then-girlfriend, Sally, who I married, both came up to Canberra, as did my stepson Adam.

It became public on that morning, so there was this whole media storm going on, which I was oblivious to. I was totally isolated from all of that. It was just total isolation. Just family members. No politicians. Then Kim Beazley came to see me four or five days later.

I was in isolation. I could only leave the hospital for walks et cetera with my mother, and then it was decided that I would go back to Canada with Mum. They were living in a place called Okanagan Valley. I had some counselling before I went.

Any meds?

For depression, but it was quite mild apparently. I had no contact with the outside world initially, even in Canada. The understanding was that I'd go to Canada, stay with Mum and her husband Ken for about four or five weeks.

How did you feel when you realised you hadn't completed your suicide?

Initially, disappointed. But once I got to Canada, and was away from everything, I actually relaxed and started to think about why I had done that, and what the future would hold, not in any great detailed sense. It was a period of time to reflect; to switch off but reflect.

Have you ever tried again?

No. Never felt close to.

People often think you have to have a mental illness to try and take your own life, but yours was a catastrophe that came out of the blue. You were tracking this brilliant career. Something went wrong. In the grand scheme of things, it was nothing, but to you it was the end of your life.

When I look back, I was far too focused on politics to the exclusion of everything else. I lacked balance in my life. I was generally content with life. On occasions I would lapse into deep worry. Whether you would classify that as depression, I'm not sure. Too deeply concerned and worried about issues that I shouldn't have been worried about.

Did the media leave you alone?

One journo attempted to contact Mum and ask for an interview after I got back. But that was it. No, they were respectful.

I came back just before Christmas, because Parliament would be resuming the following February, and I had to decide what I was going to do. In mid-January I went to Canberra. I talked with Kim Beazley and a number of other political people, some conversations with people locally, and with Sally, my girlfriend. So, quite a few people, you know, about their views and perspectives. Because it was a very unusual situation in a political context.

Did people find it difficult to talk about, as was more the norm back then?

Yes, and they really struggled with understanding. The majority of people were in favour of me not continuing politics. I think partly it was just ignorance, lack of understanding. Partly it was worry about me. The pressure of the job.

And it was rightly put to me that it's not a normal job. But there were a number who said, look, it is possible for you to rebuild and continue on doing what you're doing. Provided, you know, you're a bit more diverse and not quite as obsessed about your work focus.

Of those who said, don't come back, was there a tone of 'You'll never go anywhere in politics because of the suicide attempt'?

I think partly. But also, partly because you have to start again. Don't expect any special treatment.

Did you come across anyone who was moralistic about it or disgusted with you? You know, a moral or religious perspective?

No, no. It wasn't moral.

Was there any shunning?

No. I think it was genuinely a worry about me as a person.

When did you make the decision to push on?

'Push on' is probably the wrong term. I think it was, well, on balance I think I can still do the job. I understand the limitations going forward, but I think I can still make a contribution, I think I can still enjoy what I do. There was some trepidation, going back for the first week, into the building – all the circumstances, the reminders. Quite a bit of worry about that. I sold my flat in Canberra and I linked up with a couple of other Labor MPs – we stayed together, and I did that from then on, right through to the end of my political career.

I imagine if you'd come back after cancer or a heart attack, all sides would have spoken about it to you. But with a suicide attempt, some people wouldn't have known what to say.

No conversations at all. It was as though the world went on and nothing had changed. Nick Sherry is a back bencher. He's there. He's asking questions. He's doing his committee work, et cetera. No conversation at all with anyone. Until later in the year, I think.

John Herron, a junior Liberal Minister from Queensland, later in the year made a comment about people going and slashing their wrists. A couple of colleagues, even from his own side, were quite horrified because they could see me sitting there. I was asked about it and I said, 'Look, I'm not upset.' But that was one point when people actually thought it was okay to talk to me.

You're a quiet, determined, hard-working man, who lived through a suicide attempt at a really shitty time. My sense is that what you've achieved is a quiet way of showing you can hit the bottom and come back.

I think that's right.

But you've never really evangelised it?

No. I did do a couple of local community events on depression, where I talked about my own circumstances. But I didn't want to become a poster boy for depression or suicide recovery. I knew that was always with me. You can't get away from that.

Do you think there are benefits to having hit the bottom of your life?

Yes, there was a benefit, yeah. I wish it had been another way, but I don't know how that would have ever happened.

Today I have three beautiful kids, and I'm still in touch with my stepson, Adam. Sally and I divorced eight years ago, about the time I was thinking of getting out of politics. But we still have a good relationship. The kids are all doing well. My daughter has just finished her fourth year of medicine, the other two are first year at uni.

Mum died about six months before we went back into government in 2007. She knew I was a Shadow Minister and we thought we would win.

My life today is more diverse, more relaxed. I've got a coffee group, which started during COVID. It's a coffee group of men. They know my political background. We talk a bit of politics, but we can talk about what's happening locally in Devonport or with their families. They're very varied. A couple of guys are off the *Spirit of Tasmania*. Nothing to do with politics. A pharmacist, a guy who is a retired forester.

It came about purely by accident. During COVID you could move around Tassie, but you know, you couldn't leave Tassie. So, all my work was done at home. I'd go down and get a morning cappuccino and there was a retired journo, his son ran the coffee shop, and he'd be there helping out in the mornings. We'd go and have a conversation out the back of the coffee shop, and a cigarette, and we'd be there for half an hour or so. It just sort of grew from there, and as it grew, we moved to the car park next door. He has a trailer truck, so we meet there at nine o'clock in the morning. Seven or eight of us, around the back tray of a truck. It became quite famous, actually. The local mayor comes into the same coffee shop, the Premier drops in. They're not permanent group members.

We call ourselves the Magnificent Seven. We just yack. Just turn up every day and talk about everything and often disagree, from world events (Donald Trump, Gaza, Ukraine), health issues as we age, travel experiences, superannuation (yes, never far from my life and everyone's thoughts), the cost of the proposed AFL team/stadium in Hobart, local theft, potholes in the roads, housing and property prices and local government incompetence. Really diverse, down-to-earth, respectful conversations. We want to change the world from the back of a pick-up truck!

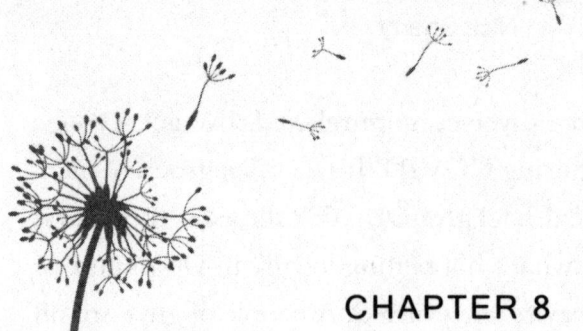

CHAPTER 8

Leilani Darwin

The Indigenous Advocate

Leilani Darwin is an impressive woman who has been touched on a personal level many times by suicide and mental illness. Leilani is a Quandamooka woman and her lived experience has led her to become a powerful advocate for Aboriginal and Torres Strait Islander people within the mental health and suicide prevention space. Leilani is an important voice we need to listen to, as she highlights understanding and acknowledging lived experience, cultural practices and intergenerational trauma when implementing and supporting mental health programs for First Nations people.

* * *

Leilani, let me kick off by asking you to tell us about yourself.

I'm forty-two. I was born in Brisbane, one of three children that my mum, Olive, had. I had an older sister and a younger sister,

Christina and Nicki, three years separating each of us. Three girls. Three different fathers.

Mum's Aboriginal. I'm a Quandamooka woman, my mob were from salt water, Straddie Island. My father is French-Indian background. So, my great-grandmother was a French woman, and my great-grandfather was an Indian man.

How do you identify then, how do you see yourself? Because that's an incredible cultural span.

It's been really tough. Identity has been something going back to when I was a little one. Mum was fair skin, blonde hair and hazel eyes. Both my sisters were fair-skinned, blonde hair and light eyes, from their fathers. Then you've got me, from my dad with his Indian background, being dark-skinned, looking very different. I knew we were Aboriginal. But I didn't know anything more than that.

We lived in housing commission in the suburbs of Brisbane. My mum had my oldest sister when she was fifteen. So, she was quite young. Three years later, she was eighteen when I came.

I went to Petrie Terrace State School for a while. We lived in Paddington. It was one of the places that I have memories of, where we actually stayed somewhere for a long time. I was getting around with no shoes on. Running everywhere.

That was where, because of my skin colour, I experienced racism – mainly kids, sometimes adults. People calling me racist names in the schoolyard: 'little Abo' or 'little black gin', stuff like that.

Were there any other dark-skinned kids at school, or was it a pretty white neighbourhood?

There were a few, and we actually had an Aboriginal teacher's aide. Aunt Jackie was her name. I was really embarrassed because my biological father was violent with my mother. There were many occasions when we'd have the police and ambulance over, so she knew.

Mum was an alcoholic and she had several males who would come over and supply her with alcohol, and drink with her. When it went quiet was the time for us kids to get worried. I remember quite a few times going down the hallway and listening, hearing slaps and yelling and stuff, then we'd ring the police or the ambulance.

How old were you when this was happening?

From a little girl, Aunt Jackie, she'd ask, 'You right, bub? I've seen the police.' I was just really embarrassed.

My younger sister was probably too young to realise. My older sister just tried to protect us all and make sure that we were safe. For a long time, my safe place was at my grandmother's. Noela Betty Smith. She was part of the Stolen Generation. Nan was in Yeronga, not too far away. She had a beautiful house. When we stayed there, we'd have breakfast, morning tea, lunch, afternoon tea, we had dinner, we had supper and dessert.

One time we came home after being at Nan's. The door was open, and we were wondering where Mum was. Everyone was looking around. I ran down the back stairs. It was one of those high-set homes in Paddington where there was nothing underneath – a Queenslander. Mum was just slumped, leaning on a pole looking straight ahead. She wasn't there. Her eyes were open. I could see a wound on her leg. I was shaking her and everything. So I ran upstairs. My Uncle Bob went downstairs and then my dad appeared. I don't know what had happened, but there was a commotion happening and we were told by our nan to get in the room. My nan had a vice-like grip for an old woman. Somehow, I got out of Nan's hold and opened the door, to see my dad being held up off the ground by his throat by my Uncle Bob.

So, you saw violence as well? It would have been frightening to watch all that happen.

When you grow up in those environments, stuff like that becomes the norm. There were lots of different things that happened there and in different places we lived. There was one place Mum used to take us, and she would sometimes disappear for a couple of weeks, or a few days. We would stay at this place, where she'd gone to drink, but we'd wake up the next day sometimes and she'd be gone.

I've reflected on the fact that this was actually a big thing for me as a child. I think it really changed me to become a people pleaser. Because then I wasn't disposable. We could tell when Mum was having a hard time. She'd be drinking more, and she'd be making us do more things. We lived off whatever the government gave her. Sometimes there wasn't any food, some days there was. We just learned to enjoy the treats when we got them. Like going to my nan's place.

Your nan never sought to intervene?

No, there was a dynamic there. My mum's biological father was an incredibly violent and abusive person. As was their stepfather. So, there was abuse of extreme amounts toward my nan, my mum and aunty, and that adversely affected my mum.

153

Was your nan a very proud woman?

Yeah. Real old-school. Had to be dressed impeccably. Her favourite place to shop was Lifeline, much to the dismay of us young kids in terms of what she was making us wear. We'd go to church, which was the other place we didn't mind going to – when Mum would send us to Sunday School – because we'd have a good feed.

One night we were woken up in the middle of the night by strangers in the room. I remember this lady telling us to get up, that our mother didn't want us anymore. This woman was pulling me and my younger sister out of the room. I remember looking back down the hallway and seeing my mother sitting in a chair, slumped over, heaving and sobbing, heartbroken. Thinking back on that now, as an adult, I wonder if she was asking for help. Was she saying she couldn't cope?

They were from Child Safety. I just thought, who actually thinks that it's okay to do that?

Mum rang them and said she wasn't okay – they didn't just rock up in the middle of the night. But to come in and say your mum doesn't want you anymore? There are such better ways to do it.

How did you feel about your mum when you heard that?

Hurt. Confused. Frightened. You know, we spent different times in foster care. Often they'd split the three of us up, sometimes together.

What was one event that you think really impacted you, with your mum?

Mum was drinking with my younger sister's biological father. Something happened, there was a commotion, and I woke up.

Mum was locked in the room with my younger sister. She came out of the room holding my sister, rocking and crying.

My older sister and I followed Mum into the lounge room. She was holding my younger sister, she kept repeating how sorry she was. Mum had stabbed my sister in the back. I don't really know the circumstances around how or why that happened, but I remember us all in the middle of the floor in the lounge room crying and she was just apologising. I was concerned for my sister but crying, knowing that we were going to be split up.

Did your mum ever know any sort of peace or balance in her life?

I don't think so. She used to cut her wrists. She ended up doing it so many times. We used to wake up after she'd been drinking and see blood everywhere. Sometimes she'd have to go to the hospital. She ended up with a hand that she couldn't use properly because she'd severed the nerves.

Mum killed herself when she was twenty-nine. I was ten. My sister and I found her. It was traumatic. It was unsettling, but you just go with the flow. It becomes normal. And, as I said, I became a real people pleaser. I just wanted people to be happy and not sad, and to love me and to be safe. That was really hard.

People have often said, 'Your mum didn't know how to show you love, so you don't know how to show love.' And I'm like, 'Excuse me?' I know she wasn't okay, but I know my mum loved me.

Because of all this, there was some point in my journey and in my life where I thought, I don't want to have the same life she had.

Her lesson for you was not to live the way she did?

I didn't want to live like that.

But you never hated your mum for what happened?

No, but my sisters did. Both of them, when they've been in some kind of crisis situation have said to me, 'I'm just like my mum, always have been, always will be.' I've said to both of them at separate times, 'Why? Why do you have to be just like Mum? You don't have to be. You've got choices now to live a different life.'

So, you felt sympathy for your mum?

Yeah, and understanding.

Was the fact that she'd killed herself openly talked about, or was that swept over?

I don't think anything was openly talked about. I mean, we knew it. I don't remember much of the funeral, to be honest. There are pockets of things which I have absolutely no memory of.

Why do you think that is? You don't want to remember them?

No, some of them are to protect my brain. I know that there were certain kinds of abuse that have been blocked, and different situations that I just have no memory of. But I know different things happened.

What did suicide mean to you at ten?

You don't think about it as suicide. You just think about it as a death. As a loss. And the fear of what's going to happen to us now? Where are we going to go? Who is going to look after us?

We spent some time with our nan. My younger sister ended up going to her dad and my older sister stayed with my grandparents. Uncle Ken and his wife Estella lived in Sydney, and they offered to take me.

To be taken away from everyone that you knew and had grown up with was tough. I had a little running away episode. I ran to Kings Cross, made it to my friend's place and stayed underneath her bed for about a week or so. But her mum knew. I eventually ended up going home, back to my nan's. Which was awesome.

My nan had a lot of health complications, as a lot of mob do. She had kidney failure, angina and diabetes. We got home one day and there was a casserole dish smashed on the floor, but no-one was there. The dish had dropped on her foot when it came out of the oven. She ended up in hospital and got an infection. She kept telling the staff that it smelled, but they said it was fine. It ended up being amputated. As soon as that happened, we couldn't go to the hospital to see her. She was so ashamed of not being a complete person, so she wouldn't let anyone see her. Nan died at fifty-nine, the day before Christmas, which would have been her sixtieth birthday.

When she passed away, in some ways it was worse than my mum's death. Even when I was in Sydney, Nan would ring me all the time. She used to write me letters. She used to crochet and send me things like that. I still have them. She kept that communication with me, and that love and care.

You didn't get to say goodbye to either of them, your mum or your nan?

No.

After your nan died, did you go back into foster care?

No, my aunty had three teenage kids herself, so she took me and my older sister in. And that was where I had my first suicide attempt. I was thirteen.

What brought you to that point at such a young age?

There was a lot of grief, a lot of unprocessed thoughts, feelings and emotions. It was a shitshow having five teenagers in a house. But on top of that, we'd been brought into a house where we grew up with our cousins and spent time with them, but now we were imposing on their space. I was literally the black sheep of the family. I put my aunty on a pedestal, because she took us in. I was just so bloody grateful that we didn't have to get split up or taken anywhere.

I would hide underneath the house, talking to the animals because that's all I felt that I had. After trying to do something nice and ruining some clothes, one of my cousins saw me and called me stupid, said that I was dumb and couldn't do anything right. That all I had were the animals to talk to. I thought, I'm done. So, I went and did the same thing that my mum did.

Did you end up in hospital?

Yeah, and my aunty organised for me to see a professional. Then she wanted to know what we talked about. I told her we just played games, as you do at that age with a professional. Later on she would complain about how much money that cost her. 'All you ever used to do is sit there and play games. There's nothing wrong with you.' She didn't realise I was someone who had been involved with Child Safety. I'd learned there's particular things that you share and there's stuff you don't share if you want to stay together, and because of that, I wasn't sharing this with her.

I had another attempt on my life, I must have been fifteen or sixteen, and then I moved out.

Were you out of school as well?

The deal was you go to school or you work. I couldn't stand school. So, over the school holidays I enrolled myself in a certificate in retail. That went into the beginning of the school year and I was like, well, I'm studying. Then I got myself a part-time job and then after that I got myself a full-time job in retail, and that was the end of school.

Where did you move to when you left your aunty's?

Another shitshow. I moved in with a best friend. We were drinking and she had some kind of meltdown episode and couldn't stay there anymore. I had to get other people to live there. It was not good. I was running amok. I was drinking too much alcohol, still going to work. I met my partner when I was there. He and I moved out. I fell pregnant, at seventeen, but lost the baby.

Did you ever get a diagnosis of mental health issues back then?

When I was twenty-one, after my third suicide attempt, I found the right person who helped me. I really didn't know who I was and where I came from, but I knew how much I felt like I belonged when I was with mob.

I'd got a traineeship in government at nineteen, in Brisbane, around this time. Because of where it was, I'd see blackfellas around. So, I had basically finished everything for my traineeship about six months in. Then I saw this Indigenous middle management program advertised. Through the application and interview process I really got to spend more time with blackfellas, and build some really strong relationships.

I felt comfortable with my mob. I felt safe. I felt like I had when my nan was around. I was like, these are my family. I get it. If I'd grown up with this, things would have been really different. Because I still at that stage didn't know where my mob were from. So it was hard.

Can you tell us about what led to your suicide attempt at twenty-one?

I was living for the first time on my own. I was working in a different area, always on temporary contracts. Then I was working in the Department of Public Works, in the community renewal team. I had some amazing experiences there. I travelled over to Palm Island with the consultants after the riots. It was about helping them choose how they responded initially after the riots. I was chosen because I had a relationship with some of the locals. The dance troupe from Palm Island came down to Brisbane, and I was their host when they came down. I knew quite a few elders and young ones from the island. I had built relationships, and they thought it would be good for me to go over. Things had deteriorated. Depression had crept in and I didn't realise. I went to my doctor and talked through my symptoms with him. He told me there was good news and bad news. The good news was that I wasn't dying, but he explained that I had severe depression; that was the bad news.

Was this the first talk of mental illness with you?

It was a revelation for me. And it got worse. I was very lonely.
I felt very alone. No partner, it was just me. I had to take time off
work because I couldn't function. I felt very empty and very sad.
It was the first time in my life where I ruminated on things. I used
to think that if I died, who would come to the funeral? I would
be counting the names of the people on my fingers. How could I
conveniently and politely die, without being a burden? Put a sign
up. Warn people. Pack everything up, so people wouldn't have to
do that. That was all going through my head.

Did you want to die?

I felt like I wanted to, and that everyone would be better off
without me.

Did you go to hospital after that attempt?

Yeah. Straight in, straight out. My ex came and picked me up
and dropped me home. I was disconnected from everyone. Just
completely in a hole, with no life. I was pushing people away and
didn't even know I was doing it. Completely isolating myself and
just staying in my house. I think it was inevitable, as I'd never
dealt with any of the stuff from when I was younger.

You just buried all of that deep down?

I remember my aunty always used to say, 'I don't know what your
problem is. You act like your childhood was so bad. It wasn't
even that bad. Why have you got to make such a big deal about
it?' Acting like what happened was normal.

After my attempt, I went back to a place I'd been to before,
a women's service in Logan – the Centre for Women and Co.

I told them I really needed to see someone. They said the same as they'd told me before, that there was a waitlist. I told them I tried to kill myself on the weekend, that I needed help. I was so fucking embarrassed, but I was also angry. I tried to kill myself. Can I have some help please?! The receptionist went and spoke to someone and made something happen.

I met Chris, a counsellor. And the biggest, greatest gift that I got from her was understanding that all these things that had happened to me were actually terrible. They weren't normal. But how I felt was normal – the behaviours that I had, the patterns, the hypervigilance. Now I was understanding PTSD and recognising that I'd had PTSD since I'd been little.

I felt affirmed. I'd thought I was going fucking crazy. But actually, I wasn't.

Chris strategised with me about the relationships I'd had and how often people expected me to drop everything and save them. What was I doing to support myself?

Did you get diagnosed with depression? Did you get medicated?

Yeah, I did. Three or four years I stayed on the medication. Between that and the counselling, connecting with mob, it worked.

Work kept going in a good way, in the public sector. I met my daughter's biological father, a Torres Strait Islander, and I was blessed with my daughter, Tahlia. My relationship with her father was volatile. I had a domestic violence relationship with him but I was in love. Deeply in love. After I became pregnant, I was like, I can't do this anymore, because my daughter couldn't grow up like I did.

Did you want your daughter to know she was Indigenous from the beginning, unlike your upbringing?

Well, here's the thing. Her dad was tall, black, a dark Torres Strait Islander. And out comes this white, blonde-haired little girl. I was like, I know which side of the family you take after. She's tall and slim, and he's tall and slim. She's got long eyelashes, and he's got long eyelashes. She got the best of both worlds. She wanted for nothing. I was a different mum to my mum.

At some stage you became a counsellor.

I started off studying part time, a Diploma of Counselling at the Australian College of Applied Psychology. Then I worked out I was going to be doing it for years. I was a single mum, trying to look after a baby, studying and working. It was beyond tough, but it was worthwhile. I passed, and an opportunity came up to be a counsellor at a men's corrections facility.

It was sink or swim. I learned the ropes, but still a lot of the guys would say, 'You're just textbook upper class blackfella, aren't you, miss?' It means they think you're just uppity, snotty. You learned, you went and studied, so you think you're all that. You're better than us.

And this is coming from mob, right. And so, what I did – this was probably pivotal to where I've ended up now – I thought, I need to introduce myself in a way that tells these fellas I've got more in common with them than they think. So, when I started a group, I shared about who I was, I shared a bit about my background, about losing my mum to suicide and about how I grew up. Just little bits of what I'd been through. So that they could see I'm a person and could probably relate to me more.

My biggest drive has continued to be about what I can do so that others don't have to experience what I did. I get the pain, I get the sadness, I get the isolation and the loneliness. I get that this is all you know, and this is how you grew up. But I also get that with hard work, with really tough bloody decisions that are painful, by changing relationships, by changing patterns and behaviours, it can be different.

What do you see are the solutions to the high level of suicide among Indigenous Australians? Where do we start? What have we got to change?

There's no single straightforward answer. There's a lot that we know that's worked, and there's a lot that we know doesn't work. The biggest thing for me, the foundational piece of that is self-determination. It's the need for government to stop over-prescribing what it needs to look like and what the criteria is, and how you have to be able to report your whole life in three months. When you look across the span of funding, a majority of the money doesn't go to Indigenous organisations. It goes to non-Indigenous organisations, delivering services to Indigenous communities.

What you're doing is unashamedly, as an Indigenous woman, running a business for profit.

It's led by the community and what the community wants. Its outcomes are driven by self-determination and it's led by us. It's led by our people. It's expertise that we bring in, as First Nations people. Our leadership actually govern this and know what's best practice. It's culturally informed, it's trauma informed. We also make conscious decisions as a company around who we will work with and who we won't. It's not about just making a buck.

It's about what we can do to improve outcomes for our people and how we can show government. Everyone's always saying, 'I can't find anyone, there's no blackfellas who can do it.' Yes there are. You're just lazy or have fear to work with us. You don't want to do the work to find them. Either that or you don't like what you're told. Part of what I've done for years is work with non-Indigenous organisations to help them understand the value of working with First Nations mob. To value their expertise, value the wisdom and understand that you can't do this alone, but neither can we. It's time for us to lead change. I'm a blackfella. I don't think of myself as anyone special. I know that I'm in a very privileged position in so far as my networks and who I know, and that kind of stuff.

You've done well and you want to pass that on to others?

Yeah, it's a big part of who I truly am, but not so long ago, things got bad again. I was done. I was just so done. I will never be enough, was all I thought in my head. I'll never be enough for someone in a relationship. I'll never be enough of a mother. I'll never be good enough anywhere.

I'd been in a dark place. I had these painkillers. Strong, too. I'd been laying there for about half an hour. Tahlia was in her room. The dog was on the bed with me. I popped some music on. I'd teed up a message to four of my – I call them earth angels – people who are just there unconditionally. Who get it. Just to say, 'I tried really hard. I just need you guys to know you've always been there.' Based on what I read, I knew how much time I had. So I thought, I'll jump off flight mode. Flick this through. Be sweet. I should just go to sleep. Sustained, slow release. So, the cops came. Ambulance came.

I'd sent the message. I thought I'd be dead ...

165

Someone, something, was watching over you.

I know that now. But I wasn't happy at the time. They'd tried to ring me. Multiple times. I had to go to the hospital. But an interesting thing happened, and it was one of the scariest parts of it, which I wasn't expecting. I started to feel the side effects more and more when they were wheeling me through emergency. I was getting hot and cold flushes. One side of my body was going all tingly. I was getting dizzy head spins. I was petrified. This was very different to going to sleep.

The thing that scares me about all of this is they didn't even do an appropriate safety plan when I left hospital. They gave me the same medication when I left the fucking hospital. When I was in hospital, I was hallucinating for quite some time. I couldn't talk. I couldn't see things, you know? I couldn't walk on my own for days. I was bad. On the first morning, one of the senior doctors from the mental health unit walked over to me, got very close, and said, 'You shouldn't have done that. You and I both know that it was wrong, what you did. You really shouldn't have done that. It was wrong.' This is the system's response when I end up in the mental health unit – they didn't even have a psychologist.

Are you happy to be alive now?

Now I am, but it took me getting to that point.

I went to my uncle's place. This is Uncle Dominic, with his wife and my cousins. I haven't really known them, because my dad kept me separated from everyone. It was the best thing for me. Such a safe place. I could just relax. He's been like the dad that I never had. He said to me, 'I feel like you just don't love yourself.' He said that he was proud of me. He said, 'Look at what you've done all on your own.' I thought, fuck, why didn't someone tell me that earlier? It meant so much.

Do you see yourself as a phoenix?

That's my plan now to find the new me. That's why I've been doing the work for all these months and continuing to do it, even with the many difficulties I've had, to come back slowly. I'm not going to do what I was doing before. I need to change that sense or need to help others that's so predominant. I can still do that, but I have to do that in a way that respects me and my wellbeing, and I've never been able to do that. Which is a lifetime of changing patterns and behaviours that kept me safe. Now I want to be happy, to have peace and joy, and actually enjoy my life – surely I too deserve that?

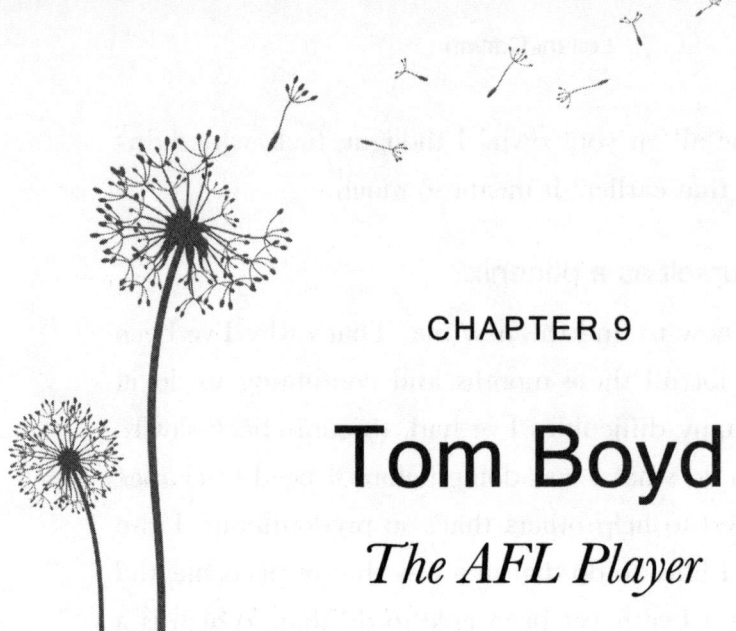

Tom Boyd

The AFL Player

Tom Boyd has an AFL/Aussie Rules story. Because I grew up in Sydney, ten minutes' walk from Leichhardt Oval, the home of the Balmain Tigers Rugby League team, AFL is a foreign sport to me. I knew very little about Tom Boyd or his world. But, during his interview, the scale of his talent and the weight of his decision to leave professional sport at his peak became clear.

Tom was the top AFL draft pick at eighteen and he signed one of the biggest deals in AFL history. And, at twenty-three, he was brave enough to walk away from it all to put his long-term physical and mental health first. His decision to walk away from the life he was born for set a new standard in Australian sport.

I travelled down to Melbourne, to the heartland of AFL, where first over coffee and then at his home, Tom told me his story.

* * *

Tom, tell us about your childhood.

I grew up in the eastern suburbs of Melbourne. It was an absolutely stereotypical suburban upbringing, in the sense that it was school, sport and family, for the most part. My dad was an electrician, he ended up operating a big commercial company. Mum didn't work in my early years. She had been in superannuation, working for AMP for a number of years, and then ended up at schools as a business manager. I have two sisters, one younger and one older.

Were you one of those kids who is good at every sport?

Yes. Basketball and football [Aussie Rules] were the primary sports I played.

At primary school I was a normal-sized kid, but by the end I grew 27 centimetres. Then every year I grew slightly more than everyone else. I was always that kid in the middle of the back row in the school photo.

At fifteen years old, I was 105 kilograms and 197 centimetres. It was challenging at times, because at school, if you knock someone over it was always your fault. If a group of guys got in trouble, it was me who got caught because I was always the one who stood out the most.

Was it a very functional home? Lots of love?

Lots of love, yep.

And you were a good kid at school?

Yeah, never perfect. There were a few kids who tried to see if my height matched my fighting skills, but for the most part I was pretty much a straight A student.

And tell me, did you always have confidence that you'd end up playing AFL professionally, that you had a big future in sport?

Yes, probably from the age of six or seven, or whenever you start being cognisant of the people running around on TV doing it as a job. That's when I knew what I wanted to do.

Did other people think you could do it?

Yeah, from a very early age. At fifteen I was the captain of the Victorian metro team.

Did you feel stress or pressure about people's expectations of you at that age? Or were you just so focused?

I put more pressure on myself than anything. I was pick number one. So, I was the first pick in the overall draft. This is at the end of my schooling, I'd just turned eighteen. I was so far ahead and certain to get drafted that the goal for me was to do really well at school and get taken at draft pick number one. Most kids are wondering how they can get drafted. I was looking at how I could not only get to where I want to get to, but absolutely excel in getting to where I wanted to get to. Which is not so much the pressure from other people, but from myself.

What's a first, or number one pick in the draft?

About sixty or seventy players are taken into the draft for AFL teams every single year. Thousands of kids nominate to be included into the draft. I was the first player selected in the country. Out of thousands of players, they chose me. 'They' being the Giants [Great Western Sydney Giants (GWS)]. The bottom team from the year before gets first pick of the new crop of players and the top team picks last. It's an equalisation thing.

A first pick gets more pressure applied to them than any other pick in the draft. Not just for the season ahead, but through your entire career. You're forever known as the first pick of that year, in my case 2013. Add to that pressure the fact that I was now going to live in a different city – Sydney – and to play at a very new club in the competition. Straight out of school, I had to try and balance those three things.

Eleven days after I sat my last school exam, and three days after the draft, I was in Sydney, about to start pre-season, moving in with two other young players who had no idea how to live by themselves.

Everything changed so quickly, one minute performing well in my exams was most important, the next education was completely on the backburner. Leaving my education behind was extremely difficult. Because I loved it, and it was really important for me.

Were you keen to go to uni and also play professional AFL?

Yes, I wanted to do both. I got into electrical engineering at Sydney Uni, but I got told not to do that by the club. They thought it would be too much of a workload. Maybe they were right, but I still to this day believe that doing something would have been better than nothing.

So, you listened to the Giants and you didn't do it?

I regret that. I thought I could be at university and play football, so that was frustrating to me. What I didn't understand when

I got drafted was how important education would be in my performance as a footballer. I always thought it was something I had to do. I soon realised that it was something I needed to do, to give me some structure in my life so that I could feel that who I am as a person is not solely based on these two hours of a game in front of thousands of people, every single weekend. Football's not who I am, it's just part of it.

How did you cope with that?

Not well. That wasn't all. During my first year, I had two major issues. Sleep, and dealing with the AFL pre-season.

The first pre-season is probably the hardest thing you'll ever do [as a player]. It was such a big jump from where I was and what pre-season looked like as a junior, to what pre-season looks like as a professional AFL footballer. You're on the training track doing extra running sessions, extra boxing, extra wrestling. We went to Cronulla sand dunes a bunch of times for workouts, bearing in mind it's the height of summer in Sydney. It is a baptism by fire, fifty to sixty hours a week.

And your other problem is sleep?

I'd never been more tired than I was, yet at 1 am almost every night, I was staring at the ceiling thinking about the problems of the next day or the next year. After a couple of months, my sleep issues changed because my body had just reached a critical point of fatigue where I started to fall asleep everywhere and anywhere.

So, now I'm dealing with that, alongside all the other changes of being away from home in a new city and being a full-time footballer for the first time.

Did you seek some help for your sleep issues?

No. The first time I mentioned anything was after the next thing that happened.

What was that?

I started to feel nervous all the time. I'd felt nervous before when I played big games on national television as a sixteen- or seventeen-year-old. The problem now was I felt this way on a Tuesday night when we had Wednesday off. In the pre-season that didn't make any sense.

When I first started talking to anyone about what I was facing mentally, they'd ask how I was going, and I'd brush it off as me just trying to find my feet. The truth of it was that I had a lack of certainty about why things were happening the way they were.

The response I got from anyone at that stage was, oh you're probably just homesick. Give yourself a few months, it'll go away.

Homesickness is a big thing in AFL. The thinking is, if you draft someone from Victoria and they move interstate, they're going to be miserable and they're going to leave because there are nine teams back in Victoria where they'd rather be.

My thinking was, why would I wait for how I felt to just go away? Why don't I just go back to Victoria? That started to pop into my mind early in my first season at the Giants.

So, you're into the season. Your sleep is still troubling you and you're still very homesick. Were there any other stresses or pressures on you?

I didn't feel I had extra energy to give, so typically speaking, on a day off I'd spend a lot of time by myself. I'd often drive to Manly, check out the beaches and go surfing. I just wanted to be alone, and I was feeling it.

What was the media saying about you?

Before I got drafted, I went from potential number one pick to probable number one pick to definite number one, to best number one pick ever, to the greatest player ever drafted. Once I arrived in Sydney, the media tone toward me went from being, 'this is amazing', to 'why is he not playing in the firsts?'

You didn't go to the first grade?

You go up and down. I played roughly half and half, with a bit more time in the reserves. I would have been dropped five times and promoted five times across the year. It's pretty common for young players. Young players take time to get there.

Right around this time, I'm stressed, I've got issues with sleep, issues with what I'd later learn was anxiety. I'm homesick. Then I get a call from my dad on a Thursday afternoon. He usually called to chat to me about last week's game and this week's game.

How often did you speak?

Probably five times a week. It was good having someone in my corner who wasn't there, and could provide me with objective and often critical feedback.

We chatted away and he told me that I'd had a contract offer. Now, in the pre-season, in January, the Giants came to me and said they wanted to extend my contract for another two seasons, effectively going from being a two-year player to a four-year player. The reason they do that is they know you're a risk of leaving, because you're a Victorian boy. And the numbers they offer you each year are much, much more.

So, you're getting into the more serious money?

Yep, very good money. But what I knew was, if I signed this deal, I'd be signing myself to Sydney for four years. To the Giants, specifically.

How locked into those contracts are you?

The first two years? Iron clad. I just wanted to wait until the end of the season and talk about it then. Let's do one year. I've still got twelve months after that. Anyway, my dad made this phone call about the contract offer.

This contract had come through my manager, to my dad. I said to Dad, I'm not interested in signing, thinking this was the contract from the Giants. He said, it's not from the Giants. I asked who it was from, but he didn't want to tell me. He didn't want to distract me because I had a really big game coming up. 'I want you to concentrate on the game and play well on the weekend. Then I'll come up, we'll have dinner on Sunday, and talk about it.'

I thought about nothing else for two days, stressed myself out and played terribly. On the Sunday, Dad nonchalantly informs me that the offer is from the Western Bulldogs.

The deal was $7 million for seven years, the second biggest deal ever in the AFL. I'm freaking out. This is amazing! How do I sign? I was thinking about how many cars I could buy and all the stupid stuff that goes through your mind when you're eighteen.

I flew back to Victoria and I met with my manager and my dad and we drove into an underground car park, at the home of the president of the Bulldogs. This was very hush-hush. It was the red-carpet treatment. They went through this process of explaining things to me and I'm sitting there thinking, you've already offered me $7 million, I don't care, but how are we going to get this done, because I'm still contracted to the Giants?

We couldn't get a deal done. We were going to wait twelve months and then the Bulldogs assured us the same offer would be in place.

When I finished that year, my one and only goal was to get away. Refresh. Get overseas. Decompress and reload to start again. And the way I was going to do that was to go to Indonesia on a surf trip with a few friends.

We were out in the middle of nowhere. No cell reception. Full-blown isolation, exactly the recovery thing I was going for. The trip coincided with the trade period for the AFL season. The grand final is the last Saturday in September, then there's a week off and then the two-week trade period. With the limited access to wi-fi that we had, I saw that the captain of the Western Bulldogs had said he wanted to be nominated to be traded with the GWS Giants. I'd signed power of attorney over to my manager. I started to get a couple of messages, but there wasn't enough reception for me to call him. My dad sent me a message saying that every good thing that had happened had been when I was willing to take a risk. I thought about that for a while and told him to pull the trigger, to get a deal done.

There's a stand-off. The first week goes by, nothing happens. I'm still in Indonesia. The night before the trade period finished I got a text message saying both clubs had gone home. This deal was going nowhere. I was staring down the barrel of going back to the Giants. This was the point when I started looking at real estate in Indonesia, to move over there. The next morning, I woke up: no news. The deadline was just a few hours away, at 2 pm. All of a sudden I got a text message at about eleven o'clock, which said it was done. The deal went through.

How did you feel?

To be clear, I chose the money. Financially, it was a life-changing opportunity. I don't regret talking about it that way. There were also a few other elements in play. The ability to be 'the man', the big forward at this club. There'd been a few other guys competing with me at the Giants, but the Bulldogs didn't have a king forward. This was my opportunity. I wanted to be part of a club with a history like the Bulldogs.

This was probably the second time in my life when I made a choice that I figured would fix everything. The mistake that I made, like many people do, is that I looked at my life and thought, this next big thing will be the antidote to all my problems. What I've learned is that the progressions we make don't fix the things that were there beforehand. In fact, the progressions often lead to more stress, anxiety and depression.

This was the best deal ever, but I don't think I understood the vitriol that I was going to face.

I was constantly fighting between whether I was a good person or not. So, for those two years, that was basically what I was living.

When you were with the Western Bulldogs, did people boo you? Did people have a go at you from the sidelines because of the trade?

Yeah, oh yeah. One hundred per cent. I was used to that, but this was a whole new form of abuse that I faced.

The players were great. The culture of AFL, generally speaking, is you don't talk about each other's contracts. You've got to live with each other, fifty or sixty hours a week. Travel with each other. Sleep in the same room. Run 400s in the blazing heat. When you're halfway up the Cronulla sand dunes, no-one cares what you're paid. They were welcoming for sure at the Bulldogs at the time. But I don't think the club knew what they'd signed up for either.

I don't think I knew just how much and how specific the condemnation would have been. By the way, don't feel sorry for me. For the first time, my on-field play started to improve. 2015 was quite a strong year for me.

How was your sleep?

I started having issues sleeping, especially around game day. Thursday nights I basically couldn't sleep at all. Much worse. You come to the club on Friday, you do the captain's run. Can't sleep on a Friday. And I know I'm playing a game of footy the next day, having hugely compromised sleep for two days.

I would just stare at the ceiling and try to work out why this was. So often I'd be thinking about a mistake that I'd made from the previous week or something someone had said to me during the day. I was just consumed by this.

Was this affecting your play?

Yeah of course, but I was trying to limit the impact these issues were having on my football.

You hadn't talked to a doctor about any of this?

No, and you don't talk to your friends.

So you're on your own? Not even your dad or your family?

God no. What was I going to do – tell people that the bloke who's getting paid a million bucks a year to play AFL footy is sad?

I didn't know who I was. I didn't know why I was feeling the way I was. The first time I can confidently say I was depressed was when I couldn't get out of bed. I couldn't face the world. If I'd played badly, the vitriol I was facing, plus the fatigue, plus waiting for the club to give me the same criticism, just did it for me. By Monday, I'd turn up and find a way to put on a brave face. Get in there, do the right thing. Tick all the boxes I was supposed to.

If I was a mate of yours, even I wouldn't have known?

Nah. I was very good at hiding it. I've been good at it since I was eighteen.

How did you feel before competing in the grand final?

In 2015 we had a very strong year. I got to three quarters of the way through the year. Again, bit tired, run down. Very common for second-year players. I played some good football in the reserves, but sort of never really threatened to get back in the AFL team. Or I did, but the coach basically wrote me off for the year – you've done your dash, get yourself ready for 2016.

I had always had issues being lean enough and being able to run enough. It was a big point of stress for me throughout my career, the ability to get my body in a position it needed to go to. During my off-season, between October and November 2015, leading into the pre-season, I hardly ate at all. I ran every day and I trained every day.

On purpose, you didn't eat?

I was militant about it. Anna, my now wife, and I started dating in 2015. She was asking me what was wrong with me? Because I hadn't eaten all day. Maybe some blueberries and a couple of scoops of yoghurt. I was preparing for it. I was mentally 100 per cent invested. My plan really worked, because I did get very thin and I did play much better.

People talking about their mental health will often tell you they were at their worst when they were succeeding the most.

We made the finals series in 2016, and won the grand final. It was the first time a team had won from seventh position on a home and away ladder, ever, in 150 years of AFL football. First team to win four finals in a row as underdogs. First Bulldogs team to win in sixty-two years, since their first and only other premiership in 1954. And also, from a fairytale point of view, one of the biggest grand final viewerships in AFL history. The whole country was behind us.

Who were you playing?

We played Sydney in the grand final. Everyone was riding the wave. We were all so invested in each other. I played an absolutely stellar game. I played an integral part. People tell me I kicked one of the most famous goals in AFL grand final history, in front of 99,981 people, and we won.

This is a fairytale story, right?

Best few days of my life, in a professional sense. You know, life comes at you very quickly. Throughout 2016 I'd dislocated my shoulder between a dozen and two dozen times. It was absolutely destroyed. But in the AFL, if you can run, you can play.

Eight days after the grand final I had a shoulder reconstruction. Two weeks after that I had surgery on my ankle. I spend the entire off-season in a sling and on a crutch.

It was so frustrating, because I was exhausted. It had been such a big year. A great year. I couldn't go surfing, couldn't recover and couldn't sleep, again. Sleep had been okay for the finals series, but then I couldn't sleep because I had my shoulder in a sling.

I was still two-and-a-bit months away from fitness. I was in the rehab group. My anxiety went through the roof. My sleeplessness went through the roof, and I didn't have the great endorphins from playing the games. Things were getting rough. Once I returned to playing in 2017, things continued to get worse and worse – and worse. I was having soft-tissue injuries, calf and hamstring injuries. I was too young to be having those sorts of injuries. I'd never had them before, and they were very obviously stress related.

I started to get sick all the time. Head colds and the like. Then I had issues with concentration. My memory was shot. I'd be standing in the gym, reading my gym program and then I'd think, what am I doing here?

Eventually I got to a stage in 2017 where I didn't sleep for two weeks and I was still playing footy at the top level. The soft-tissue injuries effectively meant I couldn't get through the game. I'd finish at three-quarter time or just after.

I couldn't run, basically. They told me they needed me to play a half in the reserves. Just to show I could get through, and then they'd play me the next week in the firsts. I remember thinking, this is the worst of it. This is like I've got nothing left. I was about to turn twenty-two, living by myself. It was raining. Middle of the year in Melbourne – miserable place to be at the best of times. I was trying to work out what I was going to do, because I couldn't play. There was no way I was getting through.

I just couldn't play that weekend. You don't get to take sick leave as an AFL footballer. I was completely between a rock and a hard place, compounded by a couple of weeks of not sleeping and stress. It had been four years of issues at this stage. I was absolutely in the mindset of: I've got no idea what I'm going to do next. Now, when we talk about suicide, was it something that floated through my mind? Sure. I felt completely trapped by my perfect circumstances, with no options. However, I never made a plan. I realised at that moment more than anything I needed help.

Tom, was that a big thing for you to admit to yourself that you needed to talk to someone about your mental health?

Oh, huge. I didn't want to burden people, because I was always so lucky with things. I didn't want to say to people, how can you help, because I don't understand this, or I can't solve this problem. I would have been telling someone that I needed help to get my life together, when I had all the resources and success in life you could possibly ask for.

You thought there would be no sympathy for you?

Right, not only that, but I felt they shouldn't have sympathy for me, and I felt like people couldn't understand me. Thankfully I'd had some interactions with the psychologist at the club, and so I picked up the phone and finally asked for help. I called her and said alright, the world is actually falling down.

The first thing I needed from her was to help me navigate the club. Which sounds stupid, but unfortunately when you're in the position I was, I had to go through this process of talking with the football club about why I wanted to take time off, why I needed a break. I wasn't worried about losing my career so much, but trying to explain to people why the number one pick, the seven-million-dollar player was upset, that he wasn't feeling that well?

I met with the club, and the psychologist was there. There was the club doctor, the executives, all of the big dogs, and she was on my side. She laid it all out because I wasn't in a state to.

These aren't exactly the blokes you talk about your feelings with. These are serious football people, who have been part of the previous generation of men. They don't have time for this stuff. They asked me what I wanted to do. The psychologist told them that I wanted to take some time off.

They said, 'Well, what do we say publicly? We're going to have to say something to the media about why you're not playing.' They said, 'We can just make a statement about personal or family issues.' I thought, bullshit. They're going to dig around. I said, 'I would like to say the truth. I want to say I've got issues with anxiety and depression, and insomnia, and I need to fix them so I can play again.'

I needed people to understand that I wasn't sitting at home sad because people were being mean to me on Twitter. There's a very big difference between feeling criticised and being incapable of working. From an authentic point of view, I needed the fan base to understand that I was trying to get better, that I wasn't giving up.

As the news broke, I took a week off and distanced myself from the club. Turned my phone off and headed down the coast.

It was just a breather, just a little valve pressure release. I had to go back and start training again, because otherwise I'd de-condition. If you de-condition, you can come back and be mentally ready, but you won't be physically ready.

I still wasn't sleeping at this stage, and I was saying, I can't be at the club all day if I haven't slept. So, I would turn up at the club and do a training session at 7 am because then I was essentially going home to rest. Then someone came out and said, 'What's wrong with you now?' It was a sign of the times. People didn't understand what this stuff was. The club was clearly supportive, but there was a very fine balance.

The real change in terms of my mood happened because I finally got a proper break from football. We didn't make the finals, so I went away through September and October and did a lot of work with a psychologist in that period. By the time 2018 rolled around, I was in a decent place. I was still dealing with the pressures of football, and I was now dealing with the added element that people were treating me differently because of my mental health.

How did the media go? Were there any articles saying this is a good thing? Finally, we've broken the taboo around mental health issues in sport.

I took a bit of control back with the narrative. In football, in Aussie Rules, no active player had really done this before. No-one had really spoken about it. No-one had ever really shared.

In 2018, after quite a strong season in the first team, I started having issues with my back, and I eventually ended up on the sideline through the back injury.

I had the off-season and my back just didn't improve, which caused a sleep issue because of the pain. I thought, is this the next chapter of my life? I'd had the knee-jerk response before, thought of chucking it all away, but never paid it any real credence. But this was different.

I was back at university. I'd started studying business and was really liking it. I talked to the doctor, Gary Zimmerman, who'd been at the club for decades. I said to him in the pre-season, 'Gaz, I think I'm going to give it away. I think I'm ready to move on.' He looked at me like I was nuts. He gave me a piece of advice, having seen this too many times. Players who were injured or out of form, they'd come to him over the years saying they were ready to give it all away. Six months later they'd come back, crying about how this was the worst thing they'd ever done. He suggested I get back out on the field, and get the back injury fixed. Which is what I did. I got to the start of 2019, played a couple of games for Footscray in the reserves coming back from this injury. Immediately, I knew this wasn't for me. So, I called the club president and I retired.

What did you say publicly about your retirement, at such a young age and in the middle of such a lucrative contract?

I had lost the passion to be an AFL footballer. I didn't have the 110 per cent required to go out and be an AFL professional athlete. There are only two choices that you have in that situation – go through the motions, take the pay cheque, playing out your games with no passion, or you make a decision that's authentic to where you're at, leave the money behind and get on with life, which is what I did. On the positive side, I was bloody excited about my future and about what I could do. I'd had a taste of what the future could look like, doing this university study, and I wanted to go out and see what the world had to offer.

Do you feel better having gone through such a difficult period, to be where you're at?

Yep. I love what I do. I left in 2019, and I had obviously made comments and told the story. Everyone wanted to know about it. Everyone wanted me to come and speak at schools, and so on. I found people enjoyed listening to it. I felt like I could make a positive contribution.

I'd always been good in the media, so I could always do that stuff. But I'd never really had a story to tell – you know, this thing that I was passionate about. So, I went down the public speaking path. I felt like I could do some great not-for-profit stuff. The lived experience is the most important thing that anyone has.

How was your mental health when you retired?

What I found was, I lost structure. Which I'd never lost before. Ever since primary school and through football, it had been: be here, do this, do that. This is how it is. It's actually the reason I went back to play community football at the end of that first year, 2019, which I enjoyed. But people know me just as much today for the mental health work that I do, as anything.

Are you happy about that?

I am. It's been an interesting space to work in. It's also one that has changed so much in the last five, six years since I've been in there. It's gone from being something we should be aware of, to something that's vitally important, that we care for people.

I feel like the way I've approached this has been authentic to me and has been very much focused on how I use my story to create context for other people to tell theirs.

You realised football wasn't the best thing for you. So you made a big change in your life. In fact, you changed the direction of your life completely.

My life wasn't going to change unless I changed something about it. I thought circumstances would fix the problems. I won a premiership. Got drafted number one. Signed a contract. But the problems were still there.

So you had to give away the thing that you had been best at for as long as you could remember.

I took time off and I changed the course of my life. That was the big moment. The second moment was, now that I was surviving and I was in a steady state, did I want to thrive and was I able to thrive in the industry I was currently in? I didn't think that was the case, so I thought that the best course of action was to do something about the future I wanted to have in forty years' time, rather than starting in seven years and maybe losing out on three quarters of what I could possibly have achieved.

If nothing else, hopefully my story will tell people that we can look across our lives and think that if I get A, B, C and D, life's going to be pretty good. And, in a lot of cases, it will be. If I have a good marriage, job and purpose, that adds up to a lot of life. But it's not all of life. If you think those things are going to be the solution to your issues, I encourage you to look at whether you're dealing with the underlying problem. Try to find solutions. That is my main message, along with this: don't feel like you can't get support, because of how your life looks to others. You can.

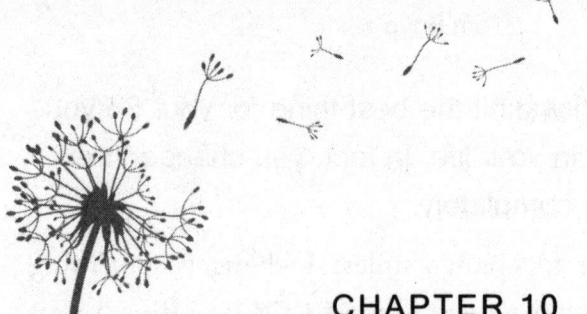

CHAPTER 10

Jacqui Lambie

The Senator

With Tasmanian and army veteran Senator Jacqui Lambie, what you see is absolutely what you get. You'd want her on your side in a fight. She is tough, driven and uncompromising. Outspoken doesn't come close to describing her. 'No fucking bullshit' does.

But for seven years, before she decided to run for Parliament to fight for veterans against the failure of government to look after them, Jacqui Lambie – a former soldier herself – was unemployed, and lived with crippling back pain and depression, reliant on a succession of pain medication, antidepressants and alcohol.

At her lowest point, she decided there was nothing to live for and no way out. She just wanted it all to end. But she survived. It changed her life – and the Australian Parliament – forever.

* * *

Tell me where you started in life. Did you have a normal childhood, a happy childhood?

For me it was normal. There was no abuse in my family or anything like that. If there's one person my dad was ever scared of, and the only person, it was my mother. You didn't get to bend the rules around Mum – not even Dad did.

You grew up in Tasmania?

In Devonport. Dad, Tom, was a truck driver. Had been for forty-five years. Mum, Sue, was working in the factories around Devonport. Then Mum hurt her back, so she went to TAFE for three years, to learn admin. They separated when I was thirteen. She had her first baby when she was seventeen. She lost that baby to cot death. I think by the time they separated, they'd been together for about fourteen or fifteen years and I think they just outgrew each other. Another thing that probably put the pressure on their marriage was both of them pulling down double shifts. After Mum separated from Dad, we had to move into public housing.

A hard-working family?

Just your average, blue-collar, working family, trying to pay their rent.

Brothers and sisters?

One brother, Bobby. He's four years younger than me. I moved my dad in with me, but Dad had a massive heart attack eighteen months ago and we lost him. Which was better than the alternative, because he used to say to me, whatever I did, I was not to put him in the meat market. That's what he called aged care. If the worst came to the worst, I was to smother him with a pillow. So, I thought I actually got out of that quite lightly. He went himself.

And your childhood?

I grew up back in the days where you came home from school, got out of uniform and they didn't see you again until five o'clock. Piss off, get out on your bikes, go hang around with your mates. Mum and Dad's thing was to try to keep us kids, as long as they possibly could, without the worries of the world. My life was pretty carefree, to be honest. We used to go out on Friday night and we were allowed to go to the bowling alley and you had to be home by ten. Just that normal stuff.

Did your parents' divorce affect you?

Not really, because Dad was still in town. So it felt exactly the same. That first twelve months might have been a bit hard. But it was always amicable. If we wanted to go to Dad's for the weekend, we'd just go down there. It was no big deal for Mum. Just because they weren't married anymore, they were still good parents.

What did young Jacqui want to do with her life?

Young Jacqui had no idea. Young Jacqui was chasing boys by the time she was twelve. No wonder young Jacqui was running into trouble. I actually wanted to be a police officer. Then I took a gap year through Year 11, and I was starting to hang around a bad crowd. Mum was telling me to get my shit together or get out. So I went and lived with my girlfriend and her family, up in Katherine in the Northern Territory. That was a big learning curve. I was working in the Katherine Hotel-Motel.

When I came back from there, I went back to school for a bit and really got stuck into Year 12. Then one day, I went down to Centrelink with my girlfriends, who didn't have a job, thinking I'd just tail along. And across the road there was the big green army bus, doing recruiting. We made a pact and said, let's all go and join the army.

We were each given a clipboard by this recruiting officer, a bloke in uniform, who was quite easy on the eye. I thought it sounded great, so I hand back my clipboard, saying, 'Come on, girls,' and they go, 'No, we don't want to do this now.' I changed my mind too, but the recruiting officer said, 'It'll be good for you; we'll be in touch.' The next thing I know, I'm at the Army Recruit Training Centre at Kapooka. I didn't have time to think about it.

How did you find Kapooka?

When I got off the bus with my suitcase I was a bit chirpy, and got shot down straight away by one of the corporals pointing out that this was not Club Med. I walked nearly a kilometre with that goddamn suitcase. Then up a staircase to the top floor. It near killed me. I was only allowed to keep my toiletries. The rest of it got locked away. That was my welcome to Kapooka.

It was the third week before we were allowed to make a phone call. I rang Mum, crying, going right off my head, begging her to get me out of there, telling her how much I hated it. Her response was, 'Thanks for the phone call, you'll be right. I'll see you in twelve weeks' time.' When I eventually told my dad that story, he said that if I'd rung him, he would have come and got me. He'd have come there bloody throwing fisticuffs, demanding his daughter be let out. Not my mother. 'It'll be good for you. You can stay there. See ya.'

Was Kapooka life-changing?

It was. I don't know where I'd be had I not had my experience at Kapooka. Without the army, I wouldn't be a Senator. There's no doubt about that.

So, you're doing basic training and find out you're pregnant?

Yeah, and the army tried to throw me out. This is how I know all about the army and their dirty shit, right, because I've been through it.

I went through my basic training and we were all laughing because I was the only one not losing weight. I hadn't put much on, but I certainly didn't lose any. They were all slimming down and I was like, what the hell is wrong with me? I also wasn't getting my periods, so I'd gone back to the RAP – which was the hospital back then. I'd been back there twice. The first time they took a urine test and nothing come back. I carried on about it again and went back a second time. That was at about the nine-week mark. They said, look, this is twice now, there's nothing wrong with you. Stop trying to get out of Kapooka, which I wasn't trying to do – but I knew I was bloody pregnant.

By the time I finally got to the Army School of Transport there was a real problem because I had this pot belly. If I wasn't pregnant, then that was one hell of a cyst in my stomach. Finally, they tested me and discovered I was twenty-one weeks gone. The army went ballistic. This was a whole new thing for them. Within an hour of leaving the doctors, I was sitting with the Adjutant, the person that's in charge of the recruits. A Major. She had four kids of her own, but bear in mind this was 1989. She pushed a paper toward me and said, 'If you just sign that, we'll get you out.' I didn't want to leave. She told me it wasn't a choice.

'I'm going to talk to Mum first.' I didn't ring Dad because Dad didn't handle this stuff. I rang Mum and told her I was pregnant. I think she needed time to digest the news, because she asked me to call her back in five minutes! I gave her about ten or fifteen minutes, rang her back and I explained how they were going to chuck me out.

Long story short, I walked back into the Adjutant's office and, with all due respect, ma'am, told her that they couldn't throw me out, that I was staying. She had no idea what to do. This Major had all the big boys on top of her telling her to get rid of me, because they were worried about this getting out in the paper. After about forty-eight hours of to-ing and fro-ing, someone had spoken to my mum, and my mum was threatening to sue them, telling them how she was going to the papers. That fixed that.

They decided it might be better all round if they just kept me in then. That attitude never changed the whole ten years I was there.

Where were you living?

I was still in Puckapunyal, Victoria, now doing my training to be a transport driver.

Did anyone make a moral judgement?

No, but the Army School of Transport were very smart. They were going to make sure I got through the course to become a driver, so I could go home and have the baby, have twelve months off, then go back and be posted there for the first three years.

They sent me back home to Devonport, where I had Brenton, my first son. I had him and then there's an army transport reserve unit down there, so when I was able, I was allocated to them. But, because I hadn't served twelve months in the military, they couldn't give me three months maternity leave. Even though it was their fault. They should have done a blood test but they didn't.

They gave me some compassionate leave, but what it meant was I wouldn't be paid anything for three months. But what they did do, is they somehow organised it with Centrelink that I could get a single mum's pension from thirty-two weeks. I went and lived with Mum and had the baby, but ten weeks later I needed to go back to work, for more money.

So, all your life, you've been a worker?

Yeah, I needed to provide for my son. So, I get back to Kapooka. Mum came with me for six weeks, so I could get married quarters, get settled and look after the baby, until I could find the right child care.

Along the way, I met John. He was already in the army, and he was separating from his wife. I met him nine months after being there. So, that was all fine. Lived a normal life. Moved in together. That was good. John wasn't my son Brenton's natural father, but as far as he's concerned, that's who his dad is. That's all he knows. We've still got a really good relationship, even though we separated.

Five years in Transport and that's when I went over to Military Police [MP]. That was a change. Transport is really easy. Yeah, mate, no worries. Beep, beep. In the Military Police you were dealing with men of high standing, who expected a lot more.

Thought their shit didn't stink. That sort of stuff. They were experimenting back then with us, putting females into Military Police where there are men who are used to having their own way and where half of them shouldn't be wearing an MP armband because they're arseholes.

MPs aren't loved, are they?

No, but there's a way of doing things. It depends on how you wear your 'God band' [MP armband]. Making my way as an MP just about destroyed me in the first year. I came unstuck. I lost a stripe because I went to strike at a male Corporal, who I'd had problems with on the basic course. I'm the only girl that lost a stripe in Military Police. A real badge of honour. There was an old Warrant Officer – a Vietnam veteran, one of the last there – and he just said to me, 'You know what? If you'd have done that on base, rather than in public, I'd be standing here shaking your hand. However, you're fucked. Your problem is you're not getting these men right. What you've got to do is, you've got to find their weaknesses. Trust me, we all have the same weaknesses. Work it out.'

He really did take me under his wing, and I loved him. He'd be the one sipping on his whisky at ten o'clock in the morning and still standing at four o'clock in the afternoon. Just one of those old-school types. 'Don't read that shit. I'll show you how it's done. That's not how it works in war.' All that sort of stuff.

I'd had my second son, Dylan, who was about nine months old then. So, after that first year of getting in a bit of trouble, they thought I had 'baby blues' and wanted to send me home on compassionate posting. I think the Military Police were thinking, we'll send her home like the first time, and she won't come back.

Do you think you did have postnatal depression?

Knowing what I do now at my age? Shit yeah.

So, I went home to Tassie for about sixteen months. I think the Military Police forgot I was there and were hoping I'd get out so they didn't have to deal with me. I was also going through a separation from John at the same time. It was all too much. So the compassionate posting worked for me. I had normal hours, I was on full pay, working back at Transport Reserves. I wasn't away from the kids, and had time to work out what the hell I was doing.

That was enough to get me back on track. Just having that family support around me. They rang me up about fourteen months later and asked me if I was getting out. I said no, I'm not. Their solution was to send me to Darwin, back in the combat unit. I thought, you bastards. They were trying to make me quit. I called their bluff, said, 'Sure, no worries. See you soon.'

I went up there. I met a bloke, Phil, and we were sort of going out. So, when I did go out in the field, most of the time either he'd look after the kids or the boys would go home to their dad, John, who was then in a Logistics Battalion. He'd just take time off work.

I'd had problems with my back for a couple of years because of a muscle I'd pulled. However, I didn't want to tell them the severity of it. Instead, I just took more painkillers, as it was getting worse and worse.

Why didn't you want to tell them?

They would have medically downgraded me. Then they would have tried to get rid of me. That's how it plays out. We all know that. So, I'd just sit there and deny it. Had I known what it was going to do to me later on, I probably would have just said, 'Let's see if we can get it fixed.'

So you coped by taking painkillers?

More and more. They weren't looking at my file properly, as they should have, but were just handing them out to me. This had been going on for two years.

In September we were ready to go to East Timor, and I was supposed to be one of the first females over there. I thought, beauty – finally, after ten years, I'm getting into some sort of war zone. Forty-eight hours beforehand, they went to try the flak jacket on me and I was in a lot of pain. When they put the flak jacket on, they lift it over your head and just chuck it on you – that's it. Well, that didn't go down too well for me and my back gave way. I couldn't get off the floor.

Then reality starts setting in: I'm in trouble here. I was still denying it. All I wanted to do was some war time. Send me to East Timor, it's fine. The boys were going to their dad's for three months to spend time there. So it was all organised.

They told me I wasn't going. They rushed me around to a specialist. I went to Brisbane twice and had one come up to Darwin. The verdict was, I was stuffed. There were some serious issues that had turned into chronic pain. They told me they were going to discharge me.

You were out of the army?

I was in denial, but they said you're leaving either way.

I went to the Department of Veterans' Affairs [DVA] to have my claim processed. They were on base, but said they were so stacked up with claims that it would be quicker if I went back to Tasmania and started my claims process once the army discharged me.

How did you feel? Were you devastated about leaving the army?

I don't think I'd really thought about it because I was too high on painkillers. I was off my face. I was chucking them down my throat and starting to drink more, just to get through the pain.

I left in the first week of December, and then of course everything closes down over the Christmas period so I had to wait. In the new year I put in a claim and within a week they said that they didn't think there was anything wrong with me, that I could get a job as a security guard. I'm like, what the fuck is going on here? You just threw me out because I'm medically unfit. I'm that medically unfit you weren't even prepared to downgrade me and give me another six months to see whether things improved.

I hassled them for about two months and then they decided to do more investigations on me. I then went to someone who was supposed to be a professor, who put cortisone shots into my back. He didn't do it in the right spot, and that made me worse.

I couldn't sit in a vehicle for long. I couldn't lift anything anywhere near heavy. Anyway, they paid me for the first year and then they said they were going to put me on the books, which means you get your normal pay – the pay rate you got out on. I was a Corporal.

Then after forty-five weeks, they drop it down seventy-five per cent. I did that first twelve months. I was with the Commonwealth Rehabilitation Service (CRS) people, who have twenty-year-olds working there. Young people straight out of school, who said they'd seen me carrying two bags at the $2 shop. 'You know, you seem to be walking okay. Now if you can carry two bags, there's nothing wrong with you.' They'd brought in video surveillance by then, which they never had authorisation to do. That was video surveillance they did on me. The bloke that did the video surveillance, when it got to the AAT [Administrative Appeals Tribunal] six years later, withdrew, which made the DVA look like a pack of shitheads. And there was no justification, apart from them calling me a malingerer. Saying I was putting it on.

They literally called you a malingerer?

That's what was in their reports. That's what the Commonwealth Rehabilitation Service decided that I was. I just could not get the specialist treatment I needed in Tasmania.

When you were that crook, Jacqui, and down to seventy-five per cent, could you have got a job?

No. I was fucked. I was a mess. I couldn't even stand up, that's how bad the pain was. That went on for the next seven years, and then they pulled out and refused to pay me anymore, saying I was putting it on.

For the next five years I was on Centrelink benefits, fighting them. Centrelink decided to put me on a Disability Support Pension because they could see the pain. They had doctors in there who obviously do this all the time, who said I couldn't work. They couldn't understand what the DVA's problem was.

Still on the painkillers and the grog?

By then I'd worked out I had a problem with the drink, so I went to Alcoholics Anonymous [AA] for a couple of years.

Would you call yourself an alcoholic?

I went to AA because I wanted to stop drinking, because I knew it wasn't helping my mind.

But the next seven years were just a blur. It took me about five years to get it through to the AAT and get it that far. The AAT said the DVA could start paying me and do the right thing, that they had not done the right thing by me.

Did you handle all this yourself?

No, I had to pay for a lawyer. I was in a tremendous amount of debt, bringing up two kids and living in a world of pain. I was taking a lot of painkillers.

Then the AAT says, let's get you back with a rehab service provider. I'd known about this provider and she was very good. She asked me what I wanted to do. This was in 2007. I told her I wanted to be in a political office. I wanted to see what was going on. Because once they pulled that funding from me, I remember sitting in the corner of my house crying my eyes out, begging God, if he just gave me a second chance at life, then I promised I'd go and help my mates and these veterans out because they were being treated badly.

Do you think you had depression all through that period?

I know I did. The reason I had the depression was the pain. I just couldn't deal with it. Over the course of those seven years, I was on antidepressants and a lot of medications.

Were you feeling better?

Not really. I went and saw a neurologist who started injecting Botox into my back. That would deaden things, but then I couldn't get any more and I was back to square one with the pain. I deteriorated so badly. I gave up then. I thought, I'm going back down the drain. There's no treatment out there to help me. Depression's taking over again. I hit rock bottom. I had given up. I couldn't do it again. I couldn't go back through all that pain like I did before.

By the middle of August 2009, I couldn't live with the pain anymore. I'd had enough. I left the kids some letters. I'd written them about three weeks beforehand, because I knew I was on my last legs. It was just about determining how I was going to do it.

Then one night, I had a slight argument with a girl at a thing that I was at. It wasn't even an argument really, it was just a fuck you. I went down to meet another girlfriend for dinner. I'd had a few drinks. It was about eight o'clock and I just remember thinking, you know what? I'm done. I'm fucking done here. I just cannot do this anymore. That's one of the last things I remember thinking, and then just walking out onto a busy street. Poor bastard. I still think about the driver. I wrote him a letter. He didn't want to see me.

Did anyone else know you were so close to suicide?

I had the same psychologist all the way through, from 2000. He used to see me every three weeks without fail. He'd already been screaming at the DVA for twelve months, saying this is not good. She really needs extra care here, I suggest you put her in a psych unit. Well, they didn't fucking do any of that. He had written them three different, long letters to say she needs some serious fucking help here. She's going to take her own life. They were warned.

What happened after your suicide attempt?

I woke up in hospital. I ended up with about eight stitches down my face. Cut my lip open. When they found me they could hardly find a pulse or anything. They thought I was gone. When I came to, my two sons were standing there. They'd been told I was being brought out of the coma they'd put me in for the forty-eight hours. I had my two sons standing there and my father. And the looks on their faces, I'll never forget it. It was just ghastly. They were like, why?

Did you say to anyone else, 'I've had it, I'm going to kill myself'?

No. My friends were the ones that picked up on it. My inner circle. It didn't surprise them. It surprised Mum and Dad. Dad didn't know how to handle it. His best way was just to say, 'Okay, she'll be right, she'll be right.' And the boys … because I guess I was in their faces all the time, they'd become desensitised to watching any of it, as this had been going on for nine years, off and on. It was just shock on their faces. Hardly anything came out of their mouths. I just told them it was okay, that I was fine, that I wouldn't try it again. Within about ten days they had me in a psych unit.

So, they worked it out, finally …

… that I needed some help. This is why I wanted a royal commission into the DVA. Because I had been through the worst of it. This is what they do to you.

So, you're in a psych unit for the first time?

That's when things started to get better for me. Within seventeen hours, they had me ready to go to a new pain management specialist. They had extra psychology. Once I tried to kill myself, if the doctor had said jump, Veterans' Affairs would have asked, how high? What do you want for her?

Did your depression improve or disappear?

It disappeared. Once the pain started to deteriorate, once I could get that under control, the depression just lifted.

But you had hit bottom to achieve this? You had to basically, from what I'm hearing ... you had to embarrass them?

I wasn't thinking about the DVA then, but that's what it comes down to. I wasn't worried about the DVA. I just wanted help. What it did was it got them off their arse and started getting me help.

You must have been proud when you made that transition from a psych unit to a Senator?

I don't know why God had taken his time, but he came through. As part of the return-to-work program, I had six months in the office of the Senator for Tasmania, Nick Sherry.

Nick Sherry's office gave me that first opportunity. But I also knew, I'd worked out by then that the only way we were going to be able to make a difference with Veterans' Affairs was that one of us had to be inside the fucking pie.

So did you get into politics to help veterans?

Yes, yep. Because I could see what happened to Vietnam veterans like my uncle and his family, and my cousins. I had no idea about politics but I had to be inside that parliament – whatever the fuck parliament was – because that was going to be the only way to make a difference. That's all I knew.

Did you want to make sure other veterans didn't have to go through what you went through?

I already knew they shouldn't have to do this. I already knew that in the first two years after I was medically discharged, because there were other people I was meeting up with and I was thinking, this is just bullshit.

I had to start from scratch. But there was a fire in the belly, because I was so fucking angry. If this is what politicians do when they're supposed to be there to help us, and this is the way they help us, they can fuck off. That was my thought. I had a purpose. Just let me get back on my feet. I can do a better job than what you bastards do.

So you decided to get into parliament?

I had to. This is what I needed to do.

Do you believe in the saying that it doesn't matter how you get there, it's what you do when you get there?

My thing was, we needed a royal commission for veterans, and I've been able to drive that, with the help of plenty of others over the years. You've got all the mums out there that have been calling for this. Before I was even elected, I said I wanted to do this.

What gets you up in the morning? Is it veterans?

No, it's everything now, because now I've seen the bigger picture. It's not just veterans that get fucking done over from up here and the decisions that are made. It's a lot of people. Just the incompetence up here, my god, it blows me away. I wouldn't employ most of these people – the staff, the public service, the politicians. Most of them I wouldn't look twice at a resume.

People love you, I reckon, because there's no filter.

What you see is what you get. The first two years I was in, I couldn't make contact with Tasmanians. They were like, oh my god, what have we done? How have we put her in there? Now I get told, darling, you might have been a wrecking ball when you first came in, but now you're like a bottle of our Pinot Noir. You just get better with age!

And, Jacqui, are you well now? Mentally well?

My back's still fucked. I still go and have shots for that. I still struggle. I try to walk and swim. My nerve pain goes right through the roof during the four months of winter when I can't really swim, but you just try and manage it as best you can.

I am very aware of my pain. I'm very aware of my limitations, what I can and can't do. All the travelling that you do sometimes, it really pulls me up. I try not to have late nights – you won't see me going to the dinners of a night-time and stuff like that. Unless it's going to be maximum press there and maximum people there that I can hit at once I'm not interested.

With mental illness, it doesn't matter how wealthy you are, or not, how famous or unknown, does it?

Suicide doesn't discriminate. It's like drugs. They don't discriminate either.

It affects a lot of sporting identities because we put them on a pedestal. Veterans are the same. You put them out in a war zone, they're special. They're out there to do a job. They get addicted to the adrenaline, and when they get back here, that's gone. When I talk to a lot of them – and I talk to a lot of them – they can't replace it, they can't get the same thing. They come back here and they don't feel their worth anymore. It's really quite sad.

If they're medically discharged, they instantly lose their military family, then they lose their finance. Once that last line of defence is taken off them – especially men – they can no longer provide for their family. That's when they're gone. So, if you cut their payments off, if you do that, then you'd better watch them really carefully.

Do you think that trying to take your own life turned your life around? Are you better off?

What I do know is, had I not tried to suicide I wouldn't be where I am today, because I wouldn't have got the help I needed. That's what I do know. As for here, and politics? I'm one of those people that goes, I'll just open the door and I'll deal with it when I get inside. I guess as you get older, you get more knowledge and you get more confident.

CHAPTER 11

Peter Moloney

The Farmer

Every morning, on his beef farm, a nine-hour drive from Brisbane, Peter Moloney meditates, practises qigong and has a three-minute ice bath – in a deep freezer. Getting to this stage of having a morning routine has been quite a journey.

But not so many years ago it all became too much for the husband and father of three. A life lived in fear of being branded stupid because of his crippling dyslexia and thinking he had to prove himself as a hard-working farmer took him to the edge.

He found a way through. And found inspiration in many people and a particular poem, 'Man in the Mirror'. Now this shy, quiet man is dedicated to helping other farmers open up about their mental health and stay alive. He now believes that this is a far superior form of toughness, as opposed to being tough by working hard and showing little emotion and going inwards.

* * *

Tell us about where you were born, where you grew up?

We lived in Geebung, Queensland. North side of Brisbane. When I say 'we', I mean Mum and Dad – Jim and Karen – and my older sister, Tina. It was a great childhood, old-school in many ways. I rode my bike to school or walked to school and everything in between.

Mum's a teacher's aide. Dad's a plumber. We're a blue-collar family. Dad would work hard so we could get away for two holidays a year. It was always to Mooloolaba, to the beach. Childhood swimming, football. I just loved the surf. Just a great, Aussie family life.

Did you like school?

I had a lot of trouble, I struggled from early on. I had hearing problems and dyslexia. I also see numbers back to front.

Did the school realise there was something wrong?

Mum did, but I didn't get help until I was in Grade 11, going into 12. I got a reader and a writer, for exams, because I knew the answers, I just could never get them on paper. I really struggled, and it's taken me a long time to come to terms with that.

To be open about it?

I was always worried about being called dumb. It'd be devastating for me. But I was lucky, because I was good at sport, and no matter what your deficiencies as a kid, you get accepted if you're good at sport. That said, I'd have given any coordinated bone in my body to be able to put pen to paper. It's taken me until just recently to be more open about it.

I'm forty-two now. When I was thirty-eight, I was sorting bulls out with a great mate on the farm. You've got to read their tag numbers and I'm getting them all back to front, and he picked up on it. He let it go a couple of times and then he jokingly called me a dyslexic cunt. If someone else had said that to me, I would have written them off. That was the first time I'd ever laughed about it.

My wife, Katie, knew, but my kids had no idea. That was the hard part of being a father with them growing up. I didn't want them to see what I considered a weakness.

It sounds like dyslexia dominated your life.

I wouldn't go anywhere. Wouldn't challenge myself. Even going to the airport, it's a challenge. I've worked through that now. No-one minds if you ask for help.

Did that affect your mental illness? Do you think it caused depression or anxiety?

It did. Because in my head, I had to be able to work harder to prove I wasn't dumb. It ended up with me having a breakdown, because I just couldn't keep that up. Just a few years ago, when I was thirty-nine or forty.

What did you do when you left school?

I was one of the first to get a school-based apprenticeship. I had no idea what I wanted to do. So, because Dad was a plumber, I went straight into a plumbing apprenticeship. I never liked it, but back then you had to get something behind you, and if you had an apprenticeship – they weren't just handed out – you had to stick to it and get it done. I had a terrible boss. He was very critical of me in front of all the other workers. So, pretty vulnerable, but I stuck it out for four years. The day I finished my apprenticeship, I left.

Looking back now, at that age, you're trying to be someone while still working yourself out. Into surfing, football, Rugby League, but I just had that worthless feeling about myself.

Did you get on the grog?

I never drank through the week. I wasn't looking for alcohol at the end of the day, but I was a party binge drinker come the weekend. I was still fit and loved keeping fit. But once Friday and Saturday swung around, it was party time.

After the apprenticeship finished, I went bush. I laugh because I had what I call my midlife crisis when I was twenty. I was a long-haired surfie, living a city life, then I chopped off the hair, went bush and fell in love with it. Maybe not so much a crisis! I continued plumbing. I still remember the day working on a high-rise when I got a job as a jackaroo at Augathella. I resigned on the spot and headed west.

I worked as a stockhand, a jackaroo, on a 600,000-acre property at Augathella, about eight and a half hours' drive out of Brisbane. I couldn't find a start to begin with, because I had no experience. I got through that, and I was playing football with a fella who took me to a country music festival. I'd never listened to country in my life, but we went there, had a hoot, met some blokes who were rodeoing, fancied having a go and so I started doing that. It didn't end well. I chipped a disc in my back and had a bull horn me in the back of the head. That was a night in Intensive Care. It was always going to happen. I was going to get hurt.

Rodeoing is a bloody dangerous thing to do. Do you think you were self-destructive?

Nah. I enjoyed the adrenaline. I thought I could ride, until I went out to Augathella and hopped on a station horse. It would have been quite humorous that first day, watching me. A lot of horses are just really soft. You pull on the rein and they go where you want. Whereas a station horse, that's chased a lot of cattle in its time. It knows where it's going, and if you're inexperienced on the back of it, you go where it wants to go.

Happy times?

Great. First time I didn't have to worry about the dyslexia. I could just work hard and not worry about numbers or letters. I fell in love with animals. Loved being with them, whether it was a horse, a dog or cattle.

Did you feel isolated out there, in the middle of nowhere?

Not at all. I had a great boss and fantastic bushmen as mentors. It was a fun environment to be working in. Although I stayed there one Christmas to look after things and that was probably the first time I thought, would anyone miss me? That was the first of me going inward, I reckon. I don't know why.

I was on that property for five years, and then I went back to plumbing to get an interim licence so I could go back out to the bush and start my own plumbing company.

But you hated plumbing? Why did you do it?

I could see there was money there. In the end I only did a couple of jobs and then I went into contract fencing and contract mustering.

I worked my way up to be head stockman. We'd go and organise the muster, weigh cattle, draft cattle. Then I met my wife, Kate, at a State of Origin night, at a barbecue before the game. We dated for a while. Katie had just come back home from Toowoomba.

You're originally from Brisbane and you married a country girl?

Yeah, I never thought I'd end up going bush. Growing up, all I wanted was a blue heeler and a Queenslander house, but to live on the coast. Today, I am living in a Queenslander with a blue cattle dog, but as far away from the sea as I could possibly be.

You went back to Katie's family farm then?

Yes. Katie's folks split the place up between Katie and Katie's sister.

All of a sudden you're a proper farmer?

It was only Katie and myself. No kids yet. I went from handling cattle and mustering to the day-to-day planning of it all and breeding decisions. It was an eye-opener. We farm organic beef.

I love it, but you do become emotionally attached to the animals. When it's dry and they're struggling, it's hard. Rural small businesses are as susceptible to the weather as we are. We are as proactive as possible to ensure we maintain the health of our animals and environment. You need to be very much aware to average out your income from more buoyant years to assist in the more challenging ones.

Was that a big stress for you? Did anything stress you in the farming life?

I think I can handle the big things better than the smaller things. With the cattle, it was always manageable. We'd try and move quickly by selling. But when it was bad, I was always caught in my own head, trying to be the property owner, the farmer. It's taken me fifteen years to realise that's not who I am. And that I was simply feeding a false ego to prove myself.

And kids?

We've got three incredible sons who I am very proud of, each a special character of their own. Jimmy, who's fourteen, Sid, who is eleven, and Ardie, nine.

So, you were running a farm, trying to be Mr Farmer when deep down inside you didn't think you were. Was there a point where it all went to shit?

I masked it for a fair while. I lived with it, depression. I was trying to be someone else and doing that silly thing of attempting to prove yourself. You've got to work harder than your next-door neighbour. You've got to work hard. Day, night. We bought another place in a terribly dry time that was in need of a lot of work. And it's about 112 kilometres from us, so it's about an hour and a half drive.

I just kept pushing it down. Pretty much worked until I dropped. In the end it caught up with me.

Were you bad company?

Yeah, yeah. Never aggressive or anything, but never present. I still would hit the grog hard of a weekend. I knew something was going on. I had a fair crack at pushing everyone away too. That was part of it. I just went inward. But, Katie, the kids, Mum and Dad – they always stood by me.

What happened? Was there a big event? Did something go wrong?

Nah, I just think the fatigue of being something I wasn't caught up. I did have a breakdown. There were a lot of tears. Before that I used to run a lot. So, I'd just run my problems out. Put the sneakers on and run, clear my head. I just had to do something. But I never had the tools to share it with anybody. I didn't know how to share it. I went to some counsellors, but never clicked with them, so I just fobbed it off. I thought it was bullshit, not for me.

Were you having suicidal thoughts?

I was questioning myself. Why was I here? I was lying in bed at night just wishing there was something wrong with me. You see someone suffering with cancer or you see a sick kid, and the parents are dealing with that. And here I am. I've got a great life, a great family, I love what I do. But I'm stuck, inside.

I now know it's called depression and it's manageable, as long as you talk about it, but back then, I could never say that word. It was judgement by me, of me. Weakness. All those things that are running around in your head.

Did it feel like dyslexia all over again? Did you feel the same sort of embarrassment and shame?

Yeah. Katie couldn't understand it.

Did something push you to the edge?

One day, we had a water leak from one of the reservoir tanks on the property. I think it was New Year's Eve and we were about to head to a party. We'd lost a heap of water and the cattle were running out. So, there was pressure. I said I was going to need a hand, but the kids, they'd had enough. I thought, oh well, I'll just go and do it myself. It was that moment I felt at my darkest.

What pulled you back?

My eldest son, Jimmy, came up on a bike to help out. He would have been thirteen. I'd left in a huff. And here's this little thirteen-year-old, riding up on his bike, coming to help. That made me realise what I had.

Have you reflected on the randomness of him appearing at that moment?

Yeah, definitely.

Had he come to find you to ask a question, or something?

No, no, he just came up to help.

We talk about 'sliding doors' moments. That was one, wasn't it?

It wasn't a coincidence. It was meant to be.

We're all sent messages.

You've just got to be open to them. The next day, I cried in front of the kids, which was the first time.

Was that the turning point, where you decided you needed to get help?

I'd had turning points before, but this was different. Katie and I knew I had to get help. My running coach is all over health, and so I rang her and said, look, I need to have a personal conversation with you. Straight away she thought, oh no, is this about erections, men's problems? I said no, it's about depression. We had a laugh, and then she put me in touch with Brendan [Brendan Cullen, Broken Hill farmer and Lifeline Ambassador].

Fantastic guy.

Excellent bloke. Brendan and I talked on the phone for a fair bit and he put me in touch with a counsellor in Brisbane. There's no-one out in the bush for someone to talk to. We had to go back into Brisbane.

That's nine hours' drive each way, to see a counsellor.

We hit it off straight away. She put it to me that if it can be taken away from you, it's not who you are, meaning if your farm can be taken off you, then what are you left with? Yourself. You've got to know who you are when you strip everything away. Which really was an awakening.

I could never talk about things like this. I would break down in tears, even with Kate. Even at the mention of my dyslexia, I'd cry and shut down. I had no tools to get it out. I went onto medication and I felt great, but it didn't fix things. In my head I hadn't solved anything, I had just band-aided it with the medication. The only way it could work for me was talking about it, through conversations with Brendan and my counsellor.

So, I opened up and started to have conversations with people. Then it just got better and better.

You now talk a lot about what you do, tell your story. Does that help?

Previously, if someone mentioned depression or anxiety, I wouldn't have known how to talk about it. I would shut it down and talk about the weather, talk about something else. I was going through it too and I didn't want to look vulnerable. Now, today, every open conversation is like therapy to me. Doing this interview with you, today, I'll walk out of here feeling great, because I've shared something, hopefully something that helps someone else.

I've seen big changes in my family. But it's because I've changed too. I'm a lot more open. I'm present. My mind's not off thinking about what I should be doing or what I haven't done. I'm not thinking of an answer before someone has finished their question, from that fear of being dumb. Now I'm just there, and I'm there to listen.

Do you feel like a farmer now? How have you reconciled that?

Yeah, that's just my job now. It's not who I am. I'm passionate about caring for the land, for our animals. I have the biggest respect for both. Our aim is to have our land in optimal condition in order for our animals to thrive. I'm really passionate about sharing with other farmers that you're not by yourself – when you're going through it, the depression. But the only way out of it is, you have to put your hand up and ask for help.

Are you part of anything formal or do people say, go and talk to Peter?

I just have a group of mates. I think it's through your conversations that people open up.

We're in this farm owners' group. I'd feel challenged just walking into the conferences, because I'd feel like it was a classroom. I reverted back to the scared dyslexic kid, with the teacher at the front of the class. After the three-year course, I was supposed to do a graduation speech. I really wanted to face my fears, get up in front of 300 people and share my story of the dyslexia.

I had it all planned, what I was going to say, but we couldn't get down there. All the way we kept getting obstacles put in front of us. We got right to Brisbane Airport and I got a text message to say we had a fire at our place. It had been hit by lightning. So, nine hours back to the farm, driving all night. The neighbours had put it out, but logs smoulder for days and it's your responsibility to deal with, which meant we had to monitor. We couldn't leave, we had to stay there. We had time to kill, so I asked my family if they wanted to hear a poem.

When you get what you want in your struggle for self,
And the world makes you king for a day,
Then go to the mirror and look at yourself,
And see what that man has to say.

For it isn't your father, or mother, or wife,
Whose judgement upon you must pass,
The fellow whose verdict counts most in your life,
Is the one staring back from the glass.

He's the fellow to please – never mind all the rest,
For he's with you, clear to the end,
And you've passed your most difficult, dangerous test,
If the man in the glass is your friend.

You may fool the whole world down the pathway of years,
And get pats on the back as you pass.
But your final reward will be heartache and tears,
If you've cheated the man in the glass.

I love this poem – 'The Guy in the Glass' [by Peter Dale Wimbrow Sr, first published in 1934]. It should be on every mirror, I think. So, I told them that and I said, 'I'm supposed to be doing a speech tonight. I was going to recite this, would you like to hear it?'

So, you gave the speech to the boys?

Yep. That was the first time I ever told them I had dyslexia.

Did they understand?

They're deep little thinkers. I can't remember which one said it, but one of them said, 'Everyone has their challenges, Dad.' That's from a little kid. And as soon as we sat down on this log, this bloody massive tree just fell to the ground. I was like, holy shit. In that moment I realised, if I had flown down there, I would have told 300 people all my fears – bloody unloaded – but I still would have been hiding from the people that are most important to me. Now, they know.

Did you feel relieved, telling the boys?

Oh, shit yeah. I guess the message to them was they can talk about anything, there is no shame in talking about this stuff. Being tough is actually sharing your emotions, not avoiding them.

I was a dead man walking, and then the whole world opened up to me. I had better relationships. I became a better father, better husband, better farmer, better friend. It's just all a chain reaction.

So, would you still say you've got depression? How are you managing it?

I would say that. I'm off the meds I was on. You're still going to have bumps along the way, though.

It's interesting. There is a view that too many people reckon they've got depression, that there are too many antidepressants out there, because we all think every day should be a happy day. Why do we think every day should be a good day? When did we think that was normal? It's normal that you have good days and not so good days. To be on a constant high is unsustainable and everyone will have setbacks and challenges to deal with. You cannot compare your story or situation with someone else's.

You've got to have the bad ones, to appreciate the good ones.

Today I have a toolbox. If I feel myself starting to go down again, I'll have a conversation, to get out of it, but that doesn't mean I've fixed anything. I might only have scratched the surface of it, and had a little bit of relief. The biggest thing is, you've just got to keep ripping that band-aid off and keep talking about it. One thing I reckon is, you've got to have a mate. You don't even have to know the bloke. Or you don't have to be sitting there face to face with them, but you need a mate that you can talk to. Someone who's been through it themselves.

I have an ice bath every week, and I do a breathing practice every morning, a breath meditation. I'm in the ice for three minutes, lying in an old freezer chest. I don't have a timer, I listen to a song. But these are the things in my toolbox. I do qigong – movement for body, mind and spirit. I still do my running. I love my running. Not every day. I have a dicky knee, so it won't cop it every day.

You've had an extraordinary transformation.

Yeah, massive. Massive change.

Do you feel your life is better for getting to that incredibly dark point?

Yeah, otherwise I'd have just kept flogging along, doing the same thing. Gratitude, it's the most powerful thing, I think. Yeah, when you wake up and can be grateful and be kinder to yourself.

CHAPTER 12

Ian Thorpe

The Swimmer

Ian Thorpe AM is an Australian swimming legend who grew up under Australia's gaze to become our most successful male Olympian in the pool, winning five gold medals and carrying the expectations of the entire nation. He won his first Olympic Gold Medal at the 2000 Sydney Olympic Games at barely eighteen. That kind of pressure is bound to take a toll, and it did. Hearing from someone like Ian about his struggles will hopefully help others facing dark times to know there is a way through.

* * *

Would you say you had a happy, normal, Aussie childhood before swimming? Before fame?

I think it was very normal, or what I knew as a normal childhood. A loving family, an older sister who bossed me around. Both parents working. We went on the same kind of holidays most kids went on, which was a drive up to the northern part of the New South Wales coast.

What did your mum and dad do?

Dad was a landscape gardener and my mum's a school teacher. Milperra was where I grew up first, then we moved, for swimming.

What did you want to be as a kid?

I wanted to be a fireman, because I liked the colour red. When I was at high school I actually wanted to be a neurologist.

And then swimming took over?

You don't realise it's taking over. I think I was thirteen, about to turn fourteen. It was taking over that much, my parents made me take a considerable amount of time off swimming, two or three months.

Out of the pool?

Two weeks would be normal to have a bit of a break, but I was getting too good, too quickly. It actually had the reverse effect on me, because the following year, when I was fourteen, I made the national team.

They were worried it was all moving too fast for you?

They didn't tell me they were worried, but there's no other logical reason for it. A fourteen-year-old should not be on the national team. I think they did it to protect me, to make sure I had some sense of normality at that stage.

What's the average age of people on the national team?

There are some female swimmers that are in their teens. It's rare, it's smaller now, the percentage of people that are in their teens, than it was earlier. It's once in a blue moon when there's a male under the age of sixteen.

Did you feel young?

Physically, I looked similar to the other older athletes. I was younger than them, but I was a very mature fourteen-year-old.

Socially mature? Talking to adults?

Absolutely. But I'd been able to do that since I was younger. I also know that I was able to do it very effectively, even though it was at a superficial level. Nothing of more substance than that. I just knew how to do it.

It's putting on a mask, a front to be able to protect yourself. Being in your teens is uncomfortable. You're adjusting to becoming an adult. You're incredibly awkward and uncomfortable within yourself. You're trying to work out how to fit in, not stand out. I was able to do that in some ways – blend into an adult crowd – while transitioning to being an adult myself.

What does joining the national team involve?

The national team is the team that will travel to all the major competitions – World Championships, Commonwealth Games, the Pacific Championships [Pan-Pacs] and the Olympics. Once you're in that group, it involves training camps with the rest of the top athletes around the country in different locations. We'd travel to training camps around the world as well. Then there's all of the sports science that goes with it – physiologists, biomechanics, dietitians – all of those things.

And when you went overseas, did your parents go, because you were young?

I went by myself, but I never felt like I was by myself. I knew I was the youngest, but I was never treated as the youngest. I saw people ten years older than me as my peers.

How did all that work with school back in Sydney?

In 1997, I missed 102 of 200 days of school. I'd have to try and fit school in when I was overseas. When I was at home I was efficient. I'd spend time in the library during lunchtime, doing most of my schoolwork. I was still the Dux of my school every year.

Then I became world champion. I'd just turned fifteen in January, and I said to my family, 'I can't do school. I can't.' I couldn't go to school but I agreed to finish it, to do it from home. My parents had a disagreement about it, as my father was advocating that I should stay at school. I was a good student and looking at doing medicine. My mum was more of the position that I could finish my education later, go to university, do whatever I wanted to do.

Were you famous overnight?

Internationally, yes, in some ways. I was doing media interviews when I was eight or nine.

What was the first great peak of your career? Was it the Sydney Olympics? When did you say 'I've arrived'?

I never thought I'd compete at the Sydney Olympics. I thought I was going to be too young at seventeen. No-one actually said that, but that's what I thought. You just don't see young male swimmers. That all changed when I won the World Championships in Perth in 1998.

My goal was to be an Olympian and my dream was to be an Olympic champion. They're two very different things. A goal is something that you can work toward. A dream is something a little loftier, an aspiration that you almost feel embarrassed to actually share with someone.

Because you sound arrogant?

We speak to young people differently to how we speak to adults. We tell young people you can do whatever you want. 'You can accomplish this. You have the platform to do anything.' But once life happens, we start to look at things in a different way. And so when we become adults, we do think differently.

How was your mental health through this? It feels like it was all going so fast.

I was actually saying to myself that I didn't deserve to be on the national team that would be competing at the World Championships. I actually broke down and cried, because I was swimming like shit. It happened one day in training where I just wasn't swimming well.

When I went on to win the World Championships at fifteen, I really didn't know if it was a fluke or not. That was kind of the question I had in the back of my mind. I then went to the Commonwealth Games that same year, and followed it up with four gold medals. Then the next year, a year out from the Olympics, I broke four world records in four days at the Pan-Pacs and won four more gold.

Consequently, going into the Sydney Olympics in 2000, people just assumed I'd win. They didn't realise the complexity of actually getting something right, to be able to deliver at that level, a level where everyone steps up. I had not had the best preparation. I was unwell in our training camp right before the Sydney Olympics. Also, I was inexperienced, in that I hadn't been to an Olympics. Most athletes may have been to one Olympics and then it will be at their next one where they do well.

So, you win a World Championship and then it all gets very serious very quickly?

I'm not the kid anymore. I'm a world champion. Things change dramatically. I'm not just this talented youngster on the rise. I'm now owning a space at the top. At the very, very top around the world.

When people were touting you as being this great swimmer, did you believe them?

I don't read anything about myself. When I was about sixteen, I stopped reading anything, never watched anything. I was neither as good or as bad as what people said. It wasn't reflective of who I was.

My lead-up into Sydney 2000 had some complexity to it in that people were assuming a result that hadn't happened yet. I would be with my mother at the shop, and people would say, 'We've got tickets to the Olympics, we can't wait to see you win your first gold medal.' I couldn't escape that part of it. Then it started being hyped up more and more and more. I was surrounded by it. Even though I tried to take myself away from it, to do what I needed to do, I couldn't avoid it.

And you knew what the expectation was.

I met a journalist afterward who was told he had to write a negative story about me beforehand and he refused to do it. He said, 'There's nothing bad to write. This is a kid going to the Olympics who grew up here.' I had an awareness of what was expected of me.

I also had an incredibly complicated first day of racing at the Olympics. I had to swim the 400-metre freestyle heats during the day and then in the evening I had the 400-metre freestyle final and the men's four-by-100-metre relay final. I had about an hour between the two finals. They had changed the schedule to put those two races on the first night in order to get the Australian team off to a good start. We hadn't won a gold medal and I was touted to be the first at the Olympics, at seventeen years old.

I didn't have a great heat swim, even though I qualified fastest. I can qualify for finals easily, that's not an issue, but I didn't feel as comfortable as I should have at that speed. The final of the 400 metres was first in the evening. I was in lane four. I was nervous and worried. Like, 'Is this too much for me? It's overwhelming. I've never seen a crowd like this.' It was incredible. I was trying to relax, trying to stay cool and calm. They announce each of the lanes to the crowd. It's really good for your ego. 'In lane four, the reigning World Champion for this event, representing Australia, Ian Thorpe.' I was in my head, which sometimes I am, sometimes I'm not. I'm overthinking things. You're trying to build your anxiety up to a level where it's manageable, before it goes beyond that. Anxiety is fantastic for performance, like putting pressure on someone to get something out of them, before they break.

It was when they announced my name and the crowd cheered. I just waved. It was so deafeningly loud that I did that thing that you do in school when you get in trouble, kind of smirk to the side. However, it was in that moment I actually got out of my head and said to myself, 'I'm ready to do this.' All the other competitors were announced and I was on the blocks ready to go, ready to control the race and have it go how I wanted it to go.

You know that saying, 'It'll be alright on the night'?

I would never trust that. I did everything in training so I never doubted myself when I performed. That was part of it, for me to say, 'I've done everything I possibly can, I have to just let go and express what that training is for.'

But before, I had a coach say to me – it wasn't my coach, it was another coach – 'You've got another race after this. If you can, conserve something for the next race.' I'm at the Olympic Games and someone is saying, 'If you don't have to try your hardest, then don't do that.' It's the fricken Olympics, like, come on!? The worst thing about it was, I'd done this before, but then I was asking myself, 'What's that person saying? What's wrong with me right now?' It's the first seed of doubt that you plant. This is what happens to people as they get older. There's all of these things that happen to us, where we start restricting the way we think, how we feel, and what we can accomplish.

I did swim the race comfortably as I intended to. I led, so I could just command things.

A lot of people, at the peak of their achievements, feel they're still a fake. How did you feel?

I think it was like I was being anointed into that position, that I then held gold for the next however many years. That was kind of where I was at that time.

Was that your right, do you think?

No, but you need this to be among the greats. It's not a technicality. You have to have it. There are a few people who are multiple world champions, but have never won gold at an Olympic Games. Then there are Olympic champions who have never won World Championships and they don't care.

And how was your mental health at that point?

It was mostly good. But I couldn't celebrate winning the 400 metres. I'd just achieved my lifetime dream and I enjoyed it, of course, but I knew I had to manage my emotions, because I had another final coming up. So I was suppressing celebrating even after receiving my first gold medal. I look at, it's shiny and nice, but I'm on a very specific schedule.

I had to swim-down, warm-up for the next race, and get in a swim suit. It was full length, from hand to ankles. These take more than ten minutes to put on. Well, I broke the one I was putting on and so I had to use the wet one that I'd just won the 400 metres in. No-one puts them on wet. They're that tight. I had six people trying to pull a swim suit onto me when I was supposed to be in the marshalling area. It was getting intense.

I'm late and I can hear on the walkie talkie one of the team managers, 'No, Thorpie's on his way.' I have to go through the marshalling area, I have to sign off. 'Thorpie's fine. I just saw him walk past.' I know this is going to take at least another ten minutes to get on. It was too much. I told everyone to get out, apart from Piney – Adam Pine – who swam in the relay heat to qualify us for the final. He helped me pull it on, being very careful around the zip. Finally, I zipped up.

I put on some tracksuit pants and ran down the back of the Homebush Aquatic Centre, which I shouldn't have done, because the last time I ran I actually snapped my ankle less than twelve months out from the Olympics. This was another reason why I was questioning myself in the 400 metres – I'd snapped my ankle in the lead-up. I didn't even know I'd broken it for three days. I just thought it was swollen. I saw my mum crying that day, thinking, 'This is over. He's not going to the Olympics.'

I ran down, signed off my name and walked out with the rest of the team, just in time to hear, 'In lane five, Australia.' I was that late, and it was weird because no-one asked me where I'd been. I should have been there twenty minutes ago and I just thought, *So, no love from the rest of the team*. But then I was ready to race. Which was fine, but it was a big call to put me last.

Why?

Technically I was the slowest out of all the swimmers. But there was a strategy. Our coaches studied what the US would do. The US swam the race the same way every time. We knew how to win. We worked on changeovers. In a changeover, the finger of one swimmer has to touch the wall while the toe of the other swimmer is still touching the block. As you're going in, you don't get to see your teammate touch, that's how fine the margins are. When one swimmer swims in, the other one's going. You have to trust the person to get on the wall. We knew we could make up time at the turns. Then we all had to over-deliver to win. It was tight, and we had to practise. We got it down pretty tight, but if we were any faster, we'd be too hot, and with all of that atmosphere, you're likely to dive in too quickly. If you go too quickly, you get disqualified.

On the last leg, I dove in and came up first, but that was the last time I led. At the fifty-metre turn, the roar from the crowd was louder than when I dove in for the 400 metres. It then goes from screaming to silence, because when you're underwater, you can't hear a thing. It's dead silent. Then you come up and you hear a buzz, a hiss. You have to breathe, so you know where you are. Also, if you're coming into a wall and you're about to turn that way and someone is pushing off, you can see where they are as well. I had a really good turn and I didn't lose any distance, but after the turn, I was genuinely shocked at how far behind I was. I knew I would be behind, nonetheless I felt the tone change from the crowd. It was like a collective gasp. It wasn't something that unnerved me or that I was overwhelmed by. It was an observation, and this is me being able to know, 'This is where I will come good.' Twenty-five metres to go and this is when the crowd starts to warm up again because I'm gaining. I'm very aware of where I am. It's going to be tight. With fifteen metres to go I know this is where the American – Gary Hall Jnr – is going to tire. He's going to tire, but I won't. And so it all came down to the last ten metres. With five metres to go, it was quite clear to people who know swimming that I was about to win this. I was swimming to win at that stage, but still, you don't know. I felt like I was going to win. I just needed confirmation. Which I soon got.

Like so many Australians, I remember every stroke of that race. You won two Olympic gold medals in one night. How did you handle the fame?

I don't think it changes you. I don't think you can actually change the person that you are, the person that is your authentic self. I think what fame might do is amplify certain characteristics that you may have – good and bad. I'm an introvert, I'm quite shy. So, for me, putting myself out there, exposing myself in that way, takes a lot. It would take most of my energy.

Physical and mental?

Yep, to be able to do it.

There are two Ians, right? There's the personal Ian …

Multiple, if you speak to my psychiatrist …

There's private Ian, there's swimming Ian, and there's public Ian. All of this energy you need to be public, is it a different energy to the swimming energy?

Yeah, absolutely. I was prepared to be a world champion and an Olympic champion. I had prepared. I'd done all of the work for that – the swimming part of it. But what came with it, no-one can prepare you for that.

Did anyone try?

It was too late. I was struggling with it, because I just didn't want to do it. I didn't want to be doing interviews, so I limited how many I did.

I just wanted to have my own life. I understand that what I do is very public, but I was trying to protect myself and my own wellbeing. It was managing that and being able to do it because I did realise that I had commitments that I had to fulfil.

So, we know your very public swimming story continues. When and how did your mental health go up and down?

I had mental health issues in my teens. I have depression.

Diagnosed?

Yep.

Mild, medium?

I wasn't told at the time. I was on medication.

What were the drivers to your depression back in your teens?

Isolation is probably my biggest thing. Still is, to this day, I know that I do that. I actually have to look out for myself. I'm getting to the point where I look at my mental health the same way as my physical health. I don't separate the two things.

I was trying to manage what was a very crazy world around me, where I had experiences most people will never have in their lives. Most of those things were incredibly good, you know, things where you have to pinch yourself and ask, 'Is this actually happening to me?' That, combined with a level of interest into my life that was bordering on bizarre. It is not a great place for someone who has mental health issues.

Ian Thorpe walks down the street. Ian Thorpe drives a car. Ian Thorpe goes shopping.

It's not normal. There's very few people that can relate to it. I wanted to be the best swimmer in the world, and I was that. I continued being that. It was everything that came with it that I didn't like.

So, you retired and then had the comeback.

Which was too late. I couldn't even train without being papped. When I did retire, that was actually my first major depressive episode.

The World Championships were in Melbourne that year, 2006. I was twenty-three, out of the sport and going to go watch. It was leaked to the French newspaper *L'Équipe* that I had returned an irregular test years ago. An irregular test isn't uncommon. They happen. So, firstly, no-one should know that information to begin with.

Somebody was out to get you?

I won't say who it was – for legal reasons. It was intended to inflict as much damage on me as possible, which was when every sports journalist around the world would be there. I'd just retired, I wanted to move on from swimming, and this was payback.

Did that story lead to the depressive episode?

I'm woken at 7 am by a phone call and find this out. I shudder. I feel as though everything I've accomplished, everything that I've been through, is for nothing.

Did that mean they could strip you of the Olympic medals?

No, because an irregular test means nothing. An irregular test gets thrown out.

But it's sensationalist in the media?

That's exactly it. It puts an asterisk next to your name and it never goes away. I was trying to move on from a sport, and was getting pulled back into it.

With the depressive episode, were you suicidal?

Definitely.

Did you make a plan?

Frequently. I was thinking of a way to do it that would look like an accident. The episode lasted for at least three months. I didn't leave the house. I was barely functioning. I was communicating with people, but no-one really knew how bad it was.

Did you share the fact that you were suicidal with anyone?

No. I wanted to deal with it myself. I'm used to doing everything on my own. I'm not used to putting my hand up. I used to rely on myself. But there are some things in life that are actually bigger than you, where you do actually need other people's help, and this was one of them.

In that kind of state, you're entirely irrational, your logic is warped. It's only in periods when you have clarity of mind, when your mental health is good, that you can actually reflect on things and say, 'Well I could have done this, I should have done this, I knew that I was doing that, but I didn't do this.' I realised what I was doing wasn't working, and that I needed help. So, I got that help, and even though I still was in a long-term depressive state, I got better. I wasn't at that point of suicide.

You must have been aware of the national and very public conversation about your sexuality?

I was asked by a print journalist when I was sixteen, directly, 'Are you gay?' I've since found out that the journalist was told, 'You ask the question, or it's your job.' If you asked that question to a sixteen-year-old now, you would lose your job.

Thank god.

Exactly. I didn't know how to respond. Because I really didn't know at that time, and it really wasn't important to me either. I think I said, 'Well, you know me.' And then raced off to training. It was just another thing that was quite overwhelming. I know that the front page of that newspaper was ready to be printed that afternoon, leading with, 'I'm gay!' as the headline. So, now I'm accused of being gay.

What a fascinating word, 'accused'.

It is. That's how it appeared. When you use the word 'accuse', you think there's something wrong. Then you start questioning yourself. 'How is this going to impact me?' At that stage, at sixteen, I was dealing with enough already. I had so much on my plate. That level of expectation around my performance and what I was doing. I didn't need another thing to deal with. That's how I was treating it, and that's how I thought about it.

After the Sydney Olympics, when it continued, I was like, 'No, no, fuck it. I'm not going to give this up to someone who has made my life a living hell. Who has poked and prodded me into this. I'm not rewarding bad behaviour.' And so, the more I was pushed on it, the further I withdrew from it. It's great to have that level of morality to what you do, but the consequence is that you take this all on yourself.

You dig it deeper and deeper?

You just push it further down. You push that trauma to the back of your mind. Learning to come to terms with my sexuality became even more difficult than it would have been otherwise. It wasn't important to me at the time, but it was becoming more important to who I was, and for me to be able to have that level of authenticity and honesty. Values that are really important to me – personal values – and I didn't have that with myself.

So, it began to limit the way you lived and the decisions you make?

I'd pigeonholed myself into being something that I wasn't, to spite people. Which is not really me as a person.

Did you say to yourself, 'It's none of their business'?

It isn't anyone's business. I still feel that way.

So, when you came out, did you feel that you could move on from that? Is it scarring, denying your sexuality for so long, or was there relief?

No, it was good. I came out to my family and a couple of friends, and then I was doing an interview with Michael Parkinson [legendary British television presenter and broadcaster] and I rang my agent up and I said to him, 'Look, I'm gay. I'm thinking I come out during this interview.' So, I actually spent a few days with Parky and his family before doing that interview in the UK. We went to the cricket, had family dinners at the pub just down the road. It was good. He got to know me a little bit.

What made you decide that was the time and that was the platform?

It had taken me thirty years to get to that point. I said, 'I've taken a step out of the closet, I'm not going to take a step back in.' It was easier for me to actually do an interview and speak openly about this than it was to actually tell people individually.

Did you know that Parkinson would treat you well? That he'd do the right thing by you, rather than scandalise it?

He didn't know he was going to be asking the question. Two days before the interview, I said to him, 'You should ask me if I'm gay. Because I'm going to tell you that I am.' He thanked me and digested that. He felt like my grandfather on the maternal side of my family, who I had the utmost respect for. He was the kind of man I'd like to be.

And Parky treated you well, as I remember it?

I'd been through a bad time. I'd had major episodes every eight years. I'd just been through a bad one then, before *Parkinson*.

Because of the time-zone difference my phone had blown up overnight. I woke up to that. My first thought was, *What's happened? What have I done?* As in, I thought I must have done something wrong, not something good. That's where my head goes. I think the worst. I knew the interview was going to air, I just didn't pay attention to when. I always knew it would be this way, that people would be overwhelmingly supportive.

Did you get any negative messages?

Yeah, absolutely. But not from people that I know. No-one who knows me said anything negative or would. They know what I've been through.

But you got some homophobic messages?

I did, and sometimes from the queer community as well. It's quite weird, because I don't know anyone else's individual circumstances. I grew up in a conservative Christian family, which makes it more difficult. I also had a level of fame that most people will never experience in their lives, which made it more difficult. I was also uncomfortable within myself. Again, more difficult. There were multiple factors that added to my decision. This is why people shouldn't be pressured into coming out. Young people ask me all the time, 'How do I come out?' It's hard. I don't know these kids. I don't know what to say, and I'm not an expert. I've done it once, and everyone else keeps reminding me about it, so I have to relive it. If I say something, anything, if I talk about mental health, I have to talk about it for the rest of my life and I get reminded about it. My coming out gets talked about again and again and again.

Would you say you were 'out and proud' at that time?

Maybe out, but not proud yet. I was still getting used to it. It was all new. I was the same Ian Thorpe, I hadn't changed. It's just, you get to see another facet of my life, that I've chosen to let you see. I would have loved to have come out earlier, I really would have. But knowing what I know now, knowing how difficult it would have been, I don't think it would have been wise for me to actually come out any earlier than I did.

It all would have been about the 'gay swimmer'.

That would have been the headline. If I went to a party – because there's this perception that gay people party more – I would be the party boy as well.

Which is code for drugs and promiscuity.

All of that. If I walk out with my mates, I'm dating them. All of this, and it would have been hell.

Do you yearn for the quiet, private Ian Thorpe?

Most of my life is incredibly private and I choose to have it that way. It's a personality trait. I do know people who thrive off the attention and it energises them, but for me it doesn't. I'm at the point now where I get to choose what I do and don't do.

What's your message of hope? How did you get through these difficult times, through these periods of suicidal ideation?

To begin with, when you're in a situation where your mental health is not great, you're thinking irrationally. Your thoughts in that moment are probably not reflective of how you feel most of the time. I think that's fundamental, understanding that part. Then the next part is having people around you that you can speak to when you are in a state. It doesn't have to be a professional. You should have a professional as one of these people, but sometimes just chatting to a friend can help.

With my closest friends and colleagues, I have a plan in place for when I'm not feeling well. If I'm going through a depressive episode where I've started to withdraw from what I normally do, I make the phone call. Which is basically, 'Pick me up tomorrow night, we're going out for dinner.'

That requires a level of self-awareness, doesn't it?

It does, but I've had enough experience. It's written down. It's not just something I have in my head. If something happens and I don't want to leave the house for a day, that's fine for one day, I can do that. But, tomorrow I will do something different. On the list I have, the first thing in the morning I do is walk my dog.

So you have a written list?

Yeah, absolutely. This is what works for me. It may not work for other people. If I don't write it down, I'll just go round and round in circles in my head, not helping myself, going through every scenario of what I should be doing. With it written down, I can actually look at the list: I will do this, I will do this, I will do this, because I know when I get through those things, the following day will be better. That's why I think it's important to write it down.

If I'm cancelling a dinner, when I would normally enjoy going out with friends, it's a sign. If I'm not showing up for things I enjoy, or if I stop doing them, it's a sign. I enjoy cooking, so if I stop cooking and start ordering food delivery, am I just being lazy or is something happening? Sometimes I am actually being lazy. It's knowing when to check myself.

Do you meditate or do mindfulness exercises?

I do both. I wish I'd meditated more. I'll take time out to just do breathing exercises. Not specifically meditation. I can walk away from something for five minutes and just do breathing exercises, anywhere. It's just finding a technique that works for you. For me, that recentres me into what I am and then I'm living in the moment.

Do you enjoy swimming still?

I can't swim. I had a shoulder replacement. Mechanically, I can't swim. I can catch a wave, but I can't swim laps.

How do you feel about that?

I think I have a romantic notion of swimming. I remember all of the good things. I don't remember all of the freezing cold mornings and waking up, when it was easier to work out which muscle in my body wasn't sore than which ones were. And just being exhausted.

Is that public knowledge, that you can't swim?

Well, I've said it, but I don't usually bring it up because everyone else gets really upset. People get sad. People feel sorry for me. And I don't want people to feel sorry for me.

People see me as a swimmer. It's a very big part of my life that happened a long time ago. I do other things now.

And life is good?

It's good. Life is good.

CHAPTER 13

Annas Davids

The Youth Worker

Annas Davids is a young Muslim man from Western Australia who first came to my attention via an ABC News article in 2022. For Annas to speak up about suicide, in a community where such conversations do not take place was, I thought, an act of bravery, and so I was very keen to invite him to take part in this book.

In recognition of his work in speaking out about mental health (for organisations such as Headspace, PCYC [Police Citizens Youth Clubs] and The Shaka Project), particularly in the Muslim community, Annas was a finalist in the 2023 Australian Muslim Achievement Awards for Role Model of the Year.

* * *

Can you tell us where you were born, where you grew up and a bit about your family?

I was born in Saudi Arabia. I'm the youngest of four. My dad was working for Saudi Arabian Airlines. Dad's side of the family lives in Sydney and my mum's side lives here in Perth. So, every year we would fly back and forth to Sydney, Perth, then back home. In 2005 we decided to stay in Perth because I guess it was time to be with family and settle down.

That was a very international start to life. What do you identify as your cultural background?

I'm what my parents are. I say I'm South African. My parents met in high school, but then my mum and her family moved from South Africa to Sydney when they were really young. Then my dad followed. They got married in Sydney, stayed there for a bit and then in the 1990s they went to Saudi for work.

However, I feel Australian because I don't know anything about South Africa. When I was living in Saudi, I'd tell the Saudi kids I was Australian but they'd look at me and say, 'You're not Australian.' And when I came here, I didn't look 'typically Australian' either. I've always been all over the place, but I'm slowly getting the confidence to say, 'I was raised here in Australia, born in Saudi but my parents are South African.'

How old were you when you arrived in Australia?

Ten.

Did you speak Arabic fluently?

No. I understood it if someone like my sister spoke it to me, but I didn't understand it fully.

We spoke English at home. When we were about to leave Saudi Arabia, they took me out of that school and then we came here. That's when I went to a private school here in Australia: Al-Ameen Islamic College, in Perth.

Did you struggle?

It was a lot easier because I was just a kid. But when I started high school, that's when things started to get rough. That's when the bullying started. It got really bad in Year 8, and in Year 9 it slowed down a little bit but it was still there. By Year 10, it just stopped.

I didn't understand why I was bullied. Knowing myself as an adult now, as someone who sees the world differently, as someone who only found out two years ago that he has attention deficit hyperactivity disorder [ADHD], maybe I can make sense of it? Perhaps the other kids saw something in me that I didn't understand or see in myself. I was probably different to them in a way.

The teachers weren't very helpful, so I didn't really have anyone to turn to. I struggled with homework and they pushed me aside. I didn't really have any relationships with friends back then. The moment I got home, I'd feel tired and miserable. I realised that it was affecting me when I finished Year 10 and we got a letter from that school saying I couldn't come back to do Year 11 and 12, and got taken out.

My mum homeschooled me for Year 10 again. Having that year of homeschooling made me realise just how much I'd struggled with homework, schoolwork and social interactions. It was a way of me slowing down and finding myself again.

When you started at school, did you feel different to the other kids?

If I look back now, I can see that there were things that I was doing that were not normal. I'd zone out and picture the clock falling on the teacher's head. Or I'd distract myself by chucking a pencil on the floor, picking it up and dropping it again. It's as though I was distracting myself on purpose.

I didn't feel like I was different at the time, but one friend I did make – I'm still friends with her today – said that she could see I looked very nervous. That's why she came up to me and asked if I wanted to play a game. That's how we connected. She could see on my face that I was anxious. I don't remember feeling like that, my recollection is that I was happy being on my own. Just happy to eat my lunch and go back to class. I didn't feel nervous or I didn't feel anxious when I was a kid, but she saw something different and that's why she approached me. That's why she asked if I wanted to be friends.

When you say you were bullied, what sort of bullying?

Name-calling. Thankfully it wasn't physical. There was no punching or anything like that. It was more teasing. Childish stuff.

What did you do next, after the homeschooling?

I went back to school at Cyril Jackson Senior Campus, in Perth. It was a special program for people – including adults – who hadn't graduated yet, to get back into education. I did Year 11 and Year 12, and then I graduated.

Did you feel the program was better suited to you than high school had been?

I felt more comfortable at this school. I wasn't there to make friends. All I wanted to do was graduate. Making high school friends was the last thing I wanted to do. I would sit by myself, eat my lunch in the classroom and wait until the class started. I didn't have any ambition to find friends, even though I'd occasionally feel lonely, but I didn't make the effort.

You were deliberate in not wanting to make friends. Is that because you were worried about being bullied again?

No. I think it was just because I wanted to get it over and done with.

Did you have friends outside school?

I didn't really have any friends that I connected with. I was pretty much at home, just chilling. I didn't really go out, didn't do what normal teenagers would do.

Would I have felt sorry for you had I known you then? Was that a sad time in your life?

I didn't feel sorry for me.

What did you want to do when you finished school?

For the longest time, I didn't know. I always wanted to share my story somehow. I wanted to share my story with the world. Whatever it was. Now I guess I am sharing my story in different ways. From the ABC article to public speaking and now this book. I didn't know what I wanted to do as a career. I found my passion and excitement in public speaking, where

I do get to share my story. Where I have opportunities like these.

That's interesting. When you were young you didn't have friends, but all these years later you enjoy interacting with people.

All the time I think to myself, I was really nervous and a really anxious kid, and I didn't have many friends. Why now am I talking to large groups of strangers? I think it's because when I tell my story to other Muslim kids who might be in the position I was in, they hear they don't have to go through it alone. I think that's what pushes me and that's what motivates me.

That makes perfect sense. Are you a shy person?

I am a very nervous person. Even before we started this meeting, I was very nervous. I didn't want to do this.

So, do you have to force yourself? How do you push through?

I have to remind myself why I'm doing this. It's because of that one Muslim boy, who might hopefully one day read this book. Or the parent who will see an article about my story and think, 'That's happened to my child.' Hopefully, someone picks this book up and reads my story, and maybe it will give them that hope and encourage them to get help or talk to their friends.

What did you do when you finished school?

I didn't have any passions. I didn't have any interest in anything. That's when my mental health was all over the place. All I did was lie around the house. I really didn't do anything.

And when did you find your mental health deteriorating?

When the media coverage of terrorism was on the rise on TV and it was literally in our faces. I think that's when it started.

Did you see negativity toward Muslims?

Yes, the anti-Muslim rhetoric.

Did you feel targeted? Is that the word?

You could say that. It was like I was having an identity crisis. It was a really confusing time. I didn't understand what was going on in my own head. When I first opened up to my friends about my mental health, I was literally pushed aside. I think this is when things started going downhill even more. I remember saying to them, 'I don't know what's going on in my head but I'm having these really dark thoughts.'

When you say 'dark thoughts', do you mean thoughts of taking your own life?

Yeah. That was my very first experience with suicidal thoughts, although I didn't tell my friends that. I don't really remember why I didn't tell them in detail, but I remember telling them I was having really dark thoughts. I couldn't really explain what was going on. But then a few of them told me that I just needed to 'Man up, you'll get over it'. One of my friends didn't know what to say to me, but he stood next to me and stuck by me. I remember seeing the worry on his face. I don't remember what he said to me, but him just sitting next to me, not saying anything, making sure I was alright, was much better than being pushed away.

When did you begin to feel that you had suicidal thoughts and poor mental health - how old were you?

I must have been seventeen or eighteen.

What do you think was behind the dark thoughts?

Escape. To escape the world. Escape the reality of what's going on. What was happening around the world wasn't helpful. I was worried about Islamophobia on the rise and the negativity of the broader community.

Were you experiencing any sort of prejudice at all at that point in your life?

Maybe I did, but I just didn't understand it back then, as I was so young.

Obviously you felt very marginalised and isolated as a young Muslim man. Did you worry about the future?

I wasn't worried about the future, but I did feel like it was me against the world and that I was suffering alone. I think that's one big thing, that I truly felt the anxiety of me against everyone else. Me as an individual. Me as an individual against everyone else and everyone was out to get me.

To be clear, you mean, 'me as an individual Muslim man'?

Yes.

Were you a practising or observant Muslim?

I did what I could do.

You were at Mosque on Fridays?

Yeah. I try my best to become a better Muslim every day. I try to do the things I can do, the five daily prayers and other practices.

Are most of your network and your friendship circle also Muslims?

Back then, they were.

But as for friends now, I have a lot of online friends across the globe and in person who I play video games with. Who truly care and support me for who I am as a person.

What got you out of that dark place?

My faith. I think my religion played a big part in that. Even though we know suicide is forbidden in our religion. When suicide happens in our community, yes, there's a group of people who will say, 'What he did was bad', or 'What he did was forbidden', but there will also be a group of people who say, 'We don't have the right to judge what happened.'

It's the same with suicides in any community. We don't know what happens in the last moments. We believe that God is all-merciful. What happens when someone passes is between them and God. I think it's shameful when we get groups of people who would say, 'He died in sin.' That's the wrong mindset. We can't judge what happened to that person. They did it because they were mentally unwell. When you hear people say how that person is going to burn in hell because of what they did, that's more about their own struggles of dealing with those issues, because they don't want to deal with what's happening in our communities.

Then there's the other side that suggests we pray for them, that we hope God forgives them. Even though I had friends who pushed me aside, I think they pushed me aside because they didn't understand what was going on. It was new to them. When I first opened up to my sister about my suicidal thoughts, she didn't push me aside. She ended up saying, 'Would you be able to speak to Mum about it?' Even though my mother is a practising Muslim, she was supportive. She didn't turn me away and say, 'Oh, it's a sin. Don't think like that. Keep quiet. Don't tell anyone about it.'

I've met those people who would say that. But, that's them having their issues where they don't want to face what their child or loved one said to them.

It really depends on what the person is going through. It depends on the individual and if they're willing to support you or not. Especially when it comes to friends or family. We can't tar the whole community with the one brush. It's each individual. On my journey, I know some Muslims who are holding suicide prevention workshops at schools, with imams, and with parents. For the longest time I thought what I was doing was wrong, but when I met these people and they saw me, it showed me that what I'm doing isn't wrong. I know these people who have high status or who are imams, who have actually come to me and said, 'Teach me what you're doing.'

So, what you're saying to the Muslim community is we should be compassionate about people who are suicidal, who find themselves in that situation.

Yes, of course, because we're human at the end of the day as well as being Muslim. When someone asks me, 'What advice would you give someone who knows someone struggling with suicidal thoughts?' I'll say, 'Just be there for them. That's all they need.' That's probably the most they need, someone to be on their side or to take them out for dinner, or it can be as simple as just asking, 'Are you okay?' So, yes. Have compassion and have empathy toward someone who is Muslim and who is having suicidal thoughts.

How dark did it get for you? Did you think about taking your own life?

I'm extremely grateful that I've only had dark thoughts. I've never made any plans or had attempts.

But the dark thoughts were about killing yourself?

Yep, for sure.

Because you didn't want to be here?

I felt so isolated and afraid. The pressure of my life was getting too much. I'll admit that every now and then I do still feel overwhelmed and those thoughts do come. I've noticed the thoughts come when life gets a little bit harder for me and I just want to crawl into a ball and not come out. I want to push everyone away and not talk to anyone, and just be under the ground. I will pull myself out of it. I will come out of it and then I'm okay. I think back then was probably the darkest. When I feel dark is when I hit rock bottom and those are the thoughts that come. I don't want to deal with work. I don't want to deal with my friends. I don't want to deal with my family. Things get really overwhelming for me. My thoughts begin to race. My anxiety gets really loud. I overthink the past.

I overthink me being bullied. I get those thoughts and I just ride them out.

You said when you get very pressured, you might go to those dark thoughts. What can trigger that for you?

I'm a bit of a perfectionist; I think if I mess up once, it's enough. No matter how small or how big, that can trigger it. Or if I feel like something didn't go the way I expected it to go, that I could have prevented it from happening, that also builds up pressure. I want everything to go a certain way. Even though I know we're all human and that we all make mistakes.

It sounds like you're very tough on yourself. Tougher on yourself than you are on other people, is that true?

Yeah, I'd admit that. I definitely am. I'm definitely an overthinker when it comes to those things.

How do you manage your anxiety and your suicidal thoughts?

I'm on medication for my ADHD, I don't take medication for anything else. I used to see a psychologist, but I stopped, and I've been thinking I want to see a therapist again.

Do you think your ADHD diagnosis explains a lot of what happened at school?

I think it definitely makes sense. And it has definitely been life-changing, even though I still have my struggles. I'm still trying to find coping mechanisms for it. It definitely does make sense of my struggle in school, my attention span in school and my attention span on a few things in my personal life.

You said you talked to your mum about how you were feeling. Has your family been supportive of you being more open about your health?

They definitely have. I've had mixed responses, but the majority of my family has been supportive.

So, as you get older, with the diagnosis of ADHD and the medication and support, do you have fewer dark times than you used to?

Not as much as I used to. But they do happen every now and then.

What are you doing for work now?

Youth work with the PCYC.

I've publicly spoken as part of my local Headspace centre. I did something with the culturally and linguistically diverse communities through them, when I volunteered. Then in 2021, I was part of the national staff and I did a video series. I spoke to over 1200 people on Islamophobia and growing up here. I got invited to talk on suicide prevention within our communities through Neami National. Three of us spoke about suicide prevention and what we can do regarding it, and what happens when there's a suicide in our community. What the response is like within the community.

There was also an opportunity to go to my old Muslim school. So, I took that on and I spoke about my mental health journey with them. I think that's when I really discovered that's what I wanted to do, to share my story with people.

When you're speaking to groups, is the message, 'I am a young Muslim man in a faith that says suicide is a sin. But I've been suicidal'? Is the message that no matter what your background is, you should speak up and get help?

I avoid saying suicide is a sin. I don't use that word in my stories. I say it's stigmatised and that as a community we can remove that stigma. Despite some people's point of view on it, we are able to talk about it more in community, comfortably.

How do you describe your journey in those speeches?

I say it's always a tough time dealing with that stigma as a male, living here in Australia. And even though I've been pushed away by old friends, I have still found my passion in the mental health space, and my passion for public speaking. That's pretty much it in a nutshell. I always talk about the stigma, but then the hope that the stigma can be removed and that we can talk about our mental health openly.

I tell people that there is definitely change, but it's still a very small change. I think me doing these things, even if I change just one person's mindset or one person gets help – that's enough for me. It might be an unrealistic goal to remove the stigma of suicide completely. My more realistic goal is hopefully that one person goes out and gets help or tells someone else who says, 'This is how I can help you with this because I heard this guy on the radio' or 'I read this in a book' or 'I read this article'.

Are you getting better at life? Have you worked out coping mechanisms?

I have coping mechanisms. I know when it's getting a bit rough, a coping mechanism I have is a sense of humour. I use a really dark sense of humour, with my friends. If I don't joke about it to them, then I guess that's a sign that I'm really struggling. I think that's a big one for me.

Have any of the people who turned away from you years ago changed their attitude, come back to you and apologised for pushing you away?

One guy messaged me on Instagram saying, 'Hey, I just wanted to apologise for what happened years ago. I hope you're doing well.' He actually said he was suffering with his own mental health at the time and didn't know how to deal with it. Which just shows me that it's not the attitude of what our religion says or what it doesn't say. It's what happens inside. We don't know people's stories, and if they don't open up, we don't know what's going on in their lives. When I got that message, it was an eye-opener. I wish he'd said, 'I know how you feel, it's okay. We can do this together.' I told him, 'It's all good. I forgive you. I hope you've been well.'

Do you think your life is better because you got to that terribly dark place? Do you think you had to go there in order to bounce back?

I think so, 100 per cent. And I found my passion in mental health midway through a therapy session. Like, I told my psychologist at the time, 'I don't want any other young Muslim person to face what I've faced. How can I do that?' She directed me toward the group where the public speaking started. And that made me believe that everything happens for a reason.

This is what the passion in your life is now?

Pretty much, yeah. I feel the most excited when I get these opportunities to tell my story.

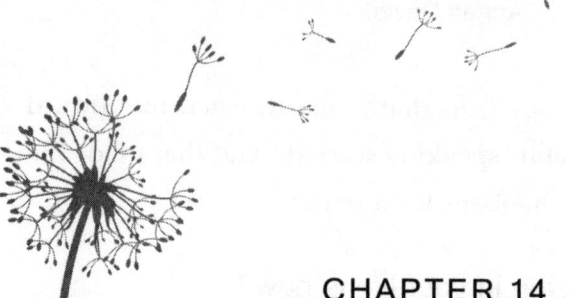

CHAPTER 14

Ellia Green

The Rugby Champion

Ellia Green OAM is an Olympian. He won gold at the 2016 Rio de Janeiro Olympic Games, and silver at the Commonwealth Games on the Gold Coast, as a member of the Australian Women's Rugby Sevens team. Born in Fiji and adopted at birth, Ellia's life has zigged and zagged in and out of the public eye. In his personal life he has experienced more trauma in his thirty-one years than most of us might in a lifetime. Physical injuries and mental illness have been part and parcel of Ellia's life, but he's never been one to take a backward step, always someone who keeps moving forward. With his sporting career now behind him and fatherhood his priority, Ellia tells his unique story of hope and inspiration.

* * *

Can we begin at the beginning?

I was born in 1992 in Fiji. In Suva Hospital. I was listed as an abandoned baby, because my birth mother was going through difficulties in her life and had no support. My mum, who adopted me – Yolanta Green – was in Fiji at the time. She was a journalist and was over there with my dad, Evan Green. She was easily spotted around Fiji because she's Polish and she's white. A local security guard in the area that she was staying in, asked her if she could help his sister, who was giving birth. She went to the hospital, without a second of hesitation, and brought in all the baby supplies that she thought my birth mother would need, paid for her to have a bed and held her hand throughout the birth.

Your birth mother, do you know much about her?

She was an Indigenous Fijian. My birth father wasn't listed. All the signs pointed toward the sex being non-consensual.

Did your mum and dad bring you straight back to Australia?

With the legislation in Fiji, if you were adopting from overseas you had to stay for a certain period of time. So we ended up staying for two years. Mum and Dad also adopted my brother, Mitchell, from another family on another island. Then Dad fell sick with prostate cancer. So, we moved back to Australia. He died not too long after, in 1996.

I'd imagine when you came back to Australia there weren't a lot of Pacific Islander kids where you grew up? And you also had parents who looked different to you.

That was a big culture shock, living on the Central Coast, with Na – our Fijian nanny – my beautiful Polish mum and my brother, who looks very different to me. He's a bit more Samoan. We looked like the United Nations. People would give us funny looks all the time. At primary school I'd make up lots of stories. I'd usually say that my mum ate way too much chocolate during her pregnancy, and that I was the result!

And you're a young girl at this stage. Were you sporty then?

I had my first athletics carnival in kindergarten. That's when I found my love for running. I won that race and when Mum saw that I could run fast, she signed me up for Little Athletics. From that moment on, I craved that feeling of winning, all the time. I wrote on my wall that I was going to be an Olympian one day.

What happened if you didn't win?

I would be so depressed. I'd feel so bad about myself. Not only that, Mum would be very hard on me. But I'm thankful for it.

It was deflating at times, but it was also very motivating because she would go off at me. She'd say that I got too distracted. That I didn't warm up properly. I didn't do this, I didn't do that. All these reasons why I didn't win. Especially if it was a national or state title.

In team sports you either win or lose, maybe draw. But in running, you can come second or third. You can still get a place. So second and third didn't matter, it was just coming first?

For me, and for Mum, winning was always the priority. No coming second or third. She bought me every Cathy Freeman and Olympic book available in Australia. I was completely fixated on my goal.

Did you have the right running gear?

No. Mum was broke, she was really struggling financially for a long time. Especially after Dad died. And then things got worse. Mum endured domestic violence during the whole of my primary school time, right up to Year 7. She'd met this person. I don't even want to say his name. Many times he'd make me watch it.

You must have hated him.

Mum taught me that you shouldn't hate anyone, because hate is a very strong word. I resent the things he has done, yes. And I never want to see his face again. But do I hate him? I don't want to say hate, it's an unforgiving thing.

It was the typical cycle of abuse. In the beginning he was very sweet, charming, lovely and funny. As soon as it seemed that my mother was locked in, everything changed.

There were a lot of changes after that relationship, and things went so badly. We had to run, we had to escape. We fled from the Central Coast. Got in the car and literally drove to Melbourne one day, because things were going from worse to bad, very quickly. Mum just said, 'Don't ask any questions. We're getting in the car and going.'

Was sport your escape as a kid?

It gave me hope toward a better life for us, for my mum and my brother. I had this vision when I saw Cathy Freeman win that iconic race at the Sydney Olympics. How effortless she looked.

Was Cathy your hero because she was a woman, or she was an Indigenous woman - or was it something else?

More so her story. I read her story multiple times. Cathy grew up with very little but a huge dream. Having been treated the way that Cathy was – her experiences with racism – and my experiences with racism at school, I saw Cathy as someone who made me believe that I could do that.

As you went into high school - I apologise if my language is indelicate - when did you begin to think you weren't female, that you were male?

It was actually well before high school, more like very early days of primary school. I was very certain that I was not in the right physical body, as a person.

Did you share that thinking with your mum and or anyone else?

I didn't talk. I didn't say a word. I didn't talk at school. Barely talked at home. That was something my mother would joke about a lot, I wouldn't talk because I was so shy. So, no, I'd have to talk to get that information out.

Did you talk in your own head, even though you didn't talk out loud?

Always. It carried on to my adult years. Talking to myself because I wasn't getting the answers from my mother, about why we were still in this situation. I wasn't getting the answers even about a lot of details about things – like what happened with my birth. And so, I think maybe the way I dealt with things was to not talk. Then, every week she said I wasn't allowed to talk to anyone about anything that was happening at home. You know, like calling the police all the time to save her. I wasn't allowed to talk about any of this at school or with anyone. And none of her friends knew either.

You would call the police?

All the time. Especially when I thought it was getting progressively worse and [she was] close to death. Yeah. My brother and I couldn't save her. I just had to call the police. A lot of people go through that situation. I really feel for children who have to watch that day-in, day-out.

But you were one of those. Do you feel for yourself?

Mum never let me feel sorry for myself. I did feel like we'd been a bit unlucky. I can't help but feel a little bit unlucky with a lot of things like that. But I also have faith that things happen for a reason. I have faith there is some kind of plan for things.

Is that a religious faith or spiritual?

I'm more spiritual than religious. I believe that there is always a reason for something happening. I think it's taught me a lot of lessons. I would channel a lot of these memories when I played Rugby, which made me a very aggressive player. When I had my most physical games is when I would think about everything that had happened. And then I'd imagine that my opponents were him.

Can we talk about your gender journey? Right back to your early days, did you want to be a boy?

It wasn't so much that I wanted to be a boy. It was just that I didn't want to be called a girl. Every time my mother would say that she wished I would be more girly, I would refuse. I'd think, stop trying to make me be something I'm not, because I don't feel like that.

When did you peak in your running career? What was your highest achievement?

Qualifying for the World School Games in Doha, Qatar. It was my first international meet. When I qualified, the first thing I stressed about was the cost, because to compete for Australia and get the uniform and everything, was going to cost $5000. Athletics Australia would fund some of it, but I just knew it was going to be way too much. Mum was telling me every single day that she had just $20 in her wallet, 'so don't ask for anything'. That's all she had left for the rest of the week. There was no way I'd be able to go. I was too scared to even show her the letter saying that I was picked. When I did eventually show her, she was in tears, just so proud. And she said, 'Well, you have to go to this.' And I'm thinking, *How? How on earth will I go to this?* Mum went to every local business in our community to ask for sponsorship and she started raising money that way.

So, you were able to get there in the end?

Yes. That was my first experience of competing for Australia. It was 1996–97. It was one of the coolest experiences of my life, I'll never forget it. However, there was something that happened on the trip that was very traumatic. I was sexually abused. I called Mum straight away when I realised what had happened was extremely inappropriate. The person had been sexually abusing multiple athletes and got sent home. I'd had a funny feeling he was a bit strange, and my gut feeling was right.

I'm so sorry. Did that affect your performance?

I came third. I was pretty upset because I won my heats and the semis. My mum was gutted for me. But she wasn't angry, which was interesting. Usually she'd get angry. She was proud but yeah, I was extremely disappointed.

How was your mental health at that time?

I was in fight-or-flight mode. Constantly. It felt like we were on the run. I'm either running on the track or I'm running with my mum somewhere. We're just running. Everything was a survival situation.

When did Rugby Union come into your life?

Rugby Australia were holding talent identification camps all around Australia. I went to a Fijian social group at a church, where all the kids met up and quite a few of them were talking about it, saying they were trying to make the Australian team. My cousin, who isn't really my cousin – everyone's your cousin when you're Fijian! – said she was going to go to the trials, and asked why didn't I go with her? We were late. On 'Fiji time'. It was so embarrassing. We did speed testing, jump testing and then skills, and they selected people from that.

I knew nothing about Rugby Union at this point so, when I got a letter saying they wanted me to go to the next stage of the trials at the Australian Institute of Sport, I couldn't believe it. I almost fainted. I showed my mum, and she was so proud. She said, 'Oh my goodness, Bub, you have to do it. Go. You're going to Canberra.' And that's where we were going to have trial games.

Was it the Rugby Sevens you focused on?

It was always Sevens, because that's what they were looking for. So, in my first games in Rugby they put me on the wing. I was told not to think about it too much, to just catch the ball and run. The coach said, 'No-one's going to catch you.' I ended up running over the try line, into the next field because I didn't know to stop.

I walked away from track, and also I left the nursing studies I'd started. I had no money because I had lied to my mum. I told her we were going to get paid a small amount, until we got full-time employment, which wasn't true. I had $200. They had offered to pay for the interstate travel, driving, from Melbourne to Sydney. I hadn't told anyone about my situation, and I slept in my car for three months.

Was this the time you started thinking about gender transition?

No. There was too much going on in my life. I could barely buy myself a meal, I was so broke. At the same time my mum was battling lung cancer. She had already battled breast cancer when I was in primary school. The doctor said it was a result of the domestic violence, the abuse and the stress she suffered over all those years. The breast cancer had spread to her lymph nodes, but she had a mastectomy and beat it. That's why I started nursing. Because I was in Year 5 then, and I was doing all her wound dressings and everything before I went to school.

And then she became sick again and the lung cancer was terminal cancer in the end?

It progressively got worse to the point it was incurable.

Did your mum get to see you play for Australia?

Yes. She came to the Commonwealth Games on the Gold Coast. For the Rio Olympics in 2016, I didn't know if she'd be able to come because she was constantly having treatment. She had to save up for that for so long. I told her, 'Mum, you know I haven't even been picked for the team yet and you've already booked a flight.' She just laughed. 'Did you think I was coming just for you? You're not that special.'

Did you medal at the Gold Coast?

Silver, and then gold in Rio.

She must have been so proud.

Seeing my mum in the crowd with this giant sombrero hat and the Australian jersey I'd given her was special. For me, at that moment, there was no-one in the stadium but my mum. I could only see Mum. It was just us and realising that moment we'd dreamed about when I was five years old in my bedroom – me being an Olympian one day with a medal around my neck. Now, I'm standing on the podium with a gold medal around my neck.

Your mum sounds like your biggest fan and your biggest critic.

One hundred per cent. Brutal. Absolutely brutal. But then, at the same time, she's telling every man and his dog about me. Yeah, she was just so proud. Couldn't be any prouder.

At this point were you a professional Rugby player earning an income?

I was starting to make good money. Endorsements came after that, which definitely changed my life a lot.

Did you have any injuries?

God, where do I start? Four knee surgeries, foot surgery, shoulder reconstruction, hand reconstruction. Out of my team, I would definitely be ranked in the top three of most surgery. It seemed as though I was spending more of my playing career in rehab than playing. It was very depressing.

Did that damage your mental health?

I became very destructive during rehab. There was this one time when I'd lost Mum and I'd just had surgery. I had all this time to think about everything that'd happened or was happening.

When you say you were destructive, how?

Alcohol. It's not good to have that with the medications I was on after surgeries. I was extremely depressed.

Did you have any thoughts of suicide?

Yeah, definitely after Mum died. The most destructive and impulsiveness in me came out around 2018.

Did you make plans to take your own life?

Yeah.

Did you try to kill yourself at any stage?

I was in the process of an attempt when the hospital called me. This was when Mum was dying. It was one o'clock in the morning and Mum had asked several nurses and doctors to call me. It was urgent. She just wanted to say good night and that she loved me, that she'd see me in the morning.

Do you think she knew something was happening?

Definitely. We'd been so spiritually connected. She could read me like a book.

Did that save your life?

Absolutely. I couldn't believe my phone was ringing at that moment. It was just bizarre. I was just going to text my mum that I loved her, and when I saw it was the hospital calling I thought, *Oh my god, don't tell me they're calling to tell me she's dead.* But it was Mum calling to tell me she loved me. I thought to myself what an idiot I was.

Your mum knew you as a woman; she didn't know you as a man?

She knew me as Ellia.

She didn't know you after your transition?

No, because she died in 2018. She knew me inside out, so I don't think it would have been much of a surprise to her. She knew everything. She said, 'Do you think I was born yesterday?' That was her response to everything.

271

Was your gender confusing to you?

Not really, no. My most effortless version of me was not as a woman. I discovered that when I was around people who loved me unconditionally, that saw me as a person, not as my gender. Once I ignored the judgement and the opinions of what society has on gender, transitioning was a very easy decision. It was when I stopped caring about what others thought and put myself and my happiness first, which I'd never done before.

Many people would not understand that, and some would judge it.

I always say you don't need to get it. There's so many things in the world that we don't understand, that we don't know. It's not about trying to get it. It's just not okay to have an opinion that hurts someone else or affects someone else. You just need to have empathy.

Were you still in the middle of your Rugby Union career when you had the surgery?

I was starting to look for different doctors and surgeons that deal with patients in transition in 2019. I was about twenty-seven. It was toward my senior years. I was one of the older players.

Did you consciously want to finish your Rugby career as a woman, before you transitioned?

Absolutely. The possibility of transitioning during a career wouldn't be possible. There's so many reasons why. I guess the main one would be because I'd have to take hormones, which would mean I would be unable to compete because I would be drug-tested. Not to mention the surgery. You'd have to ask for the time off to get that. It wasn't for performance, so it's a bit too awkward to have that conversation.

And how was your mental health going into this very important decision?

It was terrible. I'd just got told that I wasn't selected for the Australian Olympic team. That was after our trial games in Townsville. We were all put into a small room, and then if you were picked you went to the rooftop of the hotel and had drinks and celebrated. If you didn't get picked, you went to a room with a box of tissues. I got the box of tissues room. I saw my entire career end. I couldn't see a single thing that I'd done as a positive thing because that moment was a reflection of me.

Was it fair to say you hadn't prepared yourself for the end of your career?

I had definitely prepared myself for the end of my career, I just hadn't prepared myself for not getting selected then. If I have something I don't achieve, it's a massive failure. I'd developed this way of thinking from how my mum was with me, growing up with nothing. She was so tough on me if I came second in a race, not first. One time she snapped my headphones in half, threw them out the window of the car while we were driving, and then told me to get out and walk home. She said I didn't take this seriously. 'You're laughing. You're making friends, you're not there to perform. If you don't want to take it seriously, then I won't either. So get out.' As I grew older, this legacy had its positives and negatives. The negatives were that when things didn't go right, it really harmed part of my self-worth.

Who did you tell you were transitioning?

I'd told some of my closest family members and one or two teammates.

Did you want to play Rugby as a man?

No. I was tired. My body was tired and depleted.

Two big decisions - I'm becoming a man and that's the end of my Rugby career.

I was also coming off a reality show as well. One month after being dropped from the Olympic team, I went on the Channel 7 *SAS Australia* reality show. [This is a gruelling television program that follows a group of people as they progress through special forces army training.] I finished the show two weeks before I transitioned.

It was the toughest thing I've ever done in my life. I certainly was not cut out for this show at all. Not mentally or physically. I only realised when it was too late, once I was in this isolated bush area in the middle of nowhere. I ended up in hospital afterward for my mental health. The physical and emotional aspects of being on that show are extreme. I was jumping out of a helicopter, jumping from a speed boat onto a helicopter while it's moving. Getting tear-gassed, pepper-sprayed, getting a bag placed over your head and being interrogated. It tested me in ways I've never been tested before.

It was the hardest physical, emotional and mental challenge that I've ever had in my life. You don't eat, you don't sleep. You're constantly on edge. It's a show that's made to pull you apart, more so mentally than physically. I went on the show for financial reasons. I knew I was retiring. I knew I had to make some kind of income.

However, it wasn't the right time for me. It got to the point where I was so traumatised that I was disassociating to an extreme level, which eventually caused me to withdraw from the show because I was starting to hallucinate. I was very confused, starting to not really know where I was anymore.

I was disassociating so much, to the point where, as I was leaving the show, I didn't know that I had a baby on the way. [Ellia and their partner, Vanessa, were expecting a child at the time.] The doctor said to me, 'Congratulations, Ellia, an amazing effort. You must be excited with your daughter due to be born soon.' I had no idea. I didn't know that Vanessa was my partner. I couldn't speak properly. I started stuttering.

Despite all this, were you excited about the gender change?

Extremely. My partner was very excited for me as well. It was something that I had manifested for a long time, so it was really exciting.

How long did the transition surgery take?

Three to four hours. I had my chest surgery and started hormones in the same week. I was very nervous. There are a lot of things that can go wrong with the surgery – with any surgery. But especially when it comes to this one, with swelling or infection. And the placement. Is everything where I wanted it to be? Looking at myself for the first time, I was so nervous, but also really excited. When I saw myself for the first time in the mirror, I had nothing but tears of joy, of happiness, of contentment. 'Yep, that's me.'

That's now a couple of years ago. How do you manage your mental health now and how do you manage your suicidality?

It's something I've learned to manage. For me, it's meant things like going back to the gym. I'm training, especially at nighttime, when my head is busy the most. Or, if I'm overthinking, I talk to someone, like a therapist.

Are you still learning how to be proactive with your mental health?

I'd say now more so than ever. I've got more control over things, because I've learned that if I let myself stay in that space too long, it's not good. So, I am proactive about it.

I love who I am. It's got nothing to do with hating myself. It's more to do with what I haven't dealt with, a lot of my experiences as a child. I've seen so much death and trauma, I think I need to be able to process all of that, in order to heal myself in the long term.

And has becoming a man improved your mental health?

Not so much about becoming a man. It's more about having the courage to tell the world who I am without fear of judgement. It's probably been the best decision of my life – the best decision I've made for myself. To make a decision like that for me, and not to be worried about how people respond, that took time.

When my daughter was three months old I had tears in my eyes because I was looking at her and how she just looked at me; nothing else mattered at that moment. I thought to myself that I never want her to think that I was too afraid to tell the world that I'm your daddy. I didn't want her to ever think that I was too afraid or scared, so I can be the best role model. And I don't want her to ever be afraid to tell people who she is. That was a huge point that changed my way of thinking. It meant that I had to be the best role model for her, which was to be me.

Many people might start reading this chapter assuming the thing that made you mentally ill and suicidal was your gender as a woman. But that's not true, is it?

That's what pains me. That was the best part of that journey of my mental health struggle. The best. What caused all of those mental health issues was actually childhood traumas, not the gender transition.

What I've found, talking with different people who have transitioned, is that every journey is different and unique to that person. It's really hard to make an assumption that this person is having mental health issues because of that. Everyone is doing it so differently, and how their family and friends reacted is also different. Whether their lives are made public or not.

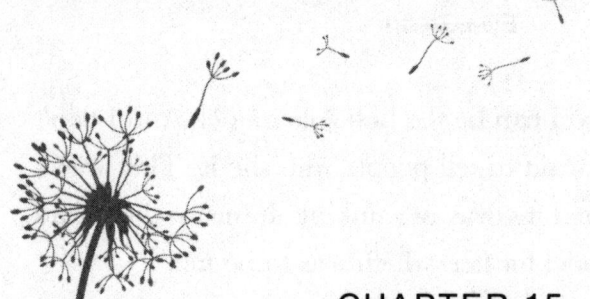

CHAPTER 15

James Packer

The Businessman

I have known James Packer for over twenty years. Over that time, we have become friends. Fifteen years ago, I spoke to him about my suicidality, and he told me, 'Mate – I've been there myself.' James is a rarity. In the world of infallibility that billionaire businesspeople tend to inhabit, he shares his struggles living with mental illness and suicidal thoughts honestly and authentically. Throughout this interview, James often acknowledges how privileged he is. Yet he is proof that no matter how much privilege or wealth you have, it doesn't guarantee good mental health.

* * *

When were you first aware of your mental health issues?

I've been depressed in my life when I've had bad times in business on several occasions. I've been caught up in bad times in business more than once. More than twice. And I've been seriously depressed. More than a couple of times. I suppose the first time would have been when One.Tel [a telecommunications company] went broke in 2001. And I was depressed for at least a year. I also had substance abuse issues alongside that.

Most businesspeople have wins and they have losses - that's business. But did you see it as a personal failure?

Yeah, I've had wins and I've had losses. I can sit here and look back and I can have more perspective now than I could as a 34-year-old. You know, then I felt as though I'd just had losses. And I was very embarrassed. I felt I'd let people down.

Family? Friends? Business partners?

All of the above. I felt I'd let family down, I felt I'd let friends down. I felt I'd let myself down. I felt I'd let my wife down. I felt I'd just let everyone down. I felt I was a failure. I felt there was no way out.

And you got to feeling suicidal?

Yeah, I got to feeling suicidal. I was abusing drugs. I was in a terrible state.

Who did you turn to then?

I had an incredibly fortunate situation. Tom Cruise came into my life, and he saw that I was unwell and he decided that he was going to help me.

It really was quite out of the blue. I have nothing but love for Tom. He's an amazing life force. He's an amazing human being. At that time in my life, and for probably ten years after that, we were very close friends. But at that time, when we really weren't, he decided he was going to help me. And he did. He helped me with my father, which wasn't simple at the beginning. He was an enormous help, and I don't know if I would have got through it without him, to be honest.

One.Tel was that first big push out by yourself, from out of the family business?

I think it probably was. I'd pushed hard for other things that we were involved in, in the business. But I'd been personally invested in one of them. I'd taken out a loan on one of them. I'd gone and spoken to Lachlan and Rupert [Murdoch] about one of them. And so one of them seemed a lot more important than the others, to me.

Investments go up and down. Was it that it went broke that really brought it home?

I think yeah, it went to zero. You know, it was not something that I bought for 100, that was worth 60. It was like putting money into a fire. It was like we incinerated a lot of money. I used to wonder whether if we'd put more money into it, would it have come good? Whereas I look back now and I'm glad we didn't put in more money, because it would have just been good money after bad.

But did James Packer need to have a stumble early?

Probably. I wish I didn't cause Lachlan [Murdoch] the problems that I caused him. You know, I love Lachlan. He's like a brother to me. He really is. And he's a good person, with a good heart. And I caused him embarrassment and I wish I didn't do that. I take responsibility for that. How much did it hurt me twenty years later in terms of making me more cynical and did it make me a better businessman? Did those scars actually help me, I think that's the question you're asking? I think that's a fair question. I'm sure people have asked you the same question. Do you actually grow in some ways from the pain of your personal failures?

My reality is I've been diagnosed with different things, by different doctors and they've given me different medications and some doctors have said definitively that I'm bipolar. And other doctors have said that they're not sure. I've found that personally confusing.

I'm not for one second implying that there's been a lack of care. I think I've been very fortunate with the people who have taken an interest in my life and have been caring. But I think it's confusing if you get different diagnoses. I practised Scientology for a period of time and it's well known that Scientology believes that psychiatry is overrated, to put it gently. I ended up disagreeing with that. There are things in Scientology that I found very practically useful as well.

Would you call it a religion?

I'd call the spirituality a religion. There are aspects that are above my pay grade. I prefer to think of the positive – my positive in terms of my time in Scientology was my relationship with Tom.

Who helped you in other dark times?

Netanyahu [Prime Minister of Israel]. In a big way. Warren Beatty has been a wonderful, wonderful friend to me. Ben Tilley's been a great friend to me through thick and thin. Jodhi [Meares] has been a great friend for me through thick and thin.

Erica [Baxter]'s been amazing. Erica's been truly amazing. My mum's been amazing. You know, I've been lucky. I've had great support and great friends. My sister's been very good.

You say how grateful you've been and how privileged you are often. Why is that so important to you?

I think humility is an attractive and an important quality. I think the ups and downs of life teach you humility. I've had a lot of people who have been good to me. I've been very lucky.

You've said you've been diagnosed with different mental illnesses from different doctors. How close to suicide did you get?

I might have ended up killing myself without realising it, if you know what I mean. Overdosing or something. So, I'm not sure how close I was, you know.

But you've thought about it?

I've thought about it. I've had dark thoughts. I've had dark thoughts but probably not that close is the truth, but I've had dark thoughts.

Do you feel you live with that darkness?

There's been certainly times in my life that I've been depressed. I was depressed in 2000. I was depressed after One.Tel. I was depressed during the global financial crisis. I was depressed in 2016 when we had people in jail and when Case 1000 happened in Israel. Those two things happened at the same time and I felt I'd rebuilt my reputation and then I felt I'd rebuilt it after the global financial crisis. Then I felt that I'd lost my reputation for a third time and fourth time and it was never going to get better again and I was very depressed. I thought it couldn't get worse, and then all of a sudden I had three Royal Commissions impact me. Maybe it was just as acute or maybe it got worse again. I had a breakdown and I went to this place called McLean, just outside Harvard in Massachusetts in 2018. So, from 2016 to 2019/20, I was seriously depressed two or three times.

And how did that manifest itself? Could you get out of bed?

I started hallucinating. It wasn't even substance abuse. I had a blood test when I went to this place in McLean and I was free of substances. That really was a bit scary because it wasn't substances. And I was seeing things that just weren't there. It hasn't happened since and they put me on medication. I was on a lot of medications from 2016 to 2022. Different doctors put me on different things, but I was consistently on medication and I'm on nothing now. I'm sure some people think I should be on medication. I'm totally serious about that. Some people think I'm mad as a hatter, and I probably am a little bit crazy. But you know, I'm choosing to live on a medication-free diet. There's no doubt in my mind, you feel better, you do better, you're more active if there's a balance in all you do.

Are you your own worst critic? Are you your own harshest critic?

No, I think... I think the *Sydney Morning Herald*'s my harshest critic. But I am a tough critic on myself. I'm a hard knocker on myself, yeah.

Where does that come from?

I've got high expectations of myself. And that's... I don't think that's a bad thing.

Are you a risk-taker?

You know, risk is a funny word. My father's business, the business that I grew up in, was a traditional media business. And my father was a genius at traditional media. He did incredibly well multiplying the inheritance that he got from his father. He did amazingly well and the majority of his wealth was in a magazine business and a free-to-air television business. If we just kept those businesses, those businesses would have reduced in value greatly. As they have. I mean ACP [Australian Consolidated Press] virtually doesn't exist today and Channel 9 is a shadow of itself. So, what's the definition of risk? By one definition, doing nothing would be not taking a risk. But history has borne out that that would be one of the biggest risks for me.

Many people will always relate to your father when they relate to you. You'll always be the son of Kerry Packer and the grandson of Frank Packer and all that comes with it. I've found a very generous and very caring streak in you. Are your roots important to you? You said to me you're very lucky or you've had a privileged life so you are not taking things for granted, are you?

I'm very conscious that I am my father's son and my mother's son. I'm very conscious of that and I'm very grateful. I think I lead a very fortunate life. I'm very conscious of that. I don't think that's a bad thing.

**People love to focus on your relationship with your dad.
I just loved watching you on TV speak at your dad's funeral.
You looked sad and proud, and it was a very beautiful
father/son reflection. Do you think of him often? Do you wish
your dad was here so I could ask him a question about you?**

Not really. I'm at peace with my relationship with my father. I'm
at peace, you know.

I think he really did it his way, you know. That Sinatra song,
he really did it his way and I think that he did all he could do for
me. I wish I could say to him that I realise he was much more
reasonable than I gave him credit for at the time.

He wasn't always right. He wasn't God. But he had some
wisdoms that were pretty special. You know, I'm so fortunate for
that blessing of ending in a good spot. And it's because of him
that we did end in a good spot. He'd obviously thought about our
last conversation. I didn't realise it was our last conversation but
he 100 per cent did.

**Can you see your future path? Are you self-aware enough
to say, I need to slow down for a couple of weeks or
months, I'm going too fast?**

It's a good question. I … yeah, I'm not great being in cities
anymore. So I don't spend too much time in a city. Silly as this
might seem, I think places have energies about them and energies
to them. And I get stimulated by the energy of a place. And I
need to be in relaxing places otherwise I get wound up.

And if you get wound up, do you risk depression?

I think more stimulants, you know. I try and stay away from
drinking and stimulants and cigarettes, and all those things.

I don't want to pretend to be better at this than I am. It wasn't so long ago that I was on a lot of antidepressants, I was drinking, I was smoking. I was all of those things. That wasn't so long ago. And I'm still overweight and so I don't want to pretend that I'm better at this than I am. I'm doing better than I was but I don't want to pretend that I've got everything worked out. I don't.

Would you say that you struggle with depression and mental illness? Is it an everyday thing for you?

No, not at the moment. At the moment, I'm doing better. I'm very happy.

But there have been times where it's a daily struggle?

In the past, when I was taking antidepressants. When I was in the middle of three royal commissions. Ab-so-fucking-lutely, it was a daily struggle. It did not make me feel better to feel like I was being portrayed as this massive bad dude. There has never been a person in Australia's history who has had three royal commissions into them before. Let alone at the same time. I'm not saying Crown was perfect, and we should have done better and I should have made sure that Crown did better. But after all that, there was not one charge. Not one criminal charge. Not one civil charge.

There's not much we don't know about you.

Well, I'm doing this with you because I think it's a good cause. I'm not doing this because I'm trying to get more publicity about who I am. I'm doing this because I think you're a good cause.

How has your mental health interacted with your personal life?

I'm proud that I get on well with my family. So, whether it's my sister or my mother, or my first wife or you know… Erica's my best friend and I get on great with my kids. I work at it with all of them. So it doesn't happen by remote control.

I'm conscious that statistically I'm toward the later part of my life, as opposed to the beginning. I might feel young. Which I do, I feel young mentally. But I've got to do a bit better job of working out and working on myself physically and all of those things. Because I'm not as young as I was. I'm happy that I've given up antidepressants, that I've given up alcohol. I'm pleased that I've managed to do those things. I'm happy with myself that I've managed to do those things.

Did it surprise you when you became depressed?

Yes, yes, absolutely. Absolutely. It surprised me how helpless I felt. The times that I've been down, how helpless I was.

It felt bottomless. Like there's no end to this. But if I look at each of those times, I can identify something that happened that began to turn things around.

Did you feel you had people who'd just back you in one hundred per cent, no matter what?

I've been very lucky. My mother's been amazing. She's been absolutely amazing. My former wives have been amazing. Erica and Jodhi have been amazing. Ben, who I lived with, has been absolutely amazing. Guy, my CEO, has been a huge help. Yeah, I've been very fortunate to have a tight core. Kerry Stokes and Lachlan Murdoch have been great to me.

How did you manage to maintain such good relationships with your ex-wives?

I'm a diplomat! But I'm very proud of that. I joke, but I'm half serious... that no-one in the world gets on better with their ex-wives than me.

What are you hoping for, for the next fifty-five years? Because you're setting yourself a lifestyle that is good. You're setting a lifestyle that is good for your mental health, that's what I'm hearing.

I like the variety, the lifestyle that I lead. So I think that that's stimulating.

Are you factoring in your mental health and the risks into your future plans? And you know, the stimulation issues when you begin to look at new places and investments?

I feel good at the moment. I think my mental health issues have invariably come from when I've lost money financially or I've been humiliated publicly. They've come from one of those two things.

Well, you're not on your lonesome there.

Yeah, and hopefully neither of those two things are on the horizon now. But you know, I've had some wins as well, as you were kind enough to say before. And so I want to see if I can get some more. I haven't really got many irons in the fire at the moment, so I've got to see if I can work up some irons in the fire going forward.

I want to go and see if I can maybe be better at the game than I've been in the past. Maybe be as good at the good things that I've done and hopefully better at not making the mistakes.

I think I've been lucky. I think I've led a very interesting life and a privileged life. And I don't think you can ask for much more in life than an interesting life and a privileged life. And if I continue doing this, what could be more blessed than that?

What would you say to somebody else having tough times?

I'd say a couple of things. I'd say see a doctor. See a doctor would be at the top of the list, you know.

So don't tough it out? Don't think that you can fix it yourself?

Well, just be careful about that. I mean, you know, do I think people are overprescribed? I absolutely don't want to pretend that people aren't overprescribed but, you know, there's a balance. There's a balance in all of that. And I guess the other thing I'd say is take deep breaths and maybe my reality doesn't apply to other cases. But my reality is I thought it would never end, and it did end. The nightmare. I'm sure my reality isn't unique in that sense. I'm sure other people have thought it will never end and it does end.

I often say to people, it'll get better. It might get worse before it gets better, but it will get better.

Yep. That's well said.

And do you think you're tougher for the next time something might go wrong?

Not necessarily.

Wow, that's very honest.

Yeah, I'm not sure. I don't know.

When you read about people who take their own life, how do you emotionally react?

I'm not one of those people who gets angry about it. If someone takes their life and there's a chance that person could have gotten through it and there's a chance that person could have lived a longer and happier life, that's a waste. And that's sad.

What makes you happy? You said you're the happiest you've ever been. What are the elements of that?

I'm not under pressure. I'm happy in my personal life. I'm happy in my business life.

I've got a sort of interesting opportunity in front of me at the moment. You know, because we sold Crown to Black Stone at the end of June. Seventy-five per cent of my net worth is liquid for the first time in a long time. And, you know, we've made a few investments in a few shares and things like that. But those investments are liquid so I could sell them tomorrow. So I'm looking to make investments, which is an interesting mindset to be in. In the past, when I've had money on one or two occasions, it's burnt a hole in my pocket. I've got to make sure that I learn from those mistakes and those experiences. But it's an interesting time. Hopefully it's a good time to have some liquidity. And to be older and wiser.

That begs the question, you could just maintain that approach, which is lower pressure. But you are looking to build something again?

I'm enjoying being curious at this stage. I'm enjoying being curious in terms of the different asset types. I'm enjoying being curious geographically. I'm enjoying being intellectually curious.

Have you had that opportunity in the past?

Not to the degree that I have now. You know, I didn't know the world the way I know it now. I've become a citizen of the world.

What did you want to be when you were twenty?

I think I probably wanted to be more successful than I have been, in a business sense. I think I would have said I still wanted to be number one on the rich list. And I'm not that.

But I think now that living an interesting life is a big prize.

And the happiest you've ever been?

Yeah, I am the happiest I've ever been. I'm having a good time. I dropped my antidepressants, but I started taking psilocybin. But I'm not taking it anymore. But I took it for the first few months after I stopped taking the prescribed antidepressants.

And why was that?

My doctor supervised it and it was his recommendation. I found it pretty painless. I had a week or two of no sleep or whatever it is. Which is coming off the antidepressants. I was coming off Xanax at the same time. I was coming off the benzo, diazepam and those things. And I was coming off benzo, which I'd done before and benzos aren't easy to come off.

How did you find the psilocybin?

I'm doing better. I'm happy. I'm happy with myself in the sense that I've given up cigarettes now. I worked it out before today and it's probably the first time since 2005 that I'm a non-smoker, I'm a non-drinker. And I'm not taking recreational drugs. I'm not doing any of those things.

Are you proud of being off all that stuff?

I feel good about that. And I feel good that it's not difficult. Apart from my weight, it's not difficult.

We talked yesterday before this interview about drugs and alcohol. I wonder if those are because of a compulsive, addictive personality?

I think it's probably a combination. I don't do well when I'm under pressure. I think there are some people who handle pressure better than other people. I just don't.

I've had the opportunity to observe myself in situations where I've been under pressure enough times now to know, that I don't do well under pressure. I'm not at my best. And so, I'm making a conscious decision to try to avoid situations where I put myself under pressure.

I'm the same. It's interesting, for years I avoided my mum when things were difficult and avoided some family situations. So I withdrew myself from those situations. Are you more aware to say, that's going to be a pressure situation, I'm not going to go into it?

I think so. Debt in the past has weighed on me. There are times when I've had too much debt and that's weighed on me.

292

Being caught up in negative publicity cycles. That weighs on me. So I'm going to try to avoid things that cause that. You know, that's easier said than done. I haven't been entirely successful at avoiding that. But, yeah, I'm more conscious of the things that I think set me off than I used to be. And I make more of an effort than I used to, to avoid them.

So is this a reset time for you?

Absolutely, it's a reset.

What do you worry about?

At the moment, not a whole lot. You know, at the moment I'm in a good spot.

Afterword from John Brogden

When I started interviewing the subjects for *Profiles in Hope*, I expected I would relate to many of their stories because I had tried to kill myself too.

I did not expect that so many of the stories would have life-saving – life-altering – sliding doors moments.

Like the bloke getting in the train and randomly asking Matt Caruana, sitting in a wheelchair after trying to kill himself, 'Well, what are you going to do about it now?'

Or Pat Hall forgetting to lock the window that is always locked, allowing a neighbour to climb into the house and save her.

And Preston Campbell's coach knocking on the door just as he decided to kill himself after his previous attempt.

I expected the journeys back to show great courage, but I was overwhelmed by what I was told and how they inspired me. I have taken away much from these discussions, including:

James Packer's openness, self-awareness and generosity to the cause of suicide prevention.

Leilani Darwin's ongoing struggles and honesty were a reminder that suicidality is not easily resolved, but with resources and support can be managed.

Peter Moloney's approach to meditation, ice baths and his work with farmers experiencing the same pain he did is inspiring, and gives practical ideas in how to manage mental health.

All the people in this book opened up about themselves with honesty and emotional truth, because they know sharing their stories will save lives.

There are tears and laughter in these pages. Some participants were very nervous. Many elements of these stories are being shared in public for the first time. That takes guts.

It was a privilege to hear the stories in this book.

And I hope you feel privileged to have read them. Each story was told willingly, and in the hope that the journey of the storyteller – the highs, the lows and the road back – will help others to see there is a way through suicide and back to wellbeing.

I thank every participant for sharing their stories of surviving suicide and finding their way back to a better life.

In my lifetime, attitudes to mental illness and suicide have changed markedly for the better. We have experienced an enlightenment. But the journey is not complete.

When I was born, we knew little about how to treat mental illness, and thought locking people away was best for them and certainly for the rest of the community. Mental health clinics were asylums. Treatment was crude, often brutal and sometimes inhumane. Many of Australia's nineteenth century sandstone asylums were built on waterways so the 'insane' could be kept off roads, away from the community. At least one of these establishments has a tunnel from the wharf to the buildings to keep the inmates out of sight.

People didn't speak openly about mental illness, and if they did, they used words like 'lunatic'. A person with what we now call clinical depression had 'bad nerves' or was in 'one of their moods'. They disappeared for periods of time – or forever – into these asylums and were not talked about. Attitudes toward suicide were even worse.

Suicide was often covered up. Compassionate police and doctors would falsify death certificates to spare the family the shame of suicide and allow them to have a religious funeral and burial. Instead of suicide, the death certificate would cite 'misadventure' or 'accidental death'. A former New South Wales Assistant Police Commissioner told me that as a young officer in the 1950s it was common practice to rearrange the body and death scene so it didn't look like a suicide.

In the 1980s, policy toward community care began to change, and many mentally ill people were returned to live in the community. My experience in life is that the greatest mistake we make is overcompensating for the last mistake we made. So in the rush to release patients from the old asylums, we failed to provide enough care in the community. Too many were abandoned by the system and found themselves in the justice system instead. Australia's gaols are the insane asylums of the twenty-first century.

My suicide attempt in August 2005 was so public I decided early on to embrace it and not avoid it. I did wonder if talking about it would hurt our children, but Lucy and I agreed that in the age of the internet they would be able to easily find out when they got older. I have talked openly about my suicide attempt and ongoing suicidal ideation for almost twenty years. In the process, I have experienced extraordinary compassion from thousands of people. And I have also experienced discrimination.

On two occasions when looking for work after my suicide attempt, I was told by executive search consultants that I would struggle to ever get a job again. I was thirty-seven. One of them was a voyeur who clearly only met me so he could brag about the fact that he'd told me I was unemployable. This was a devastating blow as I struggled to get back on my feet. The other one was rude and dismissive. He told me my only chance was to go into business for myself because no-one would employ me.

They were both wrong. I have combined my business life as a CEO, Chair and Director of commercial, mutual and not-for-profit organisations with my work for Lifeline and my passion for suicide prevention. I am grateful to my employers for their support. This extended to times as a CEO when I took leave for bouts of depression and suicidality. They showed me compassion and treated me as they would if I'd had any other physical illness. They gave the time for treatment and recovery, and then welcomed me back.

These examples of leadership from boards, and my openness to my staff about why I was on leave, sent a message that in the place where they work, it is okay to have mental illness – that you will be supported, and will return to work as a member of the team.

This has been my experience, but it is not the experience of most.

The last great battlefield of discrimination is the workplace. In the companies I know, if an employee tells their boss they have cancer, the response is compassionate and supportive.

If that same employee tells their boss they have bipolar or are suicidal, many workplaces do not know what to do. Should the employee be fired because they can't handle the job? Will they ever be able to work properly again? Could you imagine giving that response to someone with cancer?

Workplaces have improved, but far too many employers deal with mental illness with a payout and a confidentiality agreement. And when you are mentally ill or suicidal, you don't have the strength to fight to keep your job. Again – could you imagine doing this to someone with cancer? We are getting better by the day, but the principle of treating mental and physical health in the same way – a principle enshrined in work, health and safety legislation across Australia – is, in practice, mostly breached.

It is up to all of us to make a difference for those struggling. Who knows? One day it could be you.

Contacts and Resources to Save a Life
... Or to Save Your Life

I am regularly asked by people, worried or desperate that someone they know or love is going to take their own life, 'What do I do?' They feel helpless. They worry that because they are not an expert – a counsellor, psychologist or psychiatrist – they don't know what to do or say, and could actually make things worse.

Every bone in our body says we shouldn't talk about suicide. We worry that by saying the word, we may put the thought into someone's mind. Yet all our experience – supported by research – shows that this is exactly what we should do. We can't afford to be gentle. We need to be direct.

It's not a time for politeness. 'How are you?' is not enough. 'Let's go to the pub/movie/shopping/dinner' won't cut through. You need to ask the person you are worried about: 'Do you want to kill yourself?' 'Do you feel like hurting yourself?' We hope that the answer is 'no', and that they will tell you what's affecting their mood or behaviour.

But if they say 'yes', think of them as someone having a heart attack in front of you. If that were the case, you would act. Whether you knew them or not, you would call 000 and wait with them until the ambulance arrived.

Just as you don't have to be a medical professional to help save the life of someone having a heart attack, you don't need to be an expert to help someone who is thinking about killing themselves. If they answer 'yes' when you ask them if they are thinking about suicide, stay with them. Call Lifeline or another service and connect them. Sit with them if they agree to you listening to their conversation, or sit close by so you can see them as they talk to the crisis supporter. If they are highly distressed and at risk of self-harm, take them to the nearest hospital emergency department or call 000.

You wouldn't walk past someone having a heart attack, so don't walk away from someone planning to take their own life.

See over the page for important resources in a crisis.

Helplines and Services

In Australia, **in an emergency,** if you are concerned for your or another's safety call **000** at any time.

Lifeline

Phone 131 114 – 24-hour service, 7 days a week.

Chat online at www.lifeline.org.au/crisis-chat

Text on 0477 13 11 14

www.lifeline.org.au

Kids Helpline

Phone 1800 551 800 – 24 hours, 7 days a week.

www.1800respect.org.au

Beyond Blue

Phone 1300 22 46 36

beyondblue.org.au

Men's Line Australia

1300 789 978

mensline.org.au

**National Sexual Assault, Domestic Family
Violence Counselling Service**

Phone 1800RESPECT or 1800 737 732 –
24-hour service, 7 days a week

www.1800respect.org.au

Suicide Call Back Service

Phone 1300 659 467

www.suicidecallbackservice.org.au

Bravehearts

Phone 1800 272 831 – 8.30 am–4.30 pm,
Monday to Friday AEST

bravehearts.org.au

**If you or someone you love is having a mental health
crisis, please call 000 or go to your local hospital and
they can help you access care. Your GP can refer you
to a psychologist or psychiatrist.**

**Mindframe.org.au has easily accessible reference
guides on their website to assist in communicating
information about suicide safely and to reduce stigma.**

About Lifeline

In 1961, Reverend Alan Walker, the Superintendent of the Central Methodist Mission in Sydney (now the Wesley Mission), received a call at his home on a Sunday night from a stranger. The stranger introduced himself as Roy. He said he didn't know Alan Walker, but that he had called him because he was going to kill himself. Two days later at Kings Cross, police found a dead man with a letter pinned to his shirt addressed to Alan Walker. It was Roy.

To the everlasting gratitude of every Australian, Alan Walker decided at that moment that something had to be done to help people when they wanted to take their own life. On 16 March 1963, Lifeline took its first call.

What is most remarkable about this story is that in 1961, suicide was deemed a sin by most if not all religions, and attempted suicide was still a crime in most states and territories in Australia (and around the world). That a minister of religion chose to start an organisation to help 'sinners' and 'criminals' is extraordinary.

Lifeline is an anonymous service. I have often thought it interesting that people in the darkest corner of their life will speak to a complete stranger, rather than someone they know. But I guess that is the answer – they are too ashamed to talk to someone they know or love who they fear will judge them. But Lifeline doesn't judge you, or what you've done. Their focus is keeping you alive and safe.

When I meet people who tell me they called Lifeline, I always ask, 'How was it?' The answer is always, 'They listened.' Across Australia, those listeners number 4000 well-trained and highly committed crisis supporters who staff the service, of which eighty per cent are highly trained, unpaid volunteers.

Today, Lifeline provides its service by telephone, text and chat, 24 hours a day/seven days a week, and there are Lifeline kiosks at suicide hotspots around the country. For over sixty years Lifeline has been there for Australians in crisis and at risk of suicide.

For crisis support, hope and help, contact Lifeline 24/7
Call on 13 11 14
Chat at www.lifeline.org.au/crisis-chat
Text on 0477 13 11 14

Acknowledgements

Profiles in Hope is a passion for me and I am grateful to those who have shared their passion for suicide prevention.

The story starts with the drive of Nick Fordham of The Fordham Company. Nick was an instant believer in the book, its impact and its message of hope. He waved his fee to help get the book up.

Vanessa Radnidge from Hachette also believed in the importance of this book and has been an outstanding publisher. Thank you to all at Hachette Australia.

Roger Joyce joined me on the journey of interviewing the participants to get their best stories. He experienced the sadness and joy of each story with me.

Dr Jaelea Skehan, Director at the leading mental health and suicide prevention institute, Everymind, reviewed *Profiles in Hope* to ensure we applied the Mindframe guidelines on the discussion, reporting and publication of the content here that references suicide and self-harm.

I am grateful to Dr Anna Brooks at Lifeline Australia for providing me with the latest data on suicide in Australia.

Sir Peter Cosgrove was very kind to provide the foreword. It was no surprise to me that he said yes immediately. He was an outstanding soldier and Governor-General and he and Lady Cosgrove are also extraordinarily compassionate people.

Each of the fifteen participants shared their stories with conviction. For some, it is the first time they have talked publicly about their experience of suicide and suicidality. For others, the passing of time has caused greater understanding and reflection. For all, they embraced the chance to tell their story and spread messages of hope for those who find themselves in the darkest corner of their life, contemplating taking their life.

With great honesty, they helped me create a book that talks to for every Australian living with suicidality and the people who love and care for them.

hachette
AUSTRALIA

If you would like to find out more about
Hachette Australia, our authors, upcoming events
and new releases you can visit our website or our
social media channels:

hachette.com.au
🇫 HachetteAustralia
🇽 ⭕ HachetteAus